THE
DESERT
MURDERS

How Junk Science,
Witness Contamination,
and Arizona Politics
Condemned
an Innocent Man

MARY LASH

Grist Mill Press

Piedmont, South Carolina

Published by Grist Mill Press
2522 West Georgia Road
Piedmont, SC 29673

Manufactured in the United States of America

Publisher's Cataloging-in-Publication

Lash, Mary.
  The desert murders : how junk science, witness
contamination, and Arizona politics condemned an
innocent man / by Mary Lash.
    pages cm
    Includes bibliographical references.
    LCCN 2014922895
    ISBN 978-0-9858465-3-4
    ISBN 978-0-9858465-4-1

    1. Lehr, Scott Alan. 2. Judicial error--Arizona--
Phoenix. 3. False imprisonment--Arizona--Phoenix.
4. Homicide investigation--Arizona--Phoenix. 5. Rape--
Investigation--Arizona--Phoenix.   I. Title.

HV6534.P55L37 2015   364.152'30979173
                    QBI15-600004

Dedicated to the late Yvonne Lehr,
who never lost faith in her son's innocence,
and to all the victims—
both of violent crime
and of injustice

Contents

Foreword

"Here's a story for you," my brother-in-law, Steve Garcia, said in 1999. He told me about a young man—bright, a good worker and devoted father—who had been convicted of a series of rapes and murders that terrorized Phoenix in 1991 and 1992.

The man, now on Arizona's death row, was Scott Alan Lehr.

Scott Lehr, Steve added, "didn't seem the type." And Scott's mother, Yvonne, a former coworker of Steve's, passionately maintained that Scott was innocent, that his arrest and conviction were influenced by "politics."

I kept my thoughts to myself at the time. Sociopaths, I believed, are often successful predators for the very reason that they're skilled at hiding their violent tendencies. No mother wants to believe her child is capable of violence, and surely our constitutional protections would prevent the wrongful conviction and legalized murder of an innocent man.

Then I met Yvonne Lehr. We talked about her son's case, and when she entrusted to me her hefty cartons of police reports, newspaper clippings, and legal transcripts, I was honored, but wary. My own children were teenagers. I didn't want to bring the ugly facts of assault and murder into our lives, and I certainly didn't want to know anyone convicted of raping girls and women and discarding them to die in the desert. If I came to sympathize in any way with this man, wouldn't I be betraying those victims?

When I looked through the blunt, matter-of-fact police notes, I was sick over what the victims—the youngest only 10—had suffered. But even through the flat statements of the investigative reports, the facile assertions of newspaper articles, and the stylized drama of trial transcripts, I discovered shocking flaws in the investigation and prosecution. Investigators failed to follow some of the most promising leads. They disregarded glaring inconsistencies in their theory that a single man had committed this array of crimes. And when the cases came to trial, the prosecution repeatedly misrepresented evidence. Ambiguous DNA analysis, in its infancy at the time, was used to persuade the jury that Lehr had committed the crimes. Once I'd pieced together the known facts, I could no longer believe that Scott Lehr was guilty. My confidence that the innocent have nothing to fear from our justice system was shattered.

Scott Lehr is not the only victim of Phoenix's ineffectiveness in prosecuting sexual assault. According to data from the FBI's "Uniform Crime Reporting," from 1996-2000 Phoenix ranked worst among big cities in the United States when it came to rape prosecution. With less than a quarter of cases solved in Phoenix, experts suggested that two of the problems the city faced were a small staff of investigators and a highly transient population.[1]

In the years following Scott Lehr's prosecution, area authorities attempted to improve their record. A woman raped in 1998 reported that Phoenix investigators videotaped their interview with her, "in case she changed her story."[2] If such a policy ensuring the integrity of identifications had been followed in 1991-1992, Lehr would be home with his family today, for he was found guilty largely because of victims' testimony that contradicted the statements they made to police shortly after the crimes.

No appeals to logic have persuaded Maricopa County that Scott Lehr is innocent. Looking at patterns of prosecutorial behavior nation-wide, such intransigence is not surprising. Michael Baden, M.D., former New York City Chief Medical Examiner, writes, "Just how often the wrong person is arrested is nothing short of astonishing."[3] Baden cites the finding of a 1999 *Chicago Tribune* investigation "that since 1963, at least 381 homicide convictions nationwide have been overturned because overzealous prosecutors concealed evidence of innocence or presented evidence they knew to be false."[4] When it comes to "junk" scientific evidence used to secure a case, Baden writes, "My experience has shown me that even when the erroneous scientific evidence is exposed, the prosecution will be disinclined to retreat, often believing that the error was harmless because of the nonscientific evidence also available."[5]

Unacceptable as they are in non-capital cases, prosecutorial error and misconduct can be lethal when the defendant is on trial for his life. In February 2002, Columbia Law School professor James S. Liebman released a study documenting high error rates in death penalty trials. Arizona was one of the ten worst states, with a serious error rate of 79% in capital cases.[6]

The following pages reveal a tragedy of women raped or murdered and of a young man who could have been any mother's son. Gleaned from investigators' notes, legal documents, news reporting, and interviews, it's a story of outrageous victimization—not only of women who will never see justice, but also of a man wrongfully condemned to death.

1: The Baby-Seat Rapist

NOVEMBER 18, 1991

"Why are you doing this to me?" In the dark, Amy* felt as if the world had caved in on her.

This afternoon as the little girl had walked home from the bus, she remembered how she loved the sun-filled Arizona autumns. And it was great being back with her friends. She was still amazed that her dad brought her back to Phoenix to finish fifth grade at Simpson School. She'd begged him to give up on San Diego, and he finally agreed. To have him listen to her like that, it made her feel grown-up.

But Dad was so late getting home tonight that she was afraid. Only now, her worry that something bad had happened to him was very far away. Now, just this sharp pain, and relief that the man went away. And fear he'd come back.

Amy kept walking toward the lights in the distance. Just one foot, then the other; keep them moving, and she'd be safe. When he drove her out here, she'd spotted the lights of a building; it was big enough that somebody might still be there. She thought she was bleeding, but she didn't have time for that. She felt her way down the ruts in the dirt road. With the moon over the city-lit sky, she could find her way. She had to.

Now that she was alone, it was so still. If she stepped on a rattlesnake in the dark, would she hear a warning rattle before it bit? Suddenly her foot splashed into cold water; that must have been one of the puddles they drove around. Only then, it didn't seem so far from the main road before he stopped the car. Now her

---

Names have been changed to protect living victims and some witnesses, family members, and others associated with the criminal investigations or legal proceedings.

sneaker was wet and cold. She wished she hadn't lost the other sock.

Finally she could see a clearing in the cactus and shrubs in front of her. When she reached the clearing, there was pavement under her shoes. She stayed on the road and kept going. It was quicker walking on the pavement, and snakes would stay off the road. Wouldn't they?

There were headlights down the road, coming toward her fast. She jumped for the closest place to hide, just a big cactus. She lay on her stomach behind it, her head in the cold dirt. A car door slammed. She made herself so still she thought she'd stopped breathing. Minutes passed. Silence. She waited a long time, but heard only the wind. Finally she moved herself up, just a muscle at a time, until she could see. No car. Nobody at all. If she heard things that weren't there, was she crazy? Something cried out— long and wild. It sounded close. Did coyotes eat people? She hurried back onto the road and ran until she was so dizzy she had to walk.

But she could see another car's lights coming towards her. She was afraid of the desert, but if she stayed on the road he'd get her. It was like hide-and-seek when she was little, only back then, no one wanted to hurt her. Why had she ever played stupid, make-believe games? The truth was so different.

She stumbled back into the desert, just far enough that no headlight could find her. It was like a nightmare, being terrified like this. But she was awake, though it was the middle of the night.

Amy dragged her numb feet. She could see lights through the windows of a large building; she was almost there. Faster. She couldn't get caught now. There were no cars coming; it must be after midnight. A sign said Sungrove Care Center. It looked like a hospital, with wheelchair ramps. There were a couple of cars in the parking lot, but not his. She ran up into the lights.

Amy raced up to the door and yanked it toward her. It was locked solid. She knocked on the hard steel so hard her hands ached. It was rude to make a racket like that, but what if he came back? She couldn't hear anything inside. She ran around the building and up to a big door. It was locked. Wasn't there a doorbell? Nowhere. She pounded on the steel and glass with her aching hands, then listened. She thought she heard steps inside, but maybe she really was dreaming. Yes, she could see somebody. A woman in a uniform, turning on more lights, and she was coming toward the door. Maybe a nurse; surprised, but nice, peering out. Finally, in slow motion, the nurse unlocked the door. She put her hand on Amy's shoulder gently, but then almost pulled her inside, as if she was afraid, too.

As soon as the door locked behind them, Amy was so tired it was hard to speak out loud. She was panting, thirsty. But the nurse was kind, and, all in one breath, Amy told her a man took her in his car and left her in the desert.

"Did the man hurt you?"

Amy could only nod her head yes.

At 7:30 the next morning Phoenix Police Detective Malcolm Rafferty arrived to interview Amy Perry* at the Thunderbird Samaritan Hospital. There were already reports from the Peoria police who'd interviewed Amy, but Rafferty needed to get the story himself. He went into to the bare little room aware that the 10-year-old might be the latest in a series of victims. He was glad the mother had consented to letting him talk to the little girl alone; usually you could get better details when the victim wasn't worrying about upsetting her mother or boyfriend.

She looked her ten years old. She was only 4'8", but plucky, and very willing to talk. He made some chitchat, asking her about school, where she said she got "nothing but A's" on her report card. She lived with her dad in Phoenix. Her mom lived in Mesa. Then Rafferty asked her to tell him what happened to her yesterday.

After school, Amy said, she took the city bus home as usual. Her dad wasn't home, and she thought he was probably at his friend Mike's house. She made herself a snack and watched television. When her father still hadn't come home by dinnertime, she cooked herself something and watched more TV. Finally, there was nothing good on TV and she read a book. It was late for her dad to still be out, and she started to worry. When it was almost 9 o'clock she took the bus and went looking for him. But she didn't see her dad's bicycle anywhere around Mike's house, and when she looked in the windows it was dark inside. Nothing to do but go back home.

But the bus didn't come. She knew the way home, but it was chilly, and a long way to walk at night. She crossed the freeway and walked past a church. She was near a small shopping center. On the corner was a J.B.'s restaurant. A white man driving a big tan car pulled out from the parking lot and stopped near the sidewalk. He had his window down and asked Amy if she wanted a ride. She told him she could not accept a ride from strangers and kept walking.

The man continued driving beside her in the parking lot. He smiled at her. It was cold out, he said, and he would give her a ride home. She looked into the car and saw a baby-seat in the back. He seemed like a nice person. And even wearing her sweater, she was cold. Also, she needed to hurry home and make sure Dad got in safe. She asked the man if he could just drop her past the train tracks. She got in his car.

Rafferty asked her to describe the man. Tall, she said, and big and fat all over. His hair was light brown—no—orange and brown together. When the light was on inside the car, his hair kind of looked orange. At other times it looked light brown. His hair grew down to his shoulders, covering the back of his neck. It was curly and stuck to his head, but also puffed up, and he had it behind his ears. He had a beard but no mustache. His beard was long—about two inches long. No scars, no eyeglasses, no accent to his speech. He was wearing a light blue button-up shirt, gray sweatpants, and a watch or a bracelet with a large band on his right wrist; it looked like gold. His tennis shoes were white, with nylon on the top of the toes and a gray band around the soles.

His car was a big four-door, light tan. The inside was a little lighter. There were bench seats. The seats felt smooth when you rubbed them one way and rough when you rubbed the other direction. There was a thing with an ashtray and a cup holder on the floor in front between the driver's side and the passenger side. A pack of Camel cigarettes and some change lay in it. The baby-seat, in the back on the passenger's side, was dark blue and had a pad with red and green stripes down the middle. There was a small pink sweater that looked like it might fit a two-year-old. Papers, toys, and clothing littered the floor in back.

They drove only a short distance before she noticed they were heading in the wrong direction. When Amy told the man, he told her he was going a different way. He stopped at a Circle K and said he'd be right back. He returned with a bottle of regular Dr Pepper and a bottle of Vaseline Intensive Care lotion. He asked her if she wanted something to drink. She told him no, and they drove some more.

After a while, they should have gotten there, and she was very, very frightened. She said to either turn around or she would get out. She started to open the car door. But he promised he would drive her home, and she closed the door again. Then he kept driving down different streets until she had no idea where they were. Driving with him was a blur now; she was so tired. He talked to her, but she couldn't remember most of it. He did say he had a wife and children.

Amy said she would tell the man how to get there. He agreed. But when she tried to tell him the directions, they only went around in circles. She was lost. He said he knew which way to go, but they kept getting further out of the city. They went past Thunderbird Road and signs that said Sun City. Finally, there were no houses or anything. She begged him to please turn around but he said he had to go to the bathroom. After he went to the bathroom, he would take her home. She started crying.

He drove the car behind some big bushes and stopped. He got out and came around the car and opened the door on her side. He picked her up, the way a groom picks up a bride. He pulled her very close to him and said, "You're going to do what I say, right?"

"Don't kill me," she pleaded, at least 100 times.

"Don't worry, I'm not going to kill you."

He carried her around to the driver's side and put her in the back seat. She knew he was going to rape her. She thought she was too young for that. And then he kept doing things to her, though she told him it hurt.

Why, she asked, if he had children, why didn't he just do this to them, not her?

"I would never do it to my own children."

"Why are you doing this to me?" she heard herself repeating.

Out of the dark she heard, "I want the variety."

Putting together an accurate summary of the assault would have been a puzzle for Detective Rafferty. In the early hours of the morning, Amy had told Peoria police that the rapist's car was copper-colored, not tan. She'd said the suspect's beard was very long, mid-chest length. That didn't fit with what she'd just told Rafferty. Some of the details Amy remembered now were similar to five other abductions and sexual assaults in Phoenix since February. While he waited to talk to Amy that morning, Rafferty had phoned Detective Frank Dimodica, who was leading the investigation of those other cases. There were some similarities, but the attacker in the earlier cases had choked four of the women, and thrown stones at one. And then the murder ten days ago. An older woman than the others, in a different kind of scene—the edge of an orange grove. Another one of his victims? Assuming the same guy was guilty of all the crimes, his attacks were getting more violent. Yet Dr. Kezele, who examined Amy, found no evidence of physical injury. So there wasn't a clear pattern of escalating violence.

Rafferty asked whether the suspect hit Amy or anything like that. The little girl said no; he picked her up from the front seat, moved her to the back seat, and sexually assaulted her. As she put her clothes back on, he threw one of her sneakers into the desert and told her to go get it. When she ran after her shoe, he drove away.

Although it didn't look as if they had biological evidence, the man had been careless when he'd stopped at the Circle K at Grand and 99th Avenue. Customers were scarce enough between 10 and

11 p.m. that the Circle K clerk had taken a good look at the suspect and was sure he could identify him.

Having that unbiased witness was a lucky breakthrough, since the victims' descriptions of the suspect and his car weren't consistent across all the cases. Either police had the task of looking for a guy who could change his appearance dramatically, or there were more scumbags than one out there, attacking girls in similar ways.

2: A Pattern of Violence?

Phoenix Detective Frank Dimodica read through the notes on Amy Perry's case that morning. He might have had a strong hunch that the assault on Amy was the latest in the series of "baby-seat" crimes he was investigating. The car used to abduct Amy was a large American-built car, an older model, with a baby-seat in back. It sounded like the tan or beige car they were looking for in connection with the other assaults, though the copper color she described to Peoria police didn't quite jibe.

Dimodica could probably recite the police reports for the earlier cases by heart. There were some discrepancies from case to case, but it looked like the same guy. The first victim in the series was probably Wednesday, February 13, 1991. "Probably," because that case was sticky in all kinds of ways. A 47-year-old woman was found walking at 7th Avenue and Happy Valley Road at 4:30 in the morning, naked, covering herself with a cast-off doormat. A small woman, only 4'11" and 90 pounds, Shirley McClure* said a white man about thirty years old had given her a ride in the area of 27th Avenue and McDowell the night before, around 10 p.m. But then he sped north, away from town. When she objected, she said he'd choked her unconscious with one hand, while driving. If that was true, the guy was incredibly well coordinated. He stopped the car near a construction zone in the desert northeast of 7th Avenue and Alameda, about 18 miles from where he picked her up. After raping her, he dragged her out of the car by her neck and threw her in a ditch naked. He yelled at her, something degrading, she said; she couldn't remember exactly.

Trouble with that case was, Shirley had a criminal record, including prostitution and shoplifting as well as cocaine and heroin possession. And "Shirley McClure" wasn't her real name. It was Mona Barnett.* Mona probably really had been raped, but it looked as if she'd gotten into the car willingly, for prostitution. And where had she been between 10 p.m., when she said the guy had picked her up, and 4:30 the next morning, when she got help? She wasn't found that far from the crime scene, but she didn't say she'd been unconscious after he threw her out of the car.

But worse, some of the details she gave were off the wall, compared to the other victims' memories: a blond-haired man, she said, with straight hair over his ears, and a pot belly. She told the first officer who interviewed her that the suspect was clean-shaven; but later she said he had a full beard. He was wearing a green hospital smock with blue jeans, and he said his name was Dave. There was a pack of cigarettes on the dashboard; she hadn't noticed the brand. And she said his car was a light blue, American-made mid-sized sedan, with no inside door handles. No door handles, yet!

Given the lies she'd told them about her own identity, plus the strong possibility that she got into that car with the intent to commit an act of prostitution, they'd considered her case a non-crime. Still, there were some things in common with the other attacks, enough to think that Mona's story might be worth a second look. Also, she'd consented to being examined and they had biological evidence.

Then on Saturday, February 23, 18-year-old Emily Caldwell* was raped. Emily was also a smaller girl, 5'4" and 100 pounds. Picked up at about 8:30 that evening at 16th Street and East Thomas and sexually assaulted at 1100 East Alameda Road North of Deer Valley Road. That would have been within a mile of where Mona was assaulted. Like little Amy, Emily said that a man offered her a ride after she missed her bus. He was driving a large white or tan four-door car. When she was in the car he offered her a cigarette. He parked at a convenience store. While he was inside the store, she used the pay phone to call her boyfriend, but she didn't reach him. The man bought a Pepsi for her and a wine cooler for himself. After he drove several more blocks, he suddenly took I-17 North and drove away from the city. She knew something was wrong and asked him to let her out. She reached for the door, but he grabbed her by the hair. He told her, "I need you to clean my house, and I'll give you money to do it." He mentioned a wife or a girlfriend. When he slowed down on the exit ramp, she moved to jump out of the car. He grabbed her by the hair again. "You're just a little whore and you're gonna get what's coming to you." He stopped in the desert, near a mountain-bike racing track. At first she resisted his assault, but when he started choking her she had to cooperate. After he'd raped her, he pushed her out of the car without her clothes. He got out, too, and threw fist-sized rocks at her. "Run," he ordered. When she ran from him, he drove off. Two men found Emily wandering naked; they lent her a shirt and brought her in to report the crime.

The car Emily described sounded like the one used to abduct Amy: white or cream-colored, with a slightly darker tan interior (though Amy said the interior was lighter than the outside.) There was a tan plastic drink holder in the front. This time, he did not have a baby-seat in the backseat. Emily described the rapist as 35 to 40 years old; that was older than all the others, if she was right about the age. She said he was flabby, with a pot belly, and about six feet tall. He had short, straight brown hair, brown eyes, and an unshaven face with a mustache. Straight hair, where Amy said curly. He smoked cigarettes, Emily said, with a white filter.

But Emily didn't give them any more to go on. A record check turned up that she had a prior arrest for prostitution – right there at 17th and East Thomas, where she got in the car on the night of the assault. When she was asked about that arrest, she refused to be examined, or to press charges. She was out of there, and that was the end of the investigation. But prostitute or not, she probably wouldn't report being raped if she hadn't really been.

Dimodica might have made himself a note to get in touch with Emily—if she would talk to him now. Even if they had no case for prosecution here, her statement could help nail the guy on the other attacks because Emily had gotten a look at his license plate—Arizona plate ADW–515 or –519. Also, there was at least one other witness out there. Someone in a white truck with a camper was close enough to notice the rape but did not help her. Maybe not the kind of person to come forward and offer information, but at least there was a chance.

Dimodica's third case was a month after Emily. It was March 23, a Saturday, just as in the attack on Emily. Twenty-eight-year-old Nicole Churchill* said she was trying to catch a bus to meet a girlfriend around 3 p.m. He must have seen her miss the bus. "Need a ride?" he said. She got in his car at 16th Street and Glendale. As in Mona's case, he told Nicole his name was Dave. He stopped north of Joy Ranch and 12th Street, in the New River area. When the car stopped, she tried to run away; he grabbed her by her shoulders and pulled her back in. He told her to take her pants off, but she kept saying, "Take me back." He didn't say anything else; just raped her. Afterwards, he drove her to the corner of 12th Street and Joy Ranch and said, "Get out. This is close enough to civilization." She walked to a house nearby.

Interviewed a little past 5 p.m., and so within forty-five minutes of the attack, Nicole gave details that roughly corresponded to what Emily remembered. The rapist was heavyset, she said, with a beer belly. He had light brown hair (Emily had just said brown) and a day's growth of beard. Nicole said he might have worn a watch with a black band on his left wrist. She remembered he drove a four-door Chevy, brown with a light brown top. Two tones—that was different. And "brown" was more like the "copper-colored" car little Amy had mentioned. In later interviews, though, Nicole started describing the car as tan, like the others. Since Nicole had seen the car by daylight, her recollection of the color—brown with a light brown top—might be more accurate than the victims who were abducted at night. Assuming it was the same car, of course. Nicole said the car had a light brown or tan interior, with crushed velvet seats. That sounded like what Amy remembered, too. Like Emily, Nicole saw a license plate beginning with ADW or AOW. And although Nicole had been afraid he'd beat her if she didn't cooperate, he was not violent. He even drove her to a place where she could get help before he left. Unusually considerate, for a rapist. Still, the details were enough like the other attacks to think it was probably the same bastard.

It turned out that Nicole was an addict, who admitted to injecting heroin at 9 that morning. How good a witness would she be when it came to prosecuting this guy? Otherwise, they had a case this time. There was evidence in the sexual assault kit. And Nicole had held onto a Pepsi can that he'd touched. That he'd left a useable print on the Pepsi can was a long shot, but possible.

Dimodica had promising information on the plate numbers. Detective Luginbuhl analyzed records of registered Chevrolets from years before 1986 and plates beginning with ADW. That gave 15 possible vehicles, one of which was a 1980 Chevrolet Malibu, Arizona plate ADW777, registered to a Richard Donohue.* In early May, Luginbuhl had visited the Donohue home. Mrs. Donohue told him her husband was sleeping; he worked nights. That might be significant, given the range of times when the crimes took place. Mrs. Donohue showed Luginbuhl the car. Although it didn't have a drink caddy or a baby-seat, in other respects it met Nicole's, Emily's, and Amy's description. A criminal history check revealed that Richard Donohue had been arrested in 1983 for disorderly conduct (fighting, in his case) and possession of a dangerous drug. Both charges were dropped, but Donohue had been fingerprinted when he was booked. They also pulled Donohue's driver's license photo, and showed it to Nicole as part of a photo lineup. She identified Donohue as one of two possible assailants in that group. On May 8, Luginbuhl went back and interviewed Donohue. He was cooperative and allowed a quick examination of his car, which was dirty and worn, with cigarette burns inside. The seats were cloth with leather side trim. Donohue said he'd never had a drink holder installed in the car. He also said it was his wife's car, and that he normally did not drive it.

Luginbuhl showed photos of Donohue's car to Nicole, who said the interior of the car used in the crime was in much better condition. But could they count on her memory of a car interior six weeks later, if she used heroin on the morning of the crime? Too bad they couldn't have had Emily look at the car, too.

But Donohue's fingerprints turned out not to match the ones on the Pepsi can. Mark Steven Brighton* was another suspect in Nicole's case, based on physical appearance, but the comparison of his fingerprints didn't match, either. Also, Nicole didn't I.D. Brighton in the photo lineup.

Dimodica must have hoped the fourth victim could help them crack this. Nancy Caporaso* was 21 years old but tiny, 4'8" and only 85 pounds. She was raped on April 4, a Thursday. Some time after 5 p.m., she was walking home from work when a pleasant-seeming white man in a two-door cream or brown-colored car offered her a ride at 19th Avenue and Union Hills. He told her his name was Dave, and that he had a wife and two children, ages seven and nine. He needed a housekeeper and would pay her $150 a week to clean. He offered to take her to see his house. "Are you sure you're married?" she asked. Her hours had just been cut at the drugstore, and she needed the money, so she agreed to go. But he drove off I-17 and into the desert area east of the highway, near the C.A.P. canal north of Happy Valley Road. He'd said he had horses, so she wasn't afraid until the road suddenly dead-ended and he hit barbed wire. He threatened to hurt her if she didn't do what he said. After assaulting her, he pulled her out of the car by her neck. "You said you wouldn't hurt me if I would cooperate," she cried.

Nancy woke up in a grassy area, under a large tree, wearing only her socks. There were bruises on her neck indicating choking, but she couldn't have been unconscious for long: she walked the short distance to the freeway and got help from a passing driver, with two children in the car. They took her to call the police by 6 p.m.—less than an hour from the time she'd been abducted downtown. And the drive with the rapist would have taken at least 15 minutes, probably more, since it was rush hour. Another funny thing was that Nancy described the suspect as chunky, but only 5' 6" tall; all the other victims recalled a taller guy, at least 5'10" to 6'. Nancy also described his brown eyes as "sunken." His hair was "scraggly," and longish, worn layered over his ears. That was different, too, but maybe she only described him differently. People's perception of physical appearance could be quirky. She said he had an "expensive-looking" gold watch with a large square face and no numbers. She remembered a two-door vehicle, Monte Carlo/Grand Prix style, with dirty seats. "Dirty" was interesting, since Nicole said the car was clean. And all the other victims remembered a four-door model, except for Mona Barnett, who couldn't remember the number of doors. Also, Nancy said it was a "smaller" car; the other victims had said big. A silver tire rim was on the rear floorboard, Nancy added. There was a drink caddy with a McDonald's cup in it and some change. No baby-seat; no cigarettes. Still, there was enough like the other cases that Dimodica believed it was the same guy.

The crime scene was near a shooting range and a rock quarry frequented by dump trucks and tandem trucks. Criminals who were not acting on sudden impulse, who put even a little planning into their crimes, would choose a scene they were familiar with. Maybe the perpetrator once worked a job connected with the quarry. The victims all described him as on the flabby side; his job couldn't have been too physically demanding. Were they looking for a truck driver? Or even a bus driver—several times he'd picked up victims after they missed the bus; maybe he knew the bus schedules well. Or someone who drove a taxi? He was very familiar with the city streets.

It was puzzling that this guy wasn't more worried about getting caught: he ejaculated during the rape, and since Nancy had been examined so soon after the attack, the semen should be a reliable source of identification. He threw Nancy's clothes out of the car, and along with them the McDonald's cup, plastic lid, and straw. Either he wasn't too smart, or, at some level, he wanted to be stopped, and punished.

At that point, Dimodica had some leads. Stephen Glen Blondel* was arrested on a warrant for DWI on May 1. Blondel's blood type matched the semen of the man who raped Nancy, but the fingerprint on the McDonald's cup didn't match his prints.

Damn. Another investigative lead was David B. Smith.* Could he
be the guy who introduced himself as "Dave" to Mona and Nicole
as well as Nancy? But again, his prints were not a match. Of
course, they didn't know for sure that the prints on the cup really
were the perp's; could just be somebody who worked at
McDonald's.

Then on May 24, Nancy was pretty sure she saw the guy who'd
raped her, waiting in a pickup truck outside a Star Mart. And when
he noticed her looking at him, he acted guilty; he pulled down his
hat and kept putting his hand in front of his face. Before he drove
away, she got the license number of the truck. The plate belonged
to a Robert T. McGinnis.* There was no record of why they hadn't
checked him out further.

In October, police had spotted a vehicle that matched the
suspect vehicle description, near I-17 and Bell Road. Right there
in the crime scene area! And the driver looked like the suspect. It
wasn't the plate number that previous victims had given them,
though: GZR 801, where Emily remembered ADW–515 or –519
and Nicole remembered a plate beginning with ADW or AOW.
Wouldn't rule him out, though. Could be by that time—eight or
nine months later, he'd changed his plates. Guy with this GZR
plate turned out to be David Bowles.* Another "Dave"! Nancy
identified a photo of Bowles as a possibility, but again, the prints
on the McDonald's cup did not match his. So they really had no
grounds for bringing him in.

After the crime against Nancy, the rapes abruptly stopped.
Impossible to say why, but at least he was off the streets. Before
the year was out, though, he'd taken a sixth victim. On October
24, thirteen-year-old Alison Brooks* was abducted by a stranger at
8:40 in the morning at 19th Avenue and Union Hills Northeast,
right across the intersection from where Nancy accepted a ride six
months earlier. It was a Thursday, just as in Nancy's case.

The case against the man who raped Alison was complicated.
At first she'd said the man had dragged her into his car. Since
forced abduction was not the M.O. of this "baby-seat" guy, it
wasn't surprising when she later changed her story and gave the

all-too-familiar details: a man with reddish-brown hair and brown eyes offered her a ride. She'd had a fight with her mother that morning, so she asked the guy to take her to her aunt's house. First he started off in the wrong direction, but then he turned around and took her to her aunt's. She got out of the car, and her encounter would have ended there, except that her aunt wasn't home. He asked her if she'd like to come and meet his wife and kids, and she agreed.

As in Nancy's case, the man offered Alison money to clean his house; and he said he had horses. He had two packs of cigarettes in his car, Marlboro Light 100s and Marlboro Reds. Strangely, he was barefoot in October; the suspect in the other attacks was wearing athletic shoes. It sounded like the car they were looking for, though: large beige or white four-door, maybe a Monte Carlo, with a blue baby-seat in back and a drink caddy on the transmission hump in front.

The man drove Alison up 19th Avenue to Knudson Drive, within sight of the Granatelli Racing building. They were out in the desert, but he told her it was the back way to his house. Thing was, he didn't know where he was going. He started to turn into a dead-end littered with tree branches and other trash. "This isn't the way," he said, and backed out. Off a dirt road extending from West Pinnacle Peak Road, he parked in a circle of trees and raped her. Afterwards he knocked her head against the dirt road, choked her, and left her naked except for one sock. She left that sock at the site, she said, to help find the crime scene later. Then she walked to the Granatelli building for help.

The physical evidence in Alison's case had been contaminated because the girl had unprotected sex with her boyfriend within twenty-four hours of the assault. And Alison's story was a can of worms. At first she'd said the man pulled her into his car, but later, after a witness gave a different account, she admitted she went with him willingly. Even worse, she had a history of lying. Alison acknowledged that three or four years earlier she'd told a Child Protective Services worker that she'd been sexually abused by her mother's boyfriend, when in fact she had not. Still, it didn't pay to worry about whether rape victims were lying about a few details. It was better to assume that the thirteen-year-old was a victim who deserved justice. A conviction would be tough, though. Before the crime against Amy the following month, Alison had been the youngest victim.

But why the six-month break in the attacks, between April and October? Dimodica knew it wasn't that the Phoenix summers were too hot even for sexual predators; the number of rapes stayed fairly consistent across the seasons. Maybe the guy went out of town for the summer. He was someone who knew the area pretty well, though. Somebody who came to Arizona in winter to work the tourist season? Somebody who did construction in a cooler place during the summer and came back to Arizona in winter? One of thousands of college students in the area, who might go home to another state in the summer?

Or, it could be that one of the guys they questioned was guilty, after all. Letting him know he was on their list could have put enough of a scare into him to help him control himself for a few months. Possible. Or what about someone arrested on unrelated charges in April or May, who'd spent the next six months in jail?

On the other hand, he could have raped again during that period, but the victims hadn't reported it. Especially likely if the victims were prostitutes.

So what did they know? Although the crimes took place at different times of day and night, the guy seemed to have a preference for Thursdays, Saturdays, and Sundays. Also, the days he chose for attacks didn't seem random. First Mona on February 13, 1991; that would be 2/13. Then Emily ten days later, February 23—2/23. There was another possible case that bore some similarities on March 3—3/3. Nicole on March 23, twenty days later—3/23; Nancy on April 4—4/4; then the six-month break. Alison on 10/24; the homicide on 11/8; and little Amy ten days later, 11/18. Weird. Was this guy somebody who gambled, or played the lotteries? Or maybe someone with a day off from work every ten days, who spent it preying on women?

And were they looking for a family man, or someone who only pretended to be? In some ways he was smart, and smooth—could present himself as a considerate guy and serve up a line that would get a woman into his car. Yet he was dumb when it came to covering his behind. He worked unusual hours, or he went though periods of unemployment. He drove a common sort of car. Sometimes he smoked Camel cigarettes; sometimes a cigarette with a white filter; sometimes he didn't smoke. Sometimes he drank Dr Pepper, but once a wine cooler; and he bought snacks from McDonald's or Circle K. He changed his hair and beard often. And he looked like thousands of guys around Phoenix.

The M.O. was generally similar. He makes nice and offers a ride to a small-sized woman in downtown Phoenix. He drives her a little ways north of the city and rapes her, then leaves her there. In all the cases but Amy's and Alison's, he reached the crime scene by driving I-17 North. But were they making too much of that? After all, the general strategy of the crime was common sense. An unarmed rapist was likely to look for a small victim; she'd be easier to overpower. And the desert outside Phoenix was all too often the scene of rapes, robberies, and murders, for obvious reasons.

Serial criminals tend to develop a strong pattern for their crimes, but in this series of attacks, important details varied. The assaults were committed morning, afternoon, evening, and night. Usually a serial sexual predator will target a particular type of victim, but the pattern wasn't so clear here. The wide age range among the victims, from 10 to 47 years, was rare. And though some of the victims were caught up in prostitution or drug abuse, which put them at high risk for violence; others were moderate-risk victims, just young women or students who happened to be too trusting. But if, as the man who raped Amy had said, the motive for the attacks was "variety," that would explain the range.

And then there were the differences in the women's memories of the rapist and his car. If one guy did all this, you had to discount plenty of the details in the women's descriptions. Who to believe? Often victims were so traumatized you couldn't depend on the accuracy of what they said, no matter how certain they were. Not to mention, you couldn't count on most women to pay too much attention to the details of cars. Yet in most of these cases, Dimodica had nothing but eyewitness testimony to go on.

Biological evidence would be their best shot at putting this guy away, and they only had it for three cases: Mona, whose description of the man and his car was way off-base from the others; Nicole; and Nancy. They might have partial fingerprints in two cases, but they couldn't be certain the prints were those of the rapist. The prints hadn't matched any of the leads they'd looked at so far. However, just judging from blood type, one of those leads could not be ruled out as the source of the semen sample in the Caporaso case. Since the prints hadn't been a match, though, there wasn't any point in wasting money on expensive DNA analysis.

A sprawling city of countless apartment complexes, Phoenix was a place where a criminal could easily drop out of sight. It was bad enough the suspect had gone on raping girls for nine months. But now they had reason to think that his violence might be escalating to a deadly level. In four of the rapes he'd choked the victim—but not enough to endanger her life. And the choking wasn't sexually motivated; he choked victims to control them or to make his escape. He'd thrown stones at Emily to make her run away. And twice he didn't physically injure the victim after the assault.

But then, on November 8, they found that dead woman. It made sense that it was the baby-seat guy. Little Amy and Alison were lucky to be alive. If they didn't catch him soon, his next victim might not be so lucky.

3: Margaret Christorf

NOVEMBER 7, 1991

On the morning of November 8, 1991, John Curtis walked his dog in Glendale, a northwest suburb of Phoenix. Man and dog strolled through an area where people often dumped trash, on the edge of an orange grove. Curtis cut into the grove to see the ripening oranges. On an unpaved access road, he found a woman lying on her side, her hand touching her cheek.

Police called to the scene pronounced the woman dead, her head crushed by two blows. Around forty years old, she had shoulder-length brown hair and brown eyes. She was wearing jeans, a blue warm-up jacket, and worn-out tennis shoes. The accounts of the first witnesses at the scene varied: most said that her jeans were pulled down around her knees, though one said they were not. In her jeans pockets were 90 cents in change and $8 in food stamps. Her right front pocket had been pulled out.

The dirt road left evidence of the killer: shoe prints; other impressions in the earth near her body; tire tracks leaving the scene, headed west, and a freshly chewed piece of gum.

Bill McFadden called Glendale Police Saturday afternoon, November 9, to report that his girlfriend, Margaret Christorf, had been missing since Thursday night. Sandra,* a clerk at the Circle K that Bill and Margaret frequented, had told him of an article in the *Arizona Republic* about an unidentified white woman found murdered in Glendale. He called to find out if the woman could be Margaret.

That night, McFadden walked to the Circle K to speak with Glendale Detectives Tom Clayton and Chuck Jones. McFadden told them he'd met Margaret three months before, when he was driving for Ace Taxi. He drove her to the apartment of a friend she was staying with; she called him Colonel Mansfield.* Bill waited for her in the cab. Colonel Mansfield wasn't home, so Bill invited Margaret to stay with him. The two lived together after that night. When Bill showed the detectives Margaret's DES identification card, they told him that the dead woman was Margaret Christorf.

McFadden was visibly upset. The detectives asked what he remembered about Margaret's last day. Bill said that she'd just begun a new job as a housekeeper at the Budget Lodge and had the day off. After picking up her food stamps in the morning, she and Bill bought some groceries and walked home. Bill's apartment didn't have electricity, but they gave a neighbor some food stamps in exchange for running an extension cord so they could watch TV. After dark, Margaret needed cigarettes, so they walked to the shopping area at 16th Street and Indian School Road. Margaret suddenly ran into the Circle K. That was the last time Bill saw her. He went into Petsmart to buy cat food, and when he came out, she was gone.

Margaret didn't know anyone in Glendale; Bill didn't know why she'd be out in the area of 59th Avenue and Union Hills, where she'd been found dead. Bill thought Margaret might have gone over to Colonel Mansfield's in Mesa, in the southeastern metropolitan area. Bill called Colonel Mansfield when Margaret didn't come home, but the Colonel told him Margaret wasn't there. Bill added that the Colonel's two sons and Mitch Kraus, a friend of the Colonel's, did not like Margaret.

Glendale police interviewed Bill McFadden again on November 12. Elaborating on what he'd told detectives three days before, Bill said that on the day Margaret disappeared they'd gone for a walk. They stopped at Walgreens, where Margaret looked for a gift for her daughters, who were living with her sister. Margaret couldn't find a present and bought some candy with food stamps. She used the change from her food stamp purchases to buy a pint of rum. Bill hated to see Margaret drinking, but he knew he couldn't stop her. She'd worked hard for two days at a new job and deserved a reward. They returned home about 5 p.m. While Margaret drank, she sat at the table working on her astrology by candlelight. Towards the middle of the evening, Margaret abruptly said she needed cigarettes and left without Bill. When he caught up with her, he felt she was going to Colonel Mansfield's house. Bill said he hugged her and told her he loved her before she walked away.

Less than a month earlier, Margaret had gone to Colonel Mansfield's and Bill didn't hear from her for a couple of days. When Bill finally got her on the phone, she invited him over for dinner. At the Colonel's house, everyone was drinking. Bill spotted Margaret in the bathroom, clapping her hands in front of her face and talking to the air. The Colonel gave Mitch Kraus and Bill money to buy dinner and more alcohol. When they returned from the store, Bill found Margaret lying on the floor with her top off and her pants partway down. Bill asked what was going on, but no one really said anything to him. A little later, Tempe Police arrived and asked Bill to leave. Margaret stayed on at the Colonel's a day or two more.

About a week later, Bill said, Margaret started drinking again and took off during the night. She returned around 7:30 the next morning and told him she'd met someone driving a white, mid-sized car on 16th Street, just south of the canal. She'd gone to Matt's Lounge with him. Bill asked her about a mark on her forehead, but Margaret didn't want to talk about it. She just said the man told her he didn't want to hurt her.

Detective Clayton asked Bill when he and Margaret last had sex. Four or five days before her disappearance, Bill answered. Clayton responded that Margaret appeared to have had sex just before being killed, and he believed that the semen was the killer's. If they took a sample of Bill's blood, would they find that the semen was his? Bill said he didn't think so, but that he and Margaret did sleep together on the night she disappeared. Clayton pointed out that Bill first said they'd had sex 8 to 10 days before the night of Margaret's disappearance, but just a minute ago he said 4 or 5 days. Bill explained that Clayton first asked him when they were last "intimate," and Bill wouldn't use that term to describe their sex on that last night. Bill quickly agreed to have a sample taken; he said he had nothing to hide. When his blood type was compared to the crime scene evidence, it confirmed that McFadden could have been the last man to have had intercourse with Christorf.

The next day, Detective Clayton spoke to Beth,* a neighbor of Bill and Margaret's. Beth remembered that Margaret came over one night about three weeks earlier, drunk and wearing only one shoe. That would have been around the time Bill had told police that Margaret was out drinking with another man and came home with a mark on her head. Margaret confided to Beth that Bill fought with her that night; he hit her on the back of the head and locked her out of the apartment. She and Bill didn't get along when she drank; he was upset by the way she acted. Margaret stayed at Beth's for about an hour and made several calls to someone named the Colonel. Margaret told Beth that the Colonel helped her with money or whatever she needed.

Detective Clayton also talked to Marcia,* the owner of the Budget Inn where Margaret worked. Marcia recalled that on the morning when Margaret's body was found, Bill came in and asked if Margaret had come to work. After some small talk about owning a motel, Bill sat and talked for a couple of hours, telling Marcia that he and Margaret had a fight and she'd left. Bill returned the following morning and again chatted for over an hour. Out of the blue, Bill said something about never hitting a woman or never beating a woman. Marcia thought that Bill acted different, "slightly crazy." She thought that he knew Margaret would not be back.

Detective Clayton also interviewed Jack Emerson,* who was working graveyard shift at the Circle K on the night of November 7. He'd seen Margaret in the store around 10:00 that night and then again early the following morning, at about 2:30. Emerson accurately described the clothing Margaret was wearing. He remembered her because her jacket was unzipped. She'd gotten out of a light-colored vehicle that looked like a Jeep Wagoneer. The driver of the Wagoneer looked like a business type in his early to mid-thirties, with short, dark hair and wearing a white shirt.

Emerson also remembered a young man who looked Indian coming in, commenting contemptuously on Margaret's appearance. That man was slightly built, about 5'6", and looked 18 or 19 years old, with mid-chest length hair and a light mustache. Emerson added that several customers had complained lately about a man making obscene calls to women standing outside by the pay phones. Emerson thought the caller must have been watching the women from a building across the street.

Margaret Christorf lived for the party. That was the recollection of Rafe Collins,* a former boyfriend interviewed by Detective Clayton. Margaret's children had been taken away from her by the state of California two years earlier. Rafe tried to get her to join Alcoholics Anonymous, but she wasn't interested. Margaret blamed all her problems on society, he said. When Margaret began living with Colonel Mansfield, she told Rafe that the Colonel and his circle forced her to drink and take pills.

Before Rafe, Margaret had been with a man named George for about five years, and she was afraid of George. Rafe said Margaret was also afraid of Colonel Mansfield's friend, Mitch. Once Rafe had called her at Mansfield's, and she claimed that Mitch would not let her leave. She had had bruises on her arm afterwards; she said Mitch caused them.

Rafe believed that Margaret would have known whoever murdered her. He didn't think she would have gotten in a car with a stranger at night. Even when she was drunk, she walked home by herself.

Police did not investigate as suspects either Bill McFadden or the friends Margaret was afraid of. They did not try to find the unidentified men Jack Emerson saw around the Circle K just before Margaret disappeared, or the caller who'd been harassing women in the Circle K parking lot. Instead, police assumed that the "baby-seat rapist" killed Margaret Christorf. Because many murder victims know their killers, this failure to investigate suspects known to the victim deviated sharply from standard practice.

Early in the investigation of the Christorf homicide, Detective Frank Dimodica had contacted Detective Clayton and provided information on six sexual assaults that year. Dimodica thought the same unknown suspect had committed all the crimes: Mona Barnett on February 13, 1991; Emily Caldwell on February 23; Nicole Churchill on March 23; and Nancy Caporaso on April 4. After six months, Alison Brooks was raped on October 24, 1991. Ten days after the murder of Margaret Christorf, Amy Perry was raped on November 18. In describing the assault cases to Glendale police, Dimodica overstated their similarity. In all these incidents, he said, "the suspect would pick up someone hitchhiking or walking, and take them to the North Valley area near Happy Valley Road and Seventh Street, where they were sexually assaulted." In fact, that location was the scene of only two of the crimes: the rapes of Mona Barnett and Emily Caldwell. The other assaults were committed at places ranging from 2.5 miles to over 17 miles away.

"The suspect assaulted several of the victims by banging their heads against rocks or throwing rocks at them. One or two of the victims were believed to have been left for dead by the suspect in the desert area," Dimodica reported to his peers in Glendale. "Banging their heads against rocks" was misleading; the rapist had thrown fist-sized stones at one victim, in an attempt to scare her away. Only Alison Brooks reported that the attacker hit her head against the dirt road. Nor was it accurate to say that victims were "left for dead in the desert." All the victims were released near frequently traveled areas, and none were seriously injured.

In the case of the most recent rape, that of Amy Perry, the suspect looked distinctly different than the others: he had a long "Santa Claus" beard, was "fat all over," and smoked Camels. And little Amy clearly described the crimes against her as the least physically aggressive of those being attributed to the "baby-seat" rapist. Although she was terrified, the assailant reassured her that he would not kill her, and he did not hit or choke her. This was not a pattern of a serial rapist growing more violent with each successive rape. In fact, there were enough conflicting details among the victims' statements to cast doubt on whether the same person committed all the crimes.

To further complicate the investigations, widespread television and newspaper coverage following the rape of Nancy Caporaso in April 1991 created the possibility that a copycat predator was using the same general M.O. as the "baby-seat rapist." The "Real Estate Rapist" operating in Phoenix and Tucson in 1987 is believed to have been as many as three men, of which only two were ever caught.

In addition to working from a questionable pattern of evidence, in assuming that the "baby-seat rapist" was a single suspect who would grow more violent with each crime, Phoenix police were guided by questionable theory. Phoenix police's assumption that Margaret Christorf was killed by a stranger, rather than an acquaintance with a history of violence toward her, is hard to justify in retrospect. By way of explanation, the investigation may have been biased by misunderstood theory. By the early 1990s, police across the United States were influenced by the approach to identifying violent criminals developed by insightful investigators including John Douglas and Roy Hazelwood of the FBI's Behavioral Science Unit. "Behavioral profiling" begins with the principle that an objective analysis of behavioral evidence can shed light on the motives and characteristics of the criminal. Factors indicating that multiple crimes were linked to one rapist would be a consistent M.O. across the cases, such as similar characteristics of rape victims, location of the crimes, ways in which the victim was made to cooperate, weapons used, and the attacker's ways of evading capture. In the case of the theoretical "baby-seat rapist," however, the M.O. involved the expedient strategy of taking the victim to a relatively isolated area and leaving her there; a common method among rapists generally. M.O. was not a conclusive link among the "baby-seat" cases because the method was so common, the victims were different in age and other characteristics, and only two of the crimes occurred in the same area. The attacker was unarmed in all cases, but some of the victims were choked and others were not. Examined more closely, the details of the assaults were different enough to suggest that more men than one were guilty.

In addition to M.O., a unique "signature" of the offender can be a key to establishing a link among crimes. The signature is a ritual aspect, offering insight into the fantasy the crime satisfies for the offender. In the case of several of the "baby-seat" rapes, there were comparable acts: giving the victim a ride, offering her a cigarette or a soft drink before the attack, and making small talk with her. However, these gestures are not unusual enough to be considered a signature. In contrast to the brutal egotism of the rapes, the gestures implied a superficial deference to victims, a clue that the fantasy of such rapists was that they and their victims were on a "date." In their fantasies, the rapists could delude themselves that victims' cooperation was consensual. This is not unique behavior in a culture in which "date rape" is a pervasive danger.

In the typology that FBI profiler Roy Hazelwood developed from the earlier work of psychologist Nicholas Groth, the "baby-seat rapist" (or rapists) would clearly fit the type of the "power reassurance" rapist. Hazelwood described the "gentleman rapist" of this type as engaging in "pseudo-unselfish" behavior toward his victim, who, in the rapist's fantasy, is a willing participant in the sexual encounter. While the power-reassurance rapist may threaten the victim or even produce a weapon, he is unlikely to use more force than is necessary to get her to cooperate.[7] He is the psychological type least prone to commit additional violence against his victim.

Serial rapists do not usually escalate into serial killers; only a small fraction of rapists become increasingly violent in subsequent attacks. If the facts of each crime had been examined objectively, there was no good reason to conclude that, even if there was only one "baby-seat rapist," his attacks had escalated to the murder of Margaret Christorf.

The more likely scenario was that several opportunistic men were guilty of the "baby-seat" rapes and that yet another man had murdered Margaret Christorf. Reasons why police linked

Margaret's murder to the "baby-seat" attacks were superficial. She was last seen in a high-crime area of Phoenix that was 1.7 miles from the location where the nearest rape victim was picked up. Christorf was found in a secluded area northwest of the city, and she might have been raped. The vague similarities ended there.

There was more evidence that Margaret Christorf had not been murdered by the "baby-seat rapist." Christorf was killed in the early hours of the morning, between 2:30 and 7:45 a.m. None of the rape victims linked in Dimodica's investigation were attacked later than 11 p.m. She was a smaller woman, 5'3" and 123 pounds, but in other respects a different type of victim. At 40, Margaret was decades older than any of the rape victims except 47-year-old Mona Barnett, who'd described a suspect very different from the others: a blond man driving a blue, mid-size American car without inside door handles. Christorf had been shabbily dressed, while the other victims were more attractively groomed. And, with a blood-alcohol level measuring .16%, Christorf had been drunk when she was murdered, unlike any of the rape victims.

Christorf's front pocket had been pulled out, as if something had been taken from it. A dime was found on the ground at the scene. Could robbery have been a motive? Bill McFadden estimated that Christorf had at least $60 in food stamps when he last saw her, but she was found with only $8 worth. In contrast, nothing was stolen from any of the rape victims.

The grove in which Christorf was murdered was nearly 9 miles away from the nearest "baby-seat" assault. A farm supervisor remarked to police that he'd found five other dead people in that location over the years, suggesting that Christorf might have been the latest in a series of killings at that site, unrelated to the "baby-seat" attacks.

It was possible that Christorf was killed by a copycat who hoped to have his crime blamed on the "baby-seat rapist." Christorf's murderer left her on a road near residences and frequently traveled by grove workers, a spot ensuring that her body would be found soon. Two weeks earlier, the rape of Alison Brooks had been widely covered by television and newspapers in the Valley. News reports described the rapist as "beating" his victims on the head with rocks, a distortion of the facts.

Investigators had to overlook glaring differences in order to believe the man who killed Margaret had also committed the rapes. Margaret was apparently killed at arm's length by two blows from a sixteen-pound rock, many times the size of stones thrown at Caldwell. There was no sign that Margaret had struggled with an assailant. The autopsy showed no bruises or signs of being choked; unlike several of the rape victims, whose necks or arms were bruised. Margaret was found partially clothed, while the rape victims had been made to strip naked. The chewing gum on the scene gave evidence that the murderer was a gum chewer, not the smoker reported by several rape victims.

Finally, one of the most dramatic differences between the baby-seat rapes and the murder of Margaret Christorf was that, according to a police report, Christorf might have been raped *after* being murdered. The rape of his slaughtered victim would be the signature of a disordered killer, very different from a smooth-talking rapist deluded by the fantasy that he was taking his victim out on a date.

Although it was reasonable for Maricopa County investigators to consider possible patterns among crimes, it would be fatal to the investigation if unrelated crimes were linked while important leads to individual attacks were ignored. As 1991 ended, the "baby-seat rapist-murderer" investigation stalled for lack of a suspect who could have committed all the crimes.

4: Michelle Morales

FEBRUARY 7, 1992

Pretty, blond Michelle Marie Morales had recently moved to Phoenix to be with her boyfriend. Her mother had died in an apparent accident back in California, and Michelle took it hard. But when the 19-year-old did not come home the night of February 7, 1992, her roommates weren't worried. She was unpredictable; a friend described Michelle as a "hippie-type flower child."

Michelle shared a house with four young men who were students at the Universal Technical Institute. They first assumed that, after staying out all night, she was reluctant to come home and face her boyfriend, Craig Jenkins.* After two or three days, they started to ask friends and neighbors if they'd seen Michelle. One of them, Richard Green,* thought she was going back to California to visit her father, although she hadn't told anyone else she planned to leave town. On February 15, eight days after Michelle disappeared, Scott Jenkins,* Craig's brother, filed a missing person's report.

Craig and Scott Jenkins said they last saw Michelle before they drove to class the afternoon of February 7. Later that day, roommate Phil Stockman* gave her a ride to the pay phones at the Circle K at 3400 West Peoria. She told Phil she was going to call her father in California and ask him to wire money. Afterwards, she planned to go roller-skating with Rob, a friend who worked at Fry's grocery. Phil described Michelle as outgoing and friendly with everyone. He did not believe she was promiscuous, but she did hitchhike a lot and accepted rides from guys at the Circle K, often total strangers.

Twelve days later, two men on horseback were searching for
stray cattle in the Sonoran desert in an area encircled by dirt roads.
Half a mile south of Carefree Highway and 3/10 mile east of
Interstate 17, one of them spotted a woman under a shrub. She lay
on her stomach in short grass. Coming no closer than five feet on
his horse, he could see that she was dead, from a gunshot to her
head, he thought. She was partially nude. Her long blond hair was
flung above her head.

From two tattoos, a heart on her chest and a black rose on her
shoulder, police identified the murdered woman as Michelle
Morales.

Phoenix Police Detective Michael Johnson was assigned to the
homicide. As he assisted crime scene investigators, he noted a
reddish discoloration on Morales's back left shoulder. She was
wearing only a turquoise-colored turtleneck, which had been
pulled up around her neck. Her feet, legs, and back were clean,
suggesting that she'd been carried into the area. There was no sign
of a struggle. She wore a turquoise ring and a bracelet. Most
remarkably, she had a large oval-shaped tear in the skin at the top
of her head, as if she'd been scalped.

There was another unique, ritual aspect to the murder of
Michelle Morales. Twenty-three feet east of where her body lay, a
hole in the ground 5" in diameter and 7" deep appeared to be half
full of her blood. Near the hole rested a ten-pound rock, stained
with blood, with several strands of hair adhering to it. Had the
killer practiced a shocking ritual: scalping the young woman and
allowing her to bleed into the ground? He would have had to stay
on the scene for some time to fill the hole with her blood. Then, he
would have carried her more than twenty feet to where she was
found, staining himself with her blood. Someone might have seen
the bloodied murderer.

Other evidence of the killer included shoe prints, one near
Michelle's right shoulder and another near her right hip, with
cigarette ash in it; then several partial shoe prints near her right
foot. Aerial photographs were taken of the crime scene, but
nothing else was noted. A few desert squatters lived in the area.

None of them recalled anything suspicious. Unfamiliar cars came and went often; people often used that desolate area for target practice.

Detective Johnson watched Dr. Phillip Keen perform the autopsy. Dr. Keen removed hairs that were not Michelle's from her blouse and face. Those could be a solid link to the killer. Although samples were taken in an attempt to determine whether Michelle had been sexually assaulted, the biological evidence was probably too degraded to provide a clear match with the attacker. Michelle's left upper arm had some bruising, as did her right hand, near the thumb. Her lower lip was torn, as if she'd been punched. She had other abrasions and bruises consistent with having been raped. Dr. Keen also found two abrasions on Michelle's forehead, where she'd been struck with a blunt object. What had killed her, though, was a single blow to the left side of her head. Dr. Keen examined the rock found on the scene with hair and blood on it. He could not confirm that the rock had been the murder weapon because it did not have jagged edges that he could match with the wound.

Although Dr. Keen found that Michelle might have been killed on February 7, when her roommates said they last saw her, there was some evidence that her body had been left in the desert a week later. Insect samples from the remains were sent to Dr. Michael Douglas, an entomologist at Arizona State University. Based on the age of the insects, Dr. Douglas concluded that insects at the site had first come in contact with Michelle's body around February 14. Also, it rained over 1.38 inches in the area between February 7 and February 19. If her body had been there since February 7, footprints, blood, and cigarette ash found at the scene would likely have been diluted or washed away.

A neighbor described the young men living with Michelle as partying often, shouting in the early morning hours loud enough to disturb her family's sleep. According to this neighbor, eight days after Michelle's reported disappearance, her roommates were partying loudly. Arguing and screams of "knock it off!" and "stop!" could be heard.

In fact, several witnesses stated that they had seen Morales the week after her roommates said she disappeared. Barbara Keller* said she saw Michelle at the Circle K on 35th and Peoria on February 15. Barbara said Michelle was with a short, heavyset Hispanic man. Michelle had an angry conversation on the payphone with someone else. Barbara said she herself had been beaten and assaulted 10 years earlier by an unknown Indian man and abandoned in about the same place where Michelle's body was found. Barbara added that she also spotted Michelle on Valentine's Day with two Circle K employees, though no Circle K employees confirmed this. A man at a Quick Pick convenience store on 67th Avenue and Olive had also seen a woman matching Michelle's description on Valentine's Day. However, without conclusive evidence that Michelle was still alive the following week—or that her roommates were lying—investigators accepted February 7 as the date of her murder.

Cathy Holmes*, a clerk on duty at the Circle K the afternoon of February 7, called police when she heard about the murder. Holmes was used to spotting Michelle at the store two or three times a week, getting in and out of cars with various people. Holmes remembered seeing Michelle between 2 and 4 p.m. on February 7, when Michelle came in and bought a pack of cigarettes and a bag of ice. She was with a white man in a full-sized black truck in good condition. The man got out of the truck, took the ice, put it in the back, and sat in the truck as Michelle paid for it. In a later interview, Holmes told Detective Johnson that after leaving the store, Michelle walked over by the payphone and spoke briefly with a short older man standing in front of his truck. He was forty to fifty years old, possibly with a receding hairline. Holmes said that Michelle looked disgusted as she got in the truck with the man, as if she wished she could be doing something else. Although it was not unusual for Michelle to get into a car with someone, the driver was typically someone closer to her age. It struck Holmes as very unusual to see Michelle drive away with an older man.

Detective Johnson was contacted by Rob Romeski* on February 24. Rob volunteered that he'd been with Michelle early the morning of February 7. He'd driven over to her house after he got off work at Fry's at a little past midnight. Michelle came out and got into his car, and they talked for 30 minutes. She was very positive and happy, eager to find a job. Rob had arranged an appointment for Michelle to come in and apply to work as a bagger at Fry's on Saturday. She never showed up.

When Detective Johnson asked about Phil Stockman's statement that Michelle said she was going roller skating with Rob, he answered that he didn't know how to roller skate and had never gone skating with her. He told Johnson he'd met Michelle just that December, through his friend, Benjamin Cassell,* a neighbor of Michelle's. Rob added that Benjamin now lived in Minnesota but had been visiting his father in Phoenix for the holidays. One of Michelle's roommates described Benjamin Cassell as "weird" and considered it suspicious that Benjamin left town around the time when Michelle was murdered.

Johnson later interviewed Benjamin Cassell in Rochester, Minnesota, by telephone. Benjamin said he'd been visiting at his father's home in Phoenix and left in early February—around the time when Michelle disappeared. According to Benjamin, he started hitchhiking back to Minnesota on January 27, but was arrested the same day in Camp Verde, about 80 miles north of Phoenix. Benjamin had an outstanding warrant for hitchhiking in Tucson, but police held him in Camp Verde for 7 days before transporting him for trial. On February 3, police released Benjamin in Tucson and he hitchhiked back to Phoenix. He arrived around 2 a.m. on February 4 and slept in his father's car until his parents woke up. On February 5, his father drove him back north, past Carefree Highway. Benjamin explained that his father drove past this point because there was a Federal prison nearby, with signs warning motorists not to pick up hitchhikers. Remarkably, the elder Cassell dropped off his son near where Michelle's body was found. Benjamin said he resumed hitchhiking, taking four more days to reach Minnesota.

Oddly, Detective Johnson did not ask Benjamin about his relationship with Michelle Morales. Nor did Johnson interview Benjamin's father or examine the car that Benjamin said he slept in on February 4. And according to Scott Jenkins, the elder Cassell had given two contradictory versions of his son's whereabouts after Michelle disappeared—and both accounts were substantially different from Benjamin's statement. Mr. Cassell reportedly told Scott Jenkins that his son took an airplane to Minnesota on February 7, the date of Michelle's disappearance, and not on February 5, when Benjamin said he left as a hitchhiker. In another interview, Scott Jenkins told police that Benjamin's father claimed to have driven his son to Flagstaff on the day of Michelle's disappearance. Flagstaff is over 120 miles north of the spot where Benjamin told the detective his father dropped him, near the crime scene.

On February 28, 1992, an *Arizona Republic* article reported that the serial "baby-seat rapist" was "dangerous in the extreme." The article went on to report, "Police say the calm, unassuming killer has sexually assaulted at least 8 women and killed two within the past year."[8] That Christorf and Morales might have been murdered by others was a possibility the press, guided by police, did not even consider.

On March 3, Detective Johnson filed a report stating that all Michelle Morales's roommates had been eliminated as suspects. At that time, he added that Benjamin Cassell, Rob Romeski, and Richard Green had also been eliminated as having any involvement. No attempt was made to match the hairs taken from Michelle's face and shirt or the shoe prints found near her body to any of these men. There is no indication that police tried to find the 40- to 50-year-old man with whom Michelle was last seen.

On March 5, Phoenix and Maricopa County investigators requested that the FBI's National Center for the Analysis of Violent Crime do a behavioral analysis on the murders of Christorf and Morales and the "baby-seat rapes." The information that Phoenix investigators gave the FBI exaggerated resemblances among the crimes and presented the rapes as far more violent than the victims' own recollections. Based on this misinformation, Agent Thomas Salp from the Quantico, Virginia, FBI Academy agreed that all the crimes had been committed by the same suspect. Salp visited Phoenix in May 1992 and accompanied Detectives Johnson and Dimodica to the scenes of the assaults against Barnett, Caldwell, and Caporaso and the site where Morales's body was found.

5: Belinda Cronin

JANUARY 24, 1992

When Michelle Morales was saying her last goodbye to her friends, another young Phoenix woman had not been seen in two weeks. On January 24, 1992, Brenda Atchison reported her daughter, Belinda Mae Cronin, missing.

Mrs. Atchison suffered a nightmare of uncertainty since she last talked to 21-year-old Belinda on the phone on January 19. In the months to follow, Mrs. Atchison heard nothing. On June 12, Detective Charles Gregory called, saying he was following up on Belinda's case. Then Gregory asked for the name of Belinda's dentist. A woman's body had been found in the desert, and dental records were necessary for identification.

Four days later, Mrs. Atchison came to the police station with her sister. There, they quickly identified items found near the body, a wristwatch and a boot that belonged to Belinda. Detective Gregory had to tell Mrs. Atchison that dental X-rays confirmed that the dead woman was her daughter.

Belinda Cronin was last seen by her roommates on January 20. She told them she was going to the apartment of Dr. Ben Storm,* a 40-something-year-old osteopath, to get some money from him.

It wasn't until June 11 that Jeffrey Wayne Smith and Blas Ruiz Jr., two security guards patrolling the Central Arizona Project (CAP) canal, found Belinda's body. The CAP canals carry Colorado River water through the desert from Lake Havasu City through northeastern Phoenix to Tucson. The uncovered aqueduct is fenced, but people had been cutting through the fences and committing vandalism off I-17 in the area of Happy Valley Road. Smith caught sight of something by a large tree and walked toward it, investigating an odor he thought might be dead livestock. When the remains appeared to be human, Smith summoned Ruiz. Looking through binoculars from 20 feet away, the men saw a skull with long brown hair. Smith said he'd actually spotted the body approximately two weeks before, but at the time assumed it was a stump. Back in May he'd found a purple purse with a unicorn on it, later identified as Belinda's. The purse was empty, and he'd left it at the scene.

The skeletal remains of Belinda Cronin lay face down in a depression in the ground, as if unearthed by scavenging animals. Belinda's arms and legs were missing, as was most of her soft tissue. Although her arm and leg bones were later recovered, her hands and feet were never found. Belinda wore a crystal on a silver chain around her neck. Her wristwatch, still working; some of her clothing; the purse; and one black boot were recovered nearby.

Six feet above the ground in a tree near Belinda's body, a green sweater was hanging, torn under the arm. In the overhanging branches police also found gray hairs, which might have been pulled from scavenging animals—or from the murderer. A torn piece of white cloth was found about 20 feet from Belinda, in addition to two pieces of duct tape. Also in the area were smashed beer cans, apparently at the scene for some time, and expended shotgun shells. Traces of Belinda's blood were later identified in the sweater found in the tree, but not in the other clothing.

On June 23, Officer Timothy Bryant checked the crime scene with luminal for traces of blood. He found no blood where Cronin lay, or in the surrounding area. The lack of blood traces might indicate that she was murdered elsewhere and later dumped at the site. Where Cronin was killed was especially important because the remains were found in the area where Nancy Caporaso had been raped the year before. If Cronin was already dead when she was brought to the site, someone might have been disguising the murder as another "baby-seat" crime.

An additional fact should have quickly lead police to suspect that Belinda Cronin did not die where she was found. On May 18, Detectives Johnson and Dimodica had escorted FBI Special Agent

Thomas Salp to view the scene east of I-17 and north of Happy Valley Road, where Cronin would be found three weeks later. As they reflected on the rape of Nancy Caporaso at that site, surely three experienced detectives could not have overlooked Belinda's remains and her belongings if she had, in fact, been murdered there on January 20. Belinda might have been held captive elsewhere for some time, or she might have been dead since her disappearance but discarded sometime between the detectives' visit on May 18 and the discovery of her body there on June 11. Another possibility is that her remains had been buried at the scene and unearthed after the detectives' visit, possibly by animals.

Belinda had lived in northeastern Phoenix with her stepbrother, Matt Baker;* her boyfriend, Paul Garces;* and another roommate, Joe Vandecamp.* Unemployed, she did not own a car and was known to hitchhike. Family members told police that Matt Baker had had a sexual relationship with his stepsister, and that he'd violently assaulted Belinda the December before her death. Belinda had confided that she was afraid Matt would kill her. Detectives Gregory and Johnson contacted Matt five days after Belinda's body was found. By then he'd moved to a different apartment, his third change of residence within six months. According to Matt, at about 10:30 p.m. on the evening of January 20, Belinda left to go to the residence of Dr. Storm to obtain money. Half an hour earlier, she'd gone to the apartment of a neighbor, Mark Gordon, to phone Storm. Belinda owed Matt fifty dollars for rent. The two argued that night because Matt refused to lend his small, white pickup truck. He offered to take her wherever she wanted, but she would not go with him. Belinda said she would be back in two hours. Matt said that he and Paul Garces, stayed behind at the apartment.

Belinda had been meeting with Dr. Storm for approximately two months before she went missing. She told her mother she worked as his housecleaner. Matt's feeling was that Belinda might be exchanging sex for money or possibly blackmailing Storm. The most money Matt ever saw her bring home from Dr. Storm was about a hundred dollars. Belinda said Storm had lent her the money.

Matt confirmed that he'd had an ongoing affair with Belinda from the time he was 16 years old until the Christmas before she died. He denied being involved in any way with her disappearance.

For some reason, the detectives did not ask why it was Belinda's mother, and not her roommates, who'd reported her missing. Detectives also deviated from good investigative practice when they failed to interview others who had been among the last to see Belinda alive: Paul Garces; Joe Vandecamp; and neighbor Mark Gordon, from whose apartment she'd phoned Dr. Storm on January 20.

On July 13, more than a month after Belinda's body was found, Detective Gregory finally interviewed Dr. Ben Storm. It must have struck police that the osteopath's apartment was in the general area where several of the "baby-seat" rape victims had been abducted. Also, Storm was likely to have been in the habit of driving north on I-17 from his apartment near a low-rent area of Phoenix to his office near the I-17 freeway, the pattern of behavior of the "baby-seat rapist." Despite these troubling coincidences, the detective's polite questioning of Storm seemed a mere formality.

Storm told Detective Gregory that he first met Belinda Cronin some two years earlier, in the neighborhood near his apartment. Their relationship began eerily like one of the so-called "baby-seat" rapes. Storm had been parked across the street from a Circle K on 7th Street, just south of East Dunlap Avenue. Belinda walked up to Storm's vehicle, he said, and they struck up a conversation. He offered her a ride home and she gave him her phone number that night. Afterwards, Storm phoned Belinda, and she agreed to drive over to his residence in exchange for him paying for her gas. Storm said that the two developed a relationship in which he would pay Belinda forty dollars every time she had sex with him, at either his apartment or hers. For approximately nine months, Storm recalled that he hadn't had any contact with Belinda, but again in January 1992, about two weeks before her disappearance, they had one last sexual encounter. Storm said Belinda told him that she'd become addicted to cocaine during the nine months when he hadn't seen her.

Storm told Detective Gregory that on the evening of January 20, Belinda paged him at a health spa. She asked to see him, but he told her he was busy. After he left the spa, he was planning to go over to his girlfriend's place, where he had a child. He said he'd asked Belinda to contact him later that night.

If Gregory asked Storm whether he did meet with Belinda Cronin that night, or why she'd wanted to see him, there is no mention of it in the police report. Nor did the detective appear concerned that Storm's statement contradicted Matt Baker's in significant respects: Storm said he'd seen Belinda only once in the last nine months of her life, and that he'd repeatedly paid her $40. Storm also claimed that Belinda had last contacted him early in the evening on January 20, with no specific plans to meet. In contrast, Matt told detectives that Belinda obtained as much as $100 from Storm at a time, and that she'd met with Storm several times in the two months before she died. Matt said she phoned Storm twice on January 20 and was definitely on her way to Storm's apartment when Matt last saw her alive at 10:30 p.m.

Someone was lying. Police could have used phone records to determine at what time Belinda spoke to Storm on January 20, but they apparently did not.

Detective Gregory's report did not describe Dr. Storm or detail what kind of car he drove. Nor did Gregory ask Storm whether he was involved in drug use himself, or whether Belinda was in fact blackmailing him.

Storm told Gregory that his relationship with Belinda was not serious and that he was never with her for long. In April 1991, Storm's brother Michael had been living with him, although Michael had returned to New York. Michael Storm had also paid Belinda to have sex at his brother's Phoenix apartment. Gregory did not ask either for contact information for Michael Storm or for details about when and why he'd left Phoenix.

On July 30, Dr. Walker Birkby, forensic anthropologist at the University of Arizona, examined Belinda's remains and estimated that she'd been dead between three and six months. Whether Belinda was murdered where she was found could not be determined. Dr. Birkby noted numerous fractures to her forehead. He advised that she'd been struck once in the forehead, very forcibly, with a blunt object. A baseball bat might have been the murder weapon. When Detective Gregory asked whether a blow from a rock could have killed Belinda, Dr. Birkby agreed that it was possible. However, no bat, rock, or other murder weapon was ever found at the scene.

None of the three murders so hastily attributed to a single "baby-seat rapist" showed any connection to the rapes. None of the murder victims had been seen in the company of a man matching the general description of the rapist, and friends and relatives had identified acquaintances that each of the murdered women had reason to fear.

After the tragic deaths of Christorf, Morales, and Cronin, Phoenix-area detectives struggled to solve the crimes before another woman fell victim. Driven by theory and hunch, the hypothesis of a single rapist-murderer simplified their work. Detectives' motives may have been good, but the result was that the homicide investigations were hasty and superficial.

6: "Welcome to My Little World, Elaine"

OCTOBER-DECEMBER, 1989

"Hello, Scorpio. This is Cancer." It was corny, but it was the best he could do. If she laughed at him, he'd hang up, and that would be the end of it. Though it was October, the receiver was sweaty in his hand. Scott held his breath.

And she did laugh, her voice even sweeter than he remembered. When she spoke, sounding almost as nervous as he was, they got through the formalities quickly. Yes, of course, she remembered him; it had only been two weeks. No, she didn't have plans for Saturday. OK. A movie sounded like fun.

Scott Lehr lived the next few days in a bubble of anticipation, though childcare and work both gave him welcome distraction. But he didn't trust these silly feelings. In past relationships, love had always been beyond his reach. Then on that Sunday afternoon, Elaine* simply walked into his kitchen.

There he'd been on the couch, napping after the morning's work, looking like a lazy slob. A divorced father of 4-year-old twins, he slept when he could. He thought he was dreaming when he saw her. There was something familiar about her, but he couldn't place it. She had long, softly curling hair, the color of a sparrow. Her brown eyes were friendly, though a little shy. They actually sparkled. And her smile. Bright and boundless, with a little gap between her top front teeth. A "liar's gap," Grampa would have called it. But she didn't look like any kind of liar.

When he scrambled up from the couch, she didn't act disgusted that he was still dirty from pruning trees. After an embarrassingly long minute, Scott noticed that cousin Donna was with her, and good old Mitch, jumping up on him rapturously. So it wasn't a dream.

Donna said, "Scott, this is Elaine."

So, Elaine—the "good friend" Donna had gone camping with.

Scott collected himself enough to open the back door for Mitch and let the German shepherd get reacquainted with the yard. Scott was still too befuddled to come up with good manners, but Donna invited Elaine to sit down at the kitchen table.

Donna, who worked with Elaine at Smitty's supermarket, had missed her true calling as a matchmaker. As they made small talk, Donna shamelessly manipulated the conversation along flattering paths. Scott and Elaine warmed up and quickly established that they'd both gone to Washington High School, though she was five years younger. Though she looked so young, in another way Elaine seemed to be the most mature woman he'd ever met. When the subject turned to their astrological signs, Donna embarrassed them by proclaiming how compatible Scorpio was with Cancer. But then Donna and Elaine had to get home.

After he put Lindsey* and Hallie* in bed that night, Scott savored the image of Elaine. As he was about to fall asleep, a vibrant memory shook him awake. He had seen her before, but it wasn't in the halls of Washington High or while shopping at Smitty's. Elaine was the girl in the dream.

He hadn't thought about her since he was twelve. As a kid he secretly treasured that dream: the beautiful friend with long, wavy hair. He could still remember her blue denim skirt, mid-calf length, with delicate white embroidery around the bottom; her white blouse. In the dream, the girl and he never spoke, but they played happily along the railroad tracks. Together they walked back and forth, balancing on the rails for as long as they could. They weren't on his Grampa's farm, but in a desert, like a scene from a Western movie. Then abruptly the girl was sitting on a flatbed car, and the train lurched into motion. She waved to him as the train pulled her further and further away. But she was smiling, and he knew she'd come back someday.

Scott was teary-eyed. Pathetic; a twenty-nine-year-old father, getting all goofy about a little boy's fantasy.

The next day Donna called to give him Elaine's number. Donna was sure that Elaine would like to see him again. Still, it took him two weeks—and prodding from Donna—to work up the nerve to call.

On Saturday they went to a movie with Tom Selleck in the role of an innocent man who gets railroaded into prison by some dirty cops. Before and after the show, Scott found himself filling every second of silence with chatter. He knew he wasn't giving Elaine a chance to say a word, but he couldn't stop himself. When he apologized for being such a motor mouth, she thanked him, adding that she tended to be very quiet when she was nervous. That was perfect, he laughed; since when he got nervous he talked too much. He did listen long enough that night to learn she was divorced, too.

He knew he needed to get to know her slowly. When they arrived at that tense moment at her front door that night, he gave her a quick, soft kiss goodnight. She looked at him expectantly. "That's all," he added, and she smiled her wonderful smile.

Later, when he knew that Elaine wouldn't think he was crazy, he told her about the dream girl on the railroad tracks. She was delighted. His vision turned out to be on the mark: as a child she'd spent time at her grandmother's farm in Skull Valley, where she also played on the railroad tracks.

The two picked up where their forgotten dreams left off, becoming best friends and lovers. Scott had begun to believe that being a father to twin daughters would be his only share of happiness on earth, but suddenly, he had more. Hallie and Lindsey adored Elaine, and she, them. Evenings quickly fell into a peaceful routine. After they'd calmed the girls down and got them to bed, Scott and Elaine had their time together, relaxing in front of the fireplace.

Having grown up listening to his Grampa Bill's band, sometimes even helping out on the drums, Scott felt at home with music. He'd taught himself to play the guitar and loved to improvise. Now it was Elaine who inspired his music. As he strummed and put together a tune, lyrics came to him.

One evening in December, Scott felt as ready as he would ever be for her to hear his song. After the twins were asleep, Scott and Elaine settled by the fireplace. He picked up his guitar. He'd never played in front of anyone but his mother, and for sure never sang publicly, let alone poured out his guts in a love song. And he was well aware that he and Elaine weren't characters in a movie, where the girl was guaranteed to think the guy was way cool for spontaneously breaking into song. Would she run away in stitches, get on the phone, and tell everyone she knew what a moron he was? He was sweating like a hog.

He began with an introduction of open chords that gave him a chance to clear his throat. He could still duck out, but she was smiling, curious. So he went for it:

"When I was a young boy
I saw you in a dream
And I knew someday that I would find you,
Even hard as it seemed."

There were seven verses, but he thought the chorus summed it up pretty well:

"Welcome to my little world, Elaine
Hope that you're here to stay.
I want to be your friend for the rest of my life
Don't know what more I could say."

When he was through, she didn't leave him in tortured suspense. All she said was, "Wonderful," but tears on her face said the rest.

7: A Family

Elaine and Scott married on Valentine's Day, 1990.Their first adventure would be new parenthood. With another child on the way, they needed a bigger home. The sale of Scott's little house went through quickly in August. With Elaine seven months pregnant, they scrambled to find a new place. They ended up renting a four-bedroom townhouse in the Metrocenter area of Phoenix, although the expense worried them. Scott would find more work, they told themselves.

Melissa* was born in October 1990, after 12 hours of labor. Having watched the twins' birth, Scott was a confident coach for Elaine. Still, when he saw their beautiful little girl, he broke into tears.

As an experienced father, Scott could soothe his wife's worries. He was quick to jump in when Melissa needed care, and the couple agreed that he could get the best burps out of her. His major limitation was that he was a sound sleeper and couldn't wake up to help with Melissa's night feedings. Though they were proud to take on the responsibilities of parenting together, sometimes they were overwhelmed by the sudden change to raising three children.

Elaine returned to her job at Smitty's within weeks of giving birth. The family needed every dime both parents could earn. During his childhood in Wisconsin, Scott's uncle had taught him how to prune and care for trees. Before he met Elaine, "Scott's Tree Service" had supported him and the twins, with babysitting help from his mother, Yvonne. He liked being his own boss and having the flexibility of working any daylight hour he chose.

Tree service is a yearlong enterprise in Phoenix, but May through September was Scott's busiest period, when palm trees bloom and become messy. Lovely as palms are, he more than earned his fees climbing up to trim them. Any creature that bites, stings, or fouls you, lives up there. Thinning and shaping olive trees and African sumacs was safer and gave him more professional satisfaction. For the rest of the year he did tree removals, cutbacks, topping, thinning, and shaping. He also contracted with property management companies to do landscape overhauls for rentals. As long as Scott got out and hustled new business, he could usually find enough work to keep the bills paid.

To advertise, he found that his own little fliers—xeroxed on bright-colored paper and cut the size of business cards—were cheap and effective, though time-consuming to distribute. Often Scott would go out late at night with a batch of fliers, while Elaine and the girls slept. After hot desert days, he didn't mind walking the nice neighborhoods in the cool of night. He'd park his truck at the edge of a subdivision and walk up one side of the street and down the other, taping little flyers on all the mailboxes. First thing in the morning, a potential customer couldn't overlook Scott's colorful message. Most would at least read it. He often got calls in the morning from people wanting him to come give an estimate.

The winter months were sometimes lean, but Elaine and Scott made the best of a tight budget. Although they couldn't afford recreation that involved admission fees or travel, they enjoyed each other's company. When their daughters were safely asleep, the couple liked to take short walks in the neighborhood. One night Elaine insisted on dragging Scott out for a walk, even though it was starting to rain. The shower became a downpour. The two laughed as the cool water pelted them and danced barefoot like kids in the flooded street. "My bud," they called each other.

The Lehrs stayed in the townhouse until after New Year's, when they had to admit that the four-bedroom was too expensive. Temporarily they settled for an apartment near Smitty's while they saved for a better place. After nearly six months, Scott found a fixer-upper house in West Phoenix for sale on surprisingly easy terms. Scott and Elaine couldn't believe their luck. The monthly payments were again a bit more than they could afford, but in the excitement of buying a house together they overlooked that. Elaine had just accepted a good part-time job at U.P.S., a short drive from the house. In the summer of 1991 they moved into their own home. It was in poor repair, with peeling paint and bare desert for a yard. Still, they thought their hard work could get it looking cozy.

The first rainstorm in their new home taught them otherwise. As the rain drummed merrily on the roof, the family room flooded with an inch of water. Water was pouring in where the ceiling and the wall had pulled apart. The house had a serious crack in the foundation and one side of the building was sinking.

Rainstorms are not frequent in Phoenix, so the couple hoped they could live with the leaks until they could afford to move. Their home was close to the elementary school, and the convenient location would outweigh other problems. However, when Scott took Lindsey and Hallie to register for school that year, more problems surfaced. He was frustrated that the school administration would not allow the twins to be in the same first-grade classroom. The girls had been in separate classes for kindergarten, and that had not been good for them. Instead of encouraging their independence, it seemed to make them jealous and competitive. They were unusually close sisters, and Scott wanted them to keep that bond. He enrolled them in first grade across town, at the grade school that both Elaine and Dee Dee had attended. There, the twins could be in the same classroom.

Phoenix has the high crime rate characteristic of boomtowns, and that crime was beginning to cast its shadow on the family's lives. In late summer 1991, their gray-blue plastic baby-seat was stolen from the car. It wasn't expensive; Scott had bought it second-hand. Still, replacing it with a maroon car seat from a garage sale was just one more demand on their limited resources. Even worse, Scott and Elaine couldn't trust that their children were safe at home. Chilling gang graffiti staked a claim to every available wall in the neighborhood. The family often heard gunfire nearby, and a grocery store on the next street over was robbed repeatedly. At least once a week, they huddled under the roar of police helicopters, with spotlights scanning below in search of dangerous fugitives. After only four months, they let the mortgage payments on their dream house lapse.

In November 1991 the Lehrs moved into an apartment at 8848 North 8th Street, a short drive to the girls' school. It was only a two-bedroom, but Melissa and the twins could share a room. Briefly it seemed that the family had a home that would be adequate until their financial situation improved.

But it didn't take long to learn that their new neighborhood was even more crime-ridden than the last. Twice vandals broke into Scott's truck. The first time, they stole his chainsaw, the most expensive tool he had. The next time, they broke the windows on the camper shell. Maybe it was just destructive kids, but the damage weighed heavily on a family barely making ends meet. One afternoon, in broad daylight, police chased a suspect past the front window, right where the twins usually played. If the girls had been out there, they could have been killed. In December Elaine and Scott watched "Silent Witness" spots on the news, dramatizing the assault of thirteen-year-old Alison Brooks by an unknown suspect. Although their daughters were much younger than the "baby-seat" victims, hearing about those unsolved crimes added to their fear that Phoenix wasn't a safe place to raise children. Finally one night, as Scott and his daughters sat on the sofa watching TV, someone sent a rock crashing through the picture window, showering them with broken glass. Elaine and Scott knew they couldn't stay in that neighborhood, but after four moves in the two years they'd been together, it was hard to uproot again.

Liberated from years in dead-end jobs, Elaine excelled at her work at U.P.S. It was a part-time, second-shift job from 3:00 p.m. to 11:00 p.m., two or three days a week. Elaine watched the girls while Scott did tree service from early morning until early afternoon. He took the evening parenting shift when she worked at

U.P.S. While that limited their time together, the couple saved on childcare.

On December 19, 1991, it was raining hard as Elaine rushed to work. When a car in front of her slowed, she couldn't stop. Before she was even aware that she'd crashed, a truck hit her from behind. No one was injured, but the sight of her car made Elaine sick. Though already eleven years old when Scott bought it, the 1979 Chevy Caprice had been reliable. A beige car with a black vinyl top, it was decent-looking on the road and nice and clean inside. But the crash had cracked the hood and broken away the top center part of the grill and trim. The passenger side parking light and mirror were broken off and the back bumper and trunk dented. The car was drivable, technically, but the steering wheel was bent forward and the front bench seat no longer locked in place. It slid back and forth alarmingly as the car accelerated and braked. After the insurance settled for $2000 replacement value, Scott cleaned up the Chevy, put a for-sale sign in the windshield, and parked it in a Walgreens parking lot near their apartment, Days later, a man bought it for $500 cash. Scott signed over the title but didn't keep a receipt.

It was hard losing the car just before Christmas, but they got a rental for Elaine to drive to work in while they looked for an affordable replacement.

Even before the accident, the couple had agreed to put what little they money they could spare for Christmas into gifts for the children and to keep presents for each other simple that year. Scott had learned to constantly check out carport sales, as they call garage sales in Phoenix. With a good eye for quality, he also visited auction houses, sometimes finding bargains he could resell at a small profit. He'd picked up household furnishings, clothes, and toys for his daughters that he could never have afforded otherwise. Even though they were low on money, he wanted to give his wife something on their second Christmas together. Elaine had mentioned that she could use accessories to dress up a little for work. When she unwrapped a box of jewelry that Scott had found at a second-hand sale, she was as appreciative as if he'd given her gold and precious stones. Earlier in December, he'd given her something even better and wished he'd known then how lean Christmas would be: he brought home an old ring that appeared to be set with genuine diamonds. The band was broken, and the ring was just one piece in a little box of costume jewelry he bought for $5 or $10. He took the ring to a pawnshop to see if he'd made a lucky find. The pawnbroker said the ring was mass produced and offered Scott $5 for it.

By February 5, 1992, they'd found a serviceable car for sale by a neighbor of Elaine's parents, Carol* and Pete*. It was a little gray Nissan Sentra, a 1986 two-door, for only $200. The price was low because the Nissan was badly banged up on the passenger side. Though not much to look at, it was mechanically sound and got great mileage, especially compared to the old Chevy. Scott did some repairs himself, but the front passenger-side door remained buckled and hard to open.

The twins' seventh birthday was coming up on February 24, and to have time for a more leisurely get-together, Elaine and Scott invited their family over on February 23, a Sunday.

After a day in the park, Yvonne came to the apartment for a birthday dinner. Carol and Pete brought a video camera to record the occasion. While Elaine ran the children's party, Scott barbecued burgers. Lit up with energy after cake and ice cream, the twins opened their presents. They were high-spirited little girls, but unspoiled and loving.

8: Meredith Porter

FEBRUARY 23, 1992

After Yvonne, Carol, and Pete went home, Scott put his daughters to bed. Worn out from a party with lively children, he fell asleep by 10. Donna sat up late visiting with Elaine in the living room. While the friends talked and Scott slept, a teenager in downtown Phoenix faced the ordeal of her life.

At 14, Meredith Porter* was struggling with more problems than most girls her age. She'd run away from home the month before and dropped out of school. She had a court date coming up for a shoplifting charge. Now she was in and out of her parents' home, often staying overnight with friends. Her mother thought Meredith had a boyfriend.

The details of what happened to Meredith that Sunday night are sketchy. What can be confirmed is that around 7:30 on Monday morning, February 24, a man driving a dump truck stopped to help a young woman wandering 40 miles northwest of Phoenix. She wore an orange and white striped pullover and panties, black socks and one shoe. Blood covered her face and legs. She walked to the truck and opened the door. Hundreds of cactus spines pierced her body. Groaning in pain, she asked the driver to take her somewhere where she could use the restroom. Instead, he called the police.

Before she was airlifted to the hospital, Meredith Porter was able to give a few details to the first officer on the scene, Deputy Antone Jacobs. Meredith told Jacobs that, at about 7 p.m. the evening before, she was walking at Central and 19th Avenue, a neighborhood that police considered a "vice area." A young man in a newer gray pick-up, maybe a Nissan, offered to take her to South Mountain to ride his horses. She went with him. The truck had a gray interior. Meredith described the 20 to 30-year-old man as 6' 1" and of average build. He had blue-green eyes, a light brown mustache, reddish brown hair a little past his shoulders, and a beard from his sideburns to his chin, full at the chin like a goatee. He said his name was James. They drove for an hour until she was lost. Then he threatened to leave her out in the mountains if she didn't give him a blowjob. After she complied, he hit her on the head and abandoned her.

At the hospital that morning, Meredith also told Detective Bob Powers that a man in a newer grey pickup truck abducted and assaulted her.

Meredith needed to have a broken finger set, lacerations stitched, and hundreds of cactus spines removed from her body. The lost teeth, cuts, and bruises suffered as she stumbled and fell caused her severe pain. A CT scan showed no skull or facial fractures.

Police gave Meredith a day to recover. On Tuesday morning, Detectives Michael Johnson, Todd Bates, and Jerry Bruen interviewed her in the hospital—her third conversation with different investigators. The detectives described Meredith as "badly beaten," a victim of "attempted homicide" although there was no evidence that the assailant intended to kill her. Alone at night in an isolated area, he'd certainly had the opportunity. As recorded by Detectives Bates and Bruen, Meredith's recollections were startlingly different from what she'd told Deputy Jacobs the day before. She now said she accepted a ride with the suspect around 11:15 p.m., not 7 p.m. He picked her up at Indian School Road and Central Avenue, a slightly different location. And now she described the suspect as clean-cut, with short brown hair, combed straight back; with a light mustache and unshaven chin. Now she described his clothing differently, too: a black polo shirt and black shorts. The day before she'd recalled a black shirt with a Mickey Mouse logo, and blue shorts.

Most crucial to the investigation of the crime, Meredith now said the suspect drove a gray car, probably a four-door, not the gray truck she'd reported to police twice before. And now she added that the rapist had a baby-seat in the back seat of his car: blue with chrome. Before this third interview, Meredith had not described the man who assaulted her as in any way resembling the "baby-seat" suspect.

Meredith added a flood of additional details. She said that she'd asked "James" if he had any children. "Too many," he told her. She went with him because she thought he would take her to see his three horses. He seemed to know exactly where he was going as they drove away from the city. They passed a sign that said "Pleasant Lake Recreation Area" and turned onto a dirt road. Near a sign that said "Pleasant Trails" they parked. When he asked her for a blowjob, she refused.

"Listen darling, unless you want to stay out here, you have to do what I want," he told her.

She said she didn't even know him.

"Weren't you going to my house wanting to sleep with me?"

She denied it, but he repeated that, unless she wanted him to leave her there, she'd better obey. Terrified of being lost in the desert, she performed oral sex. Then he reached over to her seat to put the back down. She said the back of her seat would not recline until he removed the baby-seat from behind it. He took off her skirt and panties and raped her vaginally.

Afterwards they sat in the car for some time, with neither of them talking. Finally he asked her to go for a walk. He told her if she cooperated, he wouldn't leave her. He made her walk down with him into a rocky wash she thought was about 12 feet from the car. He was carrying a flashlight. In the wash, he told her to sit on a rock and give him oral sex again. Then he said, "Let's go," and she began to walk ahead of him. She dropped her sweater. As she bent to pick it up, he either threw rocks at her or hit her with a rock or the flashlight. She tried to cover her head with her arms, but she was knocked unconscious.

The next thing Meredith remembered was waking up in the wash. It was still dark. As she made her way out she could hear traffic. When she finally reached the roadway, about a half-mile south of the crime scene, it was daylight. A truck driver pulled over to help her.

On February 26, Detectives Bruen and Bates spoke to Meredith again; this time, with her father and grandfather present. Looking through a vehicle identification encyclopedia, she identified a 1988 Chevrolet Spectrum as being "just like" the crime vehicle. She also remembered that the handles on the outside of the car pulled upwards. In this interview, she admitted that the suspect had told her he was "looking for a date." She said she'd answered that she didn't know what that meant. After raping her, he said, "I hope you are on birth control, because I just came inside of you."

Meredith gave police several new and distinctive details during this interview. She said the suspect smoked marijuana in the wash. He appeared to be educated, and his chest was muscular. His eyebrows were very dark and met in the middle of the forehead. He had a smooth complexion, and large, smooth hands with very little hair. Most interesting, he had big, protruding ears. Evidence technician Don Ely met with Meredith to create a composite sketch of the suspect, which she agreed was a good likeness.

That Meredith's recollections changed remarkably every time she spoke to police should have raised a red flag. Did each successive interview reveal more of the truth, or lead the investigation further astray? When her description of the rapist sounded more like the "baby-seat" suspect each time she spoke to police, they should have weighed the possibility that her memories were being contaminated in the course of their interviews. Pioneering criminal portraitist Jeanne Boylan has revealed how conventional police methods can actually prompt victims to forget what they have actually experienced.[9]

In addition to the possibility that police interviews corrupted Meredith's real memories, the theory of a single "baby-seat rapist" was prominent in local news reports. Only four days before Meredith was assaulted, the media had rushed to blame the murder of Michelle Morales on the "baby-seat rapist." Meredith might have unconsciously repeated details she'd heard on the news.

Not only were Meredith's recollections of the suspect and the vehicle used in the attack inconsistent, the evidence collected after the attack was also of questionable reliability. Police first struggled even to find the crime scene in the desert, although they later identified the site as less than half a mile north of state Route 74, milepost 12.6 or 12.7. Maricopa County Detective Steve Gerlach searched for the crime scene for five hours soon after Meredith was found. Sergeant Pendergast attempted to locate the scene with scenting dogs as well. Joining in the hunt for the crime scene on that day were Sergeant Weiss and four Lake Patrol Deputies. In the area Meredith had directed them to, the seven police could not find the crime scene. The lack of evidence was not surprising, because there had recently been rain in the area.

As police searched for the crime scene, Detective Powers was at the hospital and drew a vial of Meredith's blood for typing. On the following afternoon, at least 36 hours after the assault, detectives Gerlach, Bates, and Bruen made another search for the crime scene. This time, within an hour they reported finding evidence of the assault and summoned technician Ely to process the scene. Although seven police accompanied by highly trained dogs had not been able to find evidence of the assault on the day before, Bruen, Bates, and Gerlach quickly produced a 6.6 pound rock "covered" with Meredith's blood. Ely also processed a generic cigarette butt, which might have been Meredith's, and a Marlboro cigarette, both found seven feet from the rock. In addition, the detectives reported finding a trail of blood through the dry creek bed and Meredith's sweater, covered with cactus spines.

Although the Marlboro cigarette and the bloody rock (which might have been used to strike Meredith, although she'd said the attacker might have hit her with a flashlight) were another similarity to some of the reported "baby-seat" attacks, even those similarities were vague. The "baby-seat" suspect threw stones at one of the victims, but he had not used a rock to beat anyone. Only Alison Brooks said the man who attacked her smoked Marlboros; Amy Perry distinctly remembered Camels; and Nancy Caporaso did not notice that he smoked at all. And Meredith had said the attacker smoked marijuana in the wash, unlike all the other attacks. The strongest evidence linking the crime against Meredith to the "baby-seat" attacks was that Meredith said the rapist carried a baby seat in his car, a detail she mentioned only in her third interview. Also, the man who attacked her had claimed to own horses, like the suspect in two of the earlier attacks.

In Meredith's case, some evidence pointed away from the "baby-seat" rapist. Serial rapists tend to favor a particular physical type of target, and Meredith did not fit the pattern. All of the alleged "baby-seat" victims were small-framed, but Meredith was a large young woman, 5'8" and over 200 pounds. She had also given police details, such as protuberant ears, that contradicted earlier descriptions of the "baby-seat" rapist.

The scene of the crime against Meredith was also far different: 40 miles northwest of the earlier crimes and in a remote recreational area, rather than the sparsely developed outskirts of Phoenix. Also, Meredith said she'd been assaulted both in the suspect's car and outdoors. In the "baby-seat" crimes the victims were raped inside the vehicle only. In addition, the suspect in several of the earlier attacks choked the victims, but the man who attacked Meredith did not. He took his time, walking with her into the wash and smoking marijuana. In the "baby-seat" cases, the suspects quickly released the victims and fled.

Finally, the man who raped Meredith was driving a different vehicle. Although the first two times she talked to police Meredith said the suspect was driving a gray Nissan pickup truck, she later said that he was driving a gray four-door compact car, just like a 1988 Chevrolet Spectrum. Neither vehicle could be confused with the large white or tan car reported in the "baby-seat" crimes.

The number of differences between the crime against Meredith and the "baby-seat crimes" suggested a different assailant. If Meredith's memory of a baby-seat in his car was accurate, a copycat criminal was a strong possibility. Yet, rather than pursuing that likelihood, police assumed that Meredith was another victim of the "baby-seat" rapist, and the press followed their lead. Four days after the attack, the *Arizona Republic* reported the rape of Meredith Porter as another in the series committed by the "rapist-slayer prowling freeways."[10]

As investigators focused on one theoretical serial predator, the unique characteristics of the crime were forgotten. Police portrayed the force used against the girl as more extreme than she herself described. After a thorough examination on February 24, Dr. Carl Otte diagnosed her injuries as multiple contusions and abrasions, hundreds of cactus spines embedded in her skin, facial trauma with lacerations, and a fractured finger. However, in a VICAP Crime Analysis Report that the Maricopa County Sheriff's office filed with the FBI, Detective Bruen described the blunt force injury to Meredith as "severe," defined for purposes of the report as "injury which in itself could have caused death."

In overstating the force used against Meredith, police implicitly acknowledged that the crime did not fit the pattern they expected to see from a single suspect: a progression of increasing violence. It's also possible that police followed a deliberate strategy of inflating charges that might be brought against the assailant. Aware that they could not convict anyone on the basis of Meredith's contradictory statements, they could use the threat of an attempted murder charge to pressure him to confess to rape.

9: New Leads

MARCH 5-26, 1992

On March 5, 1992, Sara Chavez,* age 31, called police after a man fitting the description of the "baby-seat" rapist offered her a ride. He was driving a gold Oldsmobile with a baby seat, she reported, when he stopped and spoke to her at 19th Avenue and Wood Drive, three and a half miles south of where Nancy Caporaso and Alison Brooks were picked up, also on 19th Avenue. Officers looking for the suspect stopped Eldon McCoy* in a tan 1979 Oldsmobile 4-door, Arizona plate GKN-352. McCoy closely resembled the "baby-seat" suspect some of the victims had described. Curly brown-haired and hazel-eyed McCoy was 5'9" and weighed 185 pounds. The unshaven face of the 38-year-old man contrasted with his polite manner. McCoy told the officers he'd left his driver's license at home, and he was found to be driving on a suspended license.

Police had spotted McCoy leaving the general area of 19th Avenue and Wood Drive, but McCoy told Detective Petrosino he had not been there. McCoy said he'd just come from 38th Street and Bell Road, where he worked as a cook. He was not working that day, he said, but had dropped by his workplace to check his schedule. His workplace was over nine miles away, but McCoy explained vaguely that he was running errands when he was stopped. The car was not his; it belonged to his in-laws. His wife, Sharon, had been driving the car for 6 or 7 months. McCoy said he had a pickup truck, which was not running. Police apparently did not closely examine the car; nor did they examine McCoy's truck.

McCoy told police they would find a compressor in the trunk of the car he was driving. Instead, they found a saddle, reminiscent of the rape of Meredith Porter less than two weeks before, as well as the rapes of Churchill, Caporaso, and Brooks, all of whom said the man who attacked them claimed to own horses. McCoy refused to say anything else until he had a court-appointed attorney.

Sharon McCoy* told Detective Petrosino she did not believe her husband was involved in the rapes or homicides. She said that they were having financial problems and that Eldon had an arrest in Prescott for DUI and other traffic citations.

Police asked several victims of the "baby-seat" crimes to look at photos of the car McCoy had been driving. They denied that the car was the one used in the crimes. Police also compared the tires of McCoy's car to photos of tire tracks at some of the crime scenes. The patterns did not match. And so, despite the facts that McCoy looked like the suspect described by several of the "baby-seat" victims, rode horses, was stopped in the area of what appeared to be an attempt at another such crime, and had lied to police at least twice, they did not consider him a suspect.

In mid March, Detective Michael Johnson interviewed Carly Sweet,* who'd been assaulted over a year earlier, March 3, 1991. No arrest was ever made, and the attack was similar to that against Nancy Caporaso a month later. As she'd come out of the Deja-Vu bar that day, 26-year-old Carly met a man on the northeast corner of 27th Avenue and Van Buren. He drove out of the parking lot of an auto repair business and called her over to his car, a white Cadillac El Dorado. Carly frankly admitted to police that the suspect asked her if she was working as a prostitute, "looking for a date." For $60 she agreed to drive to his home to have sex.

As they drove, the man said he liked living out in the area of Happy Valley Road, where it was quiet. He asked Carly if she'd ever had any bad experiences in her work. The question struck her as strange, but she told him about a time when a man pulled a gun on her. Her client continued north on the I-17 freeway and exited at Happy Valley Road. As they traveled east on Happy Valley, he pointed to a house and said, "Oh, no; my wife is home." Carly asked if he'd brought her all the way out there for nothing. He suggested that they drive out into the desert near some power lines, and she consented.

He stopped the car near the place where Nancy Caporaso would later be raped. There, he paid Carly and had sex with her in the back seat. Carly said that the suspect had behaved normally until after he climaxed. Then he grabbed her by the neck and pressed his thumbs into her throat. He laughed as she lost consciousness. She woke up on the ground, nude, as would Nancy Caporaso.

Although Carly earlier told police that the suspect's car resembled a white Cadillac El Dorado, when Johnson spoke to her the following year she identified a 1978 four-door Chevy Impala as the most similar model. The interior was green, she recalled. Carly said she saw the suspect about a month after the incident, driving the same vehicle. She thought his license place was ADW-085.

Johnson showed Carly the composite sketch of the so-called "baby-seat" rapist that was released in April of 1992. She said he resembled the man who attacked her, except that the face in the drawing was vicious and frightening. The man who choked her wasn't mean looking, she stressed. Like Nancy Caporaso, Carly described the assailant as only 5'6" to 5'8", substantially shorter than other victims recalled. As Carly herself was 5'6", she would have been a reliable judge that the man was not much taller. Carly added that the same man had also assaulted one of her friends.

It was not long before another woman was added to the list that investigators considered victims in the "baby-seat" series. On the evening of March 26, 1992, 29-year-old Teresa Martinez* was walking in the area of 24th Avenue and Buckeye, near the Saddlehorn Bar. That would have been a little more than a mile from where Carly Sweet was picked up, near another bar. A man driving a small, dark gray pickup truck offered Teresa a ride home. She accepted. Later she would describe him as white, around 40 years old. She first said that he was thin and stood 5'8", although in later police interviews she described him as around 6' tall, and of medium build. His hair was dark with some gray in it, and he had a mustache with one or two day's growth of stubble, but no beard. His hair was very straight and combed back, shoulder length in the rear. He had no scars or acne. She noticed that he wore a long-sleeved business shirt with blue vertical stripes. His pick-up was a Nissan hard body with burgundy cloth bench seats. There were cardboard boxes in the bed of the truck. The man smelled of alcohol, and he did not smoke.

The man told Teresa he had a ranch and seven horses near the north end of town. Once she was in his truck, he made a U-turn, heading back toward the freeway. She asked him why he was not driving toward her place. "You're not going home," he told her. "You know you're going to be raped, don't you?" When she begged for him to let her go, he said something like, "I'd rather rape you now and get what I can before I have to do a lot of time in prison."

Teresa started to cry. "Don't," he said. "You're gonna make me upset." He put his hand into her shirt as he drove. She was afraid to resist. He took her north on the freeway and exited at Happy Valley Road. He said he couldn't take her to his house because his roommate was home now. In a desolate area near a construction yard he stopped and ordered her to take off her clothes. He forced her to perform oral sex on him and then raped her vaginally and anally.

When a passing vehicle surprised him, he told Teresa, "We're going to go somewhere else so we can finish this." After being raped repeatedly, the terrified woman wondered what was left for him to "finish" but her life itself. In a more isolated place, surely he would kill her. She struggled to break out of the truck, but he choked her until she was too dizzy to move.

Teresa pretended to cooperate as the man drove back toward I-17, as if to travel north. When he slowed down to turn onto the freeway ramp, she got the door open. As she jumped from the moving truck, he grabbed for her throat, tearing a crystal pendant from her necklace. He sped off. Teresa dragged herself off the ground, amazed to be alive.

The *Arizona Republic* reported as a matter of fact that the unidentified woman who escaped from an abductor on March 26 was the presumed serial rapist's latest sexual-assault victim.[11] The *Republic's* source for that assumption would have been area police. Investigators of the "baby-seat" crimes must have been struck by the fact that Teresa Martinez escaped from the rapist as he drove his truck toward the scenes of two recent murders: the location 6 miles north, where Michelle Morales had been found dead; or, even closer, 3 miles away, where Belinda Cronin's body would be found in June. They must have recalled that Michelle Morales was reportedly last seen alive with a suspect similar to the man who abducted Teresa: a white man in his forties. Having revealed to Teresa that he expected to be sent to prison soon, he was likely guilty of other sexual assaults and might also have been the murderer of Cronin, Christorf, or Morales.

Martinez was a promising witness. She told Detective Frank Dimodica that she was certain she could identify the suspect. In addition, the rapist had left biological evidence. Astonishingly, however, there is no indication that Maricopa County investigators ever analyzed that evidence. For reasons lost to the public record, the investigation stopped cold. In the months ahead, police were able to locate the truck Martinez described and its owner, but they apparently did not ask him for a blood sample. His hair was not compared to the hairs that may have been left by the man who murdered Michelle Morales. The driver of the truck was never investigated as a suspect in the homicides or the other rapes. He was not even charged with the rape of Teresa Martinez.

Why the Phoenix Police and the Maricopa County Sheriff's Office ignored a suspect in a violent crime spree is a matter for speculation, but the events of the following months offer one explanation. It's a tragic example of what can go wrong when those entrusted with law enforcement bend rules, distort facts, and ultimately lose sight of the truth.

10: "There Was Too Much Alike"

Working to apprehend their suspect in the spring of 1992, investigators faced a complex puzzle. Two or more rapists might have committed somewhat similar crimes in 1991-92. Carly Sweet, Nancy Caporaso, and Teresa Martinez described the rapist as a shorter man, 5'6" to 5'9". None of them saw a baby-seat in his vehicle. Teresa Martinez recalled a suspect in a gray pickup. The man or men who attacked Carly, Nancy, and Teresa had been drinking alcohol before the attack but did not smoke cigarettes. Several other victims reported that the suspect smoked and that he drank soft drinks. The man who raped Emily Caldwell smoked filter cigarettes and drank a wine cooler, and Meredith Porter's assailant smoked marijuana.

The man or men who raped Mona Barnett, Emily Caldwell, and Amy Perry let victims go without further violence. The shorter man, who'd attacked Nancy Caporaso, Carly Sweet, and Teresa Martinez within a mile-square area, was more dangerous. Although his pleasant manner tricked the women into getting into his car, after assaulting them he abruptly became more violent and choked them. That man might have been capable of murder, although it was equally likely that Margaret Christorf, Michelle Morales, and Belinda Cronin, had been killed by other men they knew. After all, there was no sign of choking in any of the murders; the victims appeared to have been bludgeoned. No evidence linked the murders or the rapes involving choking to the "baby-seat" attacks; it was only the investigators' intuition that one man had committed them all.

Despite physical and behavioral differences among the suspects, differences in their MO, and the different vehicles used in the crimes, investigators continued to be guided by the theory that a single suspect was guilty of the series of rapes and homicides. From April 1 to April 12, 1992, Frank Dimodica oversaw a decoy operation in which women of the general physical type of the presumed "baby-seat" victims (except for Meredith Porter) strolled the streets where the victims had been picked up. But no one matching the description of the unknown predator had taken the bait.

Rather than exploring the evidence that several perpetrators drove different vehicles, the investigation adhered to the assumption that one man had committed all the crimes attributed to the "baby-seat" rapist, but that he owned more than one vehicle—the large tan or white four-door car recalled by most of the suspects, the light-blue, mid-sized American car used in the attack against Mona Barnett, the gray Nissan pickup truck described by Teresa Martinez and Meredith Porter, and the gray four-door Chevy Spectrum later described by Meredith Porter. Although it was possible that a perpetrator stole, borrowed, or rented vehicles used in the crimes, detectives began with the hope that he owned them all.

On June 22, 1992, Detective Scoville of the Maricopa County Sheriff 's Office received a printout from the Arizona Department of Public Safety listing all General Motors vehicles with a partial license plate beginning ADW whose registered owner also owned a Nissan. Scoville found only one person who met all the criteria: The General Motors vehicle was a 1979 Chevy Caprice, Arizona plate ADW-015. The Nissan was a 1986 Sentra, a two-door sedan. The owner was Scott Alan Lehr. What's more, Lehr had sold the Caprice in December 1991 and bought the Sentra in February 1992, the month when Meredith Porter was raped.

Investigators were elated. "There was too much alike. There had to be a connection," Sergeant Jordan Barber would soon tell a reporter for the *Arizona Republic*[12]

It looked as though they had their man. At 32 years old, Scott Lehr was within the age range of the unknown suspect, and his driver's license photo showed a man resembling the vague composite sketch scrapped together from victims' varying accounts. His license records gave his employer as Scott's Tree Service. Self-employed, it seemed. A tree-trimmer would have the freedom to set his own hours. Probably he'd have less work in the fall and winter, when most of the crimes had been committed. And surely he'd be busiest in the summer, when none of the baby-seat crimes had occurred. That Scott had changed his address four times in the last couple of years added to the impression that he was guilty. Moving frequently is known to be typical behavior of serial killers of the brutal "disorganized" type. However, such offenders are also low-IQ misfits who live alone. Further investigation would show that Scott did not fit that profile. Also, none of the crimes in the series was characteristic of a disorganized lust-murder attack, a crime of rage accompanied by torture, maiming, or dismemberment of the victim.

The auto-records match seemed to be a lucky breakthrough, however. On the other hand, some facts that should have urged caution in identifying Scott as the perpetrator were obvious from the start. First, even assuming the rapist used cars he had not stolen or borrowed, the fundamental criteria for the records search—owning both a General Motors vehicle and a Nissan vehicle—were fatally flawed. Meredith Porter had identified a Nissan truck or a four-door Chevy Spectrum sedan, not a two-door Nissan Sedan.

Second, Scott hadn't owned the Chevy Caprice since December 1991, but someone meeting the description of the "baby-seat" suspect had tried to pick up Sara Chavez in a similar vehicle, with a baby-seat, on March 5, 1992.

In addition, Scott's license plate number for the Caprice, Arizona ADW-015, was not a plate implicated in any of the crimes. Under hypnosis, Alison Brooks identified the license number of the man who had raped her as something like AZW or ACW-529. Emily Caldwell clearly remembered the plate number of the suspect in her case as ADW-519 or ADW-515. Emily was sure of all the numbers except the last: it was either 519 or 515. What's more, Phoenix police would soon learn that one of the exact plates being sought, ADW-519, had been stolen and could not be accounted for during the time period of the "baby-seat" crimes. That plate number had been issued to a vehicle that was subsequently repossessed, and the plates disappeared sometime between February 11 and March 7, 1991. Emily was raped on February 23. The missing plates were never found. Obviously, the "baby-seat" rapist could not be located through motor vehicle records if he was driving with stolen plates.

Then, the physical description of the suspect didn't quite fit: at 6 feet, 1 inch, Scott was taller than the suspect they were looking for, if one man had committed all the crimes in question. The victims' estimates of height had ranged from 5'6" to 6'1" with only one victim giving 6'2" as a possible upper limit on the suspect's height. Nor did Scott have the large, protuberant ears or blue eyes that Meredith Porter recalled. His eyes were brown and his ears normal. Scott's hair was not curly, as some victims had stated, and he'd never worn the long beard that Amy Perry remembered.

Police would also discover that Scott was a loving husband and father with no criminal record. Although the image of an apparently decent citizen who turns out to be a vicious criminal haunts our imaginations, statistically it's much more likely for rapists to have a history of assault, robbery, larceny, or serious traffic offenses. Finally, Scott had a solid alibi for the key crime in the series: the Meredith Porter case, the only case possibly involving a car resembling a Nissan Sentra. On the night of February 23, after his twin daughters' birthday party, Scott was sound asleep, with his wife and his cousin awake in the living room in full view of the apartment's only door.

All the same, the principal investigators of the "baby-seat" crimes lost interest in any other suspects. They convinced themselves that because Scott stopped driving his Chevy Caprice in December 1991 he must be the "baby-seat" rapist, who'd used a tan, white, or light brown car. They would soon learn, however, that Scott's Caprice was actually cream-colored, almost yellow, and had a black vinyl top. This crucial fact would be ignored. Too early, investigators laid down all their evidence for a dozen crimes on a wager that only one man committed them all. They bet on Scott Lehr as that man.

On June 23, Detective Bates showed two photos of Scott Lehr to Meredith Porter in a photo lineup. Meredith agreed that one of the pictures of Scott generally resembled the man who attacked her, although she couldn't positively identify him. That afternoon, Phoenix police put the Lehrs' apartment on North 8th Street under surveillance. Spotting Scott Lehr for the first time, Detectives Randy Chapman and Charles Gregory noted that he vaguely met some of the victims' descriptions: a white man with two or three days' growth of beard and a pot belly.

At around 6:40 pm, detectives watched Scott leave the apartment and get in an old yellow Ford pickup truck. He drove to an address on West Georgia Street, where he put two small bicycles in the back of the truck and two little blond girls got in. They bought food at a Taco Bell drive-through and returned home. A few minutes past 8:00 p.m., a young woman with long brown hair arrived in the gray Nissan Sentra.

Seeing the Lehr's Sentra, the detectives might have been puzzled. There was a baby-seat in it: not the blue one in the back seat that Meredith and other victims had remembered, but instead a maroon child's seat, in the front. Even more confusing, the passenger side of Scott's car was very obviously damaged. The area around the passenger-side door was dented; and the rear of the car on the passenger side was in bad shape: the gas tank door and the trunk could not be closed completely, and a chunk of the rear bumper was missing. And the damage was rusted; the car had looked that way for some time. If this had been the car used in the attack against Meredith four months earlier, surely she would have noticed its condition.

The following morning, Scott put a couple of quarts of oil in the truck, hitched on a trailer, and drove north on 7th Street, then west on Happy Valley Road to the Skunk Creek City Landfill. Detectives followed him. At the landfill Scott dumped pine tree trimmings and other trash from the trailer. Officers went through the trash Scott left at the dump and found a discarded Marlboro cigarette pack, a *Prescott Courier* newspaper, and a landfill fee ticket.

Just before 3 p.m., an older woman drove up to the Lehr's apartment in a white 2-door Oldsmobile. She went inside with three little girls. Police ran the plates on the Oldsmobile and found that the car was registered to an Yvonne Lehr.

At 3:25 p.m., the young woman came out and got into the Nissan. Detectives followed her to the U.P.S. building on 37th Avenue and Thomas Road. At about a quarter to 5, the older woman left alone. A little past 5, Scott walked to a nearby Walgreens and returned with two bottles of Dr Pepper.

At 6:30 p.m., the young woman returned. About an hour later she left the apartment with a toddler in a stroller and the two older girls on foot. The four walked to a park.

Carrying a Dr Pepper and a Manila folder, Scott left the apartment around quarter to 8. He drove the truck to a Kinko's copy shop. Within minutes he was in and out of Kinko's. He walked to a Drug Emporium, then got back into the truck and went for gas. He stopped at a Liquors Drive Through momentarily, then went into a Burger King for about 12 minutes. At 8:48 p.m. he returned to Kinko's and remained inside for 13 minutes. He came out carrying something that looked like business cards and drove home.

About 9:30 p.m., Scott and the brown-haired woman came out of the apartment. Holding hands, they walked down the block to the Walgreens. When they came out, talking quietly, he held a bag the size of a half-gallon of milk. Police on surveillance details are not paid to speculate about guilt or innocence, and felons may follow the same routines as the law-abiding. Still, nothing the surveillance team had seen so far suggested that Scott lived a secret life as a predator.

But at 10:44 that night, Scott left the apartment alone. He got into the old yellow truck and pulled out. Several undercover cars followed. Maybe they could catch him in the very act of picking up a victim.

11: Seplow

SEPTEMBER 1992

Phil Seplow leaned back and put his feet up on the table. In his peach-colored polo shirt, fashionably faded jeans and high top sneakers, always unlaced, he was an incredible figure as an attorney.

After three months of wearing the county jail "blues," Scott thought if he made that kind of money himself, he'd dress the part, like the other lawyers in their three-piece suits.

But Seplow really was a lawyer at heart; the uniform of a rebel was just a front. At this moment, he sounded dubious. "You were driving around to pass out fliers for your business. But you never even got out of your truck because you thought a bunch of *thugs* were following you?"

"Sure. It was late; hardly any traffic. How should I know they were police? All I knew was someone was following me. I wasn't going to stop on a dark residential street to find out why. Would you?"

"You had a *feeling* that someone was following you. And you *thought* you saw headlights behind you wherever you turned? Come on, Scott! Nobody's gonna buy that. Sounds like you made it up."

Whenever Scott felt frustrated with Seplow, he reminded himself of the public defender who'd first represented him. That Ken Doll of an arrogant young twerp actually laughed when Scott told him he was innocent. But Phil and Scott sat face to face in the little legal visitation room. Phil would come in with duplicate copies of police reports or some other paperwork. He'd throw Scott a highlighter and they'd sit reading for an hour or so. They'd talk it over. Scott could see that Seplow wanted him to understand the case. It wasn't that Scott didn't appreciate how different that was from other attorneys; it just made him nervous. True, the man was helping Scott more than he was being paid to; but he was also trying to control him. Phil had all the power. To be helpless was one more maddening thing about being in jail. "I kept seeing headlights behind me, everywhere I went. So I put it to the test and turned some corners. They followed. Somebody was always lagging behind me."

Seplow flipped through his Manila folder. Sometimes the guy looked so much like Columbo that Scott had to smile. "Yeah; they did have six unmarked cars on your tail."

"Guess it's never occurred to the cops that if they follow you at night, you can see their lights. No wonder they never catch any crooks." Scott had given up even pretending to respect the Phoenix police. He'd never been in trouble with the law. But they'd locked him up and now they were threatening to kill him. Would making nice change anything now?

Seplow tolerated Scott's digs at authorities, but he didn't get sidetracked. "So you just drove around on the night of June 23. You didn't pass out a single flier because you thought the police who were following you were actually out to hurt you?"

"Exactly. For all I knew they had guns. Would you get out and put fliers on mailboxes?"

Seplow didn't waste time answering rhetorical questions. "Where did you drive, Scott?"

"All around. Even in circles—trying to lose them. Can't remember everywhere."

"Try."

"Hm. Pretty much on the main roads. Cactus, Scottsdale, Lincoln. Made a long circle around towards home. Then up 19th Avenue, near my mother-in-law's."

"Which is?"

"22nd Drive and Glenn. Not too far from my place, but I didn't want them to follow me home. Didn't see them anymore, so I thought they'd given up. But I sure wasn't up for walking around to do flyers. I drove on home."

"But you didn't tell your wife that you were followed?" Seplow's voice was uncharacteristically sharp.

"No point whining at her. She had enough to worry about. When I got up the next morning, I thought I'd just been paranoid."

Seplow finished writing. He nodded. "OK; maybe. You headed out northeast to Scottsdale and circled through Paradise Valley; none of the crimes were anywhere near there. Nice residential neighborhoods where people can afford to pay somebody to take care of their trees. Bad place to pick up a date, last I heard. Then you came back through your mother-in-law's neighborhood because you felt safe there." He finally looked as if he believed Scott.

But then, Phil was always reassuring, so predictably that it was impossible to trust his optimism. Seplow would make a decent poker player, if former hippies played poker. When he'd told Scott about the grand jury indictments, he was downright casual. Ten victims; 39 counts. No sweat. Oh, but there was one thing. In addition to the sexual assaults, they were charging Scott with killing three women. First-degree murder in any one of them could get the death penalty. But not to worry; the State had no case.

After Scott learned what went on in the grand jury, Seplow's insistent mellowness was not reassuring. For starters, the police played fast and loose with the facts—yeah, there was a polite way to say that, if it wasn't your neck on the line—to make it sound as if they had a single case worth prosecuting, let alone ten cases. Talk about crimes! Why wasn't anybody indicting D.A. Mike Morrison and his gang?!

Phil described the prosecution's strategy as just "clearing the books." Charging one convenient suspect with as many unsolved crimes as possible was good strategy. Giving the public the appearance of effective law enforcement and "toughness on crime" is a lot easier than delivering real justice. Judges, prosecutors, and police who occasionally disregard the truth for what they may consider a higher cause stand a good chance of enjoying long, respectable careers. And defendants who are scapegoated are chosen for sound political reasons: they are people without money or connections; loners whom many "normal" people have trouble relating to. Social outsiders who can easily be made to look guilty.

When Phil voiced his cynicism about some of those in power, he seemed to be behind Scott a hundred percent. But did he actually think Scott was innocent? Maybe it wasn't part of an attorney's job description to believe in his client's innocence. Still, the suspicion that Phil didn't trust Scott was what made it hard for Scott to trust his attorney. And to Scott, it mattered deeply whether Phil believed he was guilty, and not only because Scott was dependent on the attorney to save him.

Or maybe it wasn't really about Seplow, but the years growing up with John, Mom's boyfriend, that made trusting an older man impossible. Somehow it didn't seem to matter to Scott how reliable Phil Seplow was, or that the day he was assigned the case, he visited Scott. And it was just plain "Phil" and "Scott" from the start, no formalities. Scott couldn't imagine feeling better about any attorney, except maybe Robert Shapiro or Johnnie Cochran Jr., lawyers with million-dollar price tags. So maybe it was just the man thing. Though Scott could hide it from a lot of people, older men at close range made him nervous and angry.

On the other hand, there was Grampa Bill; there were the summers Scott spent helping Uncle Randy. They were decent men, but distant childhood memories. When Scott wondered what it would be like to have a father, the image that popped up was John, drinking and bullying, or sober and mean. Randy and Grampa, in their wildest imagining, could never have understood that excuse for a man. Even so, remembering their good hearts didn't cast out the demon of John. And for years, Scott blamed Mom for loving that maggot, even moving them to Arizona to be with him. Poor Mom. She didn't know the truth until years too late. Scott was tired. "So, what's next?"

"We'll file a motion to remand your case because you were denied due process in the grand jury proceedings."

"Translation? I must have slept through that part of law school."

Phil chuckled. It was fun to throw him off guard, startled when a tree trimmer, who'd taken only a handful of college courses, could say something the attorney considered clever.

"I'll write up a request that the State send your case back to a grand jury for reconsideration. The grand jury would never have voted to indict you if they'd been given all the evidence. Grand juries can be a rubber stamp for the D.A. The usual rules of evidence don't apply and the whole process is closed to the public. If the State wants to prosecute, the grand jury will usually indict. And this one was worse than most.

"In your case, police claimed there was a striking resemblance among the crimes. The grand jurors never knew that the crimes were committed over a wide distance and at different times of day and night. They never heard that the victims described the suspect and his vehicle differently. The jurors didn't know that you really don't look much like the suspect described by most of the victims. And of course they never knew that Alison Brooks and Meredith Porter changed their stories drastically. Ditto that Nancy Caporaso actually ID'ed a guy she was sure had attacked her; obviously, not you, and he didn't look like you. All the State had was that most of the victims ID'ed you in the lineup. Of course, the grand jury wasn't told that eyewitness identification is no better than 50-50 accurate. Just a flip of a coin. And the more certain the witness is, the more likely he or she is wrong."

"That lineup," Scott protested. "I swear it was rigged. They brought those girls in so fast, one right after another; they could have overheard . . ."

"But we stick with what we can prove." There it was: Seplow dropped the pretense that he wasn't in charge here. "And you remember that Margaret Christorf's boyfriend could not be ruled out as the source of the sperm found in her body? The grand jury didn't know that, either. Plus they never knew that Carl Frederick Gardei was arrested in February and confessed to very similar crimes to the 'baby-seat' attacks. He could have done them all. And Scott, I've got to remind you, Gardei bargained. He admitted he attacked at least 20 women in northwest Phoenix, but he pled guilty to only 9 counts, total. He'll probably be out in five years."

Scott said nothing. Confessing was supposed to be a smart move, but he'd never admit to crimes he didn't commit in order to get a lighter sentence. No matter how many times he looked at the transcripts of the grand jury proceedings, Scott's disgust didn't fade. The grand jurors weren't told that Belinda Cronin was last seen on her way to Dr. Storm's and that her family believed that she was blackmailing Storm. And rumor had it that Storm had plenty to be blackmailed about, that he was giving her cocaine to have sex with him and his brother, too. Instead, the prosecution made a big deal about that old secondhand ring that Elaine gave the detectives. Detective Michael Johnson testified that the ring was "tentatively" identified as Belinda Cronin's. That "tentative" I.D. meant nothing. Actually, neither Belinda's half-brother, who lived with her, nor Belinda's mother recognized that ring. Let alone, nobody knew whether Belinda was wearing any ring at all when she disappeared. The prosecution didn't even claim that Elaine's ring was the same size as Belinda's would be! And the jury never knew that Belinda's watch, still running, and her 14-karat gold necklace were found with her body. On the contrary, Detective Johnson told the grand jury that no other jewelry of Cronin's was found with her body. If the killer stole her ring, why didn't he take her watch and necklace, too? Then there was the fact that Detective Dimodica misinformed the grand jurors that the bodies of Morales and Cronin were found a quarter of a mile apart. In fact, the two women had been found more than seven miles apart. The list went on and on.

Phil's outrage seemed sincere. "But worst of all, the foreman of that grand jury was none other than Richard Donohue, a person of interest at one point. A *person of interest* is leading the jury that charges you with the crimes!" Phil scanned his file for the photo of Donohue. A smiling guy, with curly hair and big ears. Big ears, like in the Meredith Porter case. "Worked nights and drove a 1980 tan Chevy Malibu, plate ADW 777. The car and the plate were in the ballpark, too. And, Donohue had previously been arrested for disorderly conduct and drug possession. Only at the end of the proceedings was Donohue finally disqualified from voting to indict you. If there's any justice in Maricopa County, they'll have the decency to remand."

"Why me? I just don't get it. Don't they want to find the guys who really committed the crimes?"

The answer, according to Phil, was that they had Scott in custody. Clearing the books. There had been a storm of publicity about the "baby-seat" attacks, and women felt safer with someone behind bars for all of them. And clearly, plenty of people believed that Scott had killed little Brandy Myers in May. But she'd never been found, so they'd put him away for something else. No, it wasn't legal, but, to the average citizen, it felt right.

"It's already too easy for them, Scott. Don't let them make you look guilty. Don't show anger. You have to show that you're not a violent person."

"Wouldn't you be angry? I may not be the friendliest guy in the world, but I'm good to my family and I've never hurt anyone. So my cars came up in their half-assed computer search. Once they saw my cars they should have admitted that they're not the ones they're looking for. Are they morons, or just lazy?"

Phil smiled, as if in sympathy. "Doesn't pay to speculate. You still have to treat them with respect. Just you keep being a model prisoner and I'll keep hammering away with the facts."

Phil was suddenly impatient to get back to whatever lawyers do. He had a lot of cases, and Scott knew he should be grateful for all the time Phil devoted to him. Most of the guys in here never heard from their lawyers at all.

Phil waved to the visitation officer behind the windows, like asking for the check at the end of a less than satisfying lunch – disappointing, but not bad enough to complain to the manager. When the officer came, Phil would always give Scott a casual good-bye, as if they were coworkers. As he left, he'd say the most upbeat thing he could come up with. Today it was his favorite, "Don't worry; we're gonna win this fucking case."

As he made his way out of the ugly, old building, Phil Seplow's back hurt. He likely had no doubt that Scott had the law on his side. But for all Scott's intelligence, he was a problem client. To get off as easily as they could, most guys would shut up and do whatever Phil told them. Unless they were nuts. Scott didn't seem to be nuts, and Phil actually liked him. But Scott couldn't come up with the alibis they needed to convince the D.A. of his innocence, and he wouldn't bargain. And he could be a loose cannon, with all that anger, and biting humor. It would be all Phil could do to stop him from mouthing off. Judges—and juries—don't like smart-ass defendants who don't show remorse. Nobody believes they're innocent. They have to show remorse.

But Phil wasn't worried. He just had to keep bringing up the facts, as diplomatically as he could. And save Scott from himself. All the prosecution had was a theory. There was nothing solid against Scott and plenty of evidence pointing to other suspects. Not one of these cases was strong enough to even go to trial.

12: Any Mother's Son

SEPTEMBER 1992

Scott's pod was on the top floor, the sixth. That was the secure area for inmates under protective custody, either because their cases were "high-profile," or because they were informants. Scott concluded that he was being protected not only from the families of his presumed victims, but also from other prisoners. Back in the muggy, swamp-cooled pod, he was glad he had no cellie. Most of the guys in the Madison Street Jail would lose their minds without someone nearby to bitch and moan to, but he preferred to be alone for some part of the day. Not to mention, safe—at least at night— from violent crazies.

Scott's life over the last three months would have made a good story, he thought, if it happened to someone else. On a beautiful June morning Detectives Chapman and Johnson came to call, and he hadn't seen his family since. Then, on his thirty-third birthday, he sat in jail. But just to make it an extra special birthday, he was indicted for 39 crimes, including three that could get him the death penalty.

Whenever he came back from the relative quiet of the visitation rooms, the noisiness of the pod struck him again. Everybody talked at once, until late night. When they were locked down, they talked through their doors. You could pick out different voices, but you could rarely follow what they were saying in that roaring flood of chatter.

Now, he got to overcome his lifelong shyness by living 16 hours a day in an open pod, with no privacy. A guy who really didn't like games or small talk was a captive in a social life that consisted of playing cards, chess, or checkers, or watching TV with men who'd committed every crime you could stand to name.

It surprised him at first that the other prisoners didn't challenge him, that he could survive by his wits. He quickly learned he could get away with being smart and gentle only because the other prisoners believed he was a murderer—and because at 6'1" he was a powerful-looking man. Scott had never thought of himself as tough. Back as a kid with John controlling his mother's house, Scott felt worthless and small. But he finally knew he wasn't small. No one had to know that sometimes at night he broke down in tears.

Here, most of life's enjoyments were denied—even the light of the sky or the call of a bird. There wasn't much to look forward to but eating, and Scott was always hungry. Today he made it back upstairs in plenty of time for the chow line. Thirty guys and twenty-two seats made for a rough game of musical chairs at every meal. Some just refused to compete and pretended it was their choice to take their tray to their cell, but Scott was glad to sit in the open pod and eat with the group. He felt like a crazy dog when he ate alone. Even grape Kool-Aid and cardboard "pizza" tasted better with a little company.

Lockdown wasn't until 10 p.m., and if there was something good on T.V. Scott would stay in the open pod and watch. But sometimes he would just go back to his cell and read. For the first time in his life, he understood why people actually enjoyed reading. His family could send books, magazines, and newspapers, as long as they came directly from the distributor, and he preferred reading to watching most of the stupid shows on the tube. Lots of the guys did like to read, and it helped Scott's popularity on the pod that his family often sent new books, which he shared readily.

And he wrote. Long letters to Elaine and Mom. Painting the most encouraging picture he could, he told them about his life and the latest on his legal situation. He decorated little notes to Lindsey, Hallie, and Melissa with drawings of animals. He assured them that he loved them, asked them for news, and reminded them to be good. Mom wrote back, and he saw a whole new side to her. No, she never did tell him much about her personal life, but she became his staunch advocate and second attorney. She clipped every article she could find on the case, and she was going to get her own copies of the police reports to study. And just as she'd helped him take care of the twins before he met Elaine, she did whatever she could now to help him be a father in these impossible circumstances.

But Elaine was another story. She said she believed he was innocent. Still, she wasn't sure of him; they both knew that. He could see it the first time she came to visit, with Mom. There was a single phone in the visitation booth, so only one of them at a time could talk to him through the glass. The other would gaze at him with what he thought was accusing pain. He didn't know what to tell them. Elaine hovered behind Mom in a stunned, awkward posture. She told him that she and Melissa had moved in with her parents right after his arrest. The twins were shipped off to his first wife, Trish's,* family in California.

When their half-hour was up, the tears came. "My baby," Mom said. She'd never called him that, and hearing it now brought him as much hurt as comfort. And then she put her hand up to the glass toward him; a gesture he'd seen on TV police dramas, never dreaming that ordinary people could share such a moment. Elaine had already taken a few steps towards the exit, but she hurried back and did the same.

Elaine came regularly during the first weeks and brought Melissa a few times. But by September, Elaine's visits were rare. Scott knew he shouldn't blame her. Even before the arrest, their relationship had grown tense, sad. If he could be with her, they could work it out, he was sure. But what if he was here for years?

Though it must have torn her apart, Mom kept visiting. Looking back, he blamed himself for the anger he'd felt toward her when he was a stupid kid. With time to reflect, he finally understood. What was her life like as a strong-willed young girl growing up on a farm? She was twenty-four years old when he was born, uninvited. These days, that was nothing; but in the small town of Monroe, Wisconsin, in 1959, it must have been a public humiliation for her and her family. Was that why she and Grampa didn't get along? He was twenty-five when his Lindsey and Hallie arrived. When Trish had split, he was overwhelmed by the responsibility of taking care of the babies. Back then, Yvonne must have been worn out as a single mother. No wonder the boundless energy of her little son only frustrated her. But he finally understood how she'd fought to make a living for them all.

He could still see in her the slim young beauty with short, black hair. Men couldn't keep their eyes off Yvonne. Fashionable in dark glasses, always with her cigarette in one hand, gracefully cool. No cookie baking like the other moms; no warm snuggles. And, always under the tough facade, mourning the love she never found.

Sometimes it still ate at him: why couldn't she have been the mother he needed, back then? Never mind. Life deals the cards; we can only choose to play them or throw them away. Yvonne had given her twin granddaughters a loving mother figure until Elaine joined their family. And today, as he sat in jail and Elaine seemed to be fading out of his life, his distant, cynical Mom stood strong as his dearest friend.

13: America's Toughest Sheriff

1994

Phil Seplow's stomach must have done a flip when he heard that Scott Lehr was on the evening news. What possessed Scott to set himself up as the other prisoners' representative and debate Sheriff Arpaio about jail conditions? Calling attention to himself as an inmate with an attitude. The motion to remand Scott's case had been summarily denied. Now it was going to be even harder to save him from going to trial.

Tuned in to the Channel 15 news that evening, Scott also wondered what had possessed himself. After he came into office in January 1993, Joe Arpaio liked to be called "America's toughest sheriff." The voters got a kick out of that, but they had no way of knowing the dark side of it. Scott had actually believed it might help if he made the public aware of jail conditions. He should have known better.

Not that everyone loved "Sheriff Joe." Word of his jail "reforms" spread nationally. *Dateline NBC, 20/20,* CBS's *Eye on America,* and *60 Minutes* all ran investigative features on Arpaio. But whether it was because no prisoner dared to talk openly or because nobody cared what prisoners said, the residents of Maricopa County jails weren't asked about what was going on inside.

For Scott, the issues were clear. Taking office six months after Scott was arrested, Arpaio had announced to the press, "I want to make this place so unpleasant that they won't even think about doing something that could bring them back. I want them to suffer."[13] Like 70% of the prisoners in the county jails, Scott was awaiting trial, and so presumed innocent.[14] Yet for prisoners suspected of crimes, whether great or small, Sheriff Joe's policies changed life equally in the Madison Street Jail. Arpaio took away privileges that inmates could formerly earn by good behavior, and he made obtaining necessities as frustrating as possible. He started by abruptly banning cigarettes and taking coffee off the menu. Next he censored the prisoners' magazines; no more *Playboy* or *Hustler*. Anyone who didn't have a problem with those measures was hit by the next: Arpaio reduced an already low food budget, bringing the average cost per meal from 65 cents to less than 31 cents, the cheapest in the United States.[15] Hot lunches were eliminated. Now everyone got the Ladmo bags, packed with food too old to sell—generously donated by the private sector. The overripe produce and spoiled meat gave people the runs. When complaints about the food went public, Arpaio not only agreed the food was bad, he bragged about it. "I say jail should be punishment, period."[16]

By anyone's standards, conditions in Sheriff Arpaio's county jails became much worse than in state prisons where convicted felons served their sentences. The Sheriff took control of the pod televisions by installing a cable system that offered only harangues by Newt Gingrich and Arpaio himself in the morning, and at other times the Disney Channel, A & E, ESPN, CNN, and GED classes. No more videos on Friday and Saturday nights as a reward for obeying the rules. The sheriff also changed the blue scrub uniforms in Madison Street Jail to black and white striped pajamas. It reminded Scott of the silent movies he'd seen as a kid. Convicts in their striped costumes were comic characters in those movies, dumb clowns who deserved to fall out of cars or to be knocked out cold by falling rocks. Sheriff Joe added his personal stamp to the uniform: color-coded sleeves to signify security level.

Arpaio became ever more inventive. Claiming that underwear supplied by the jail was being stolen, Arpaio spent $180,000 of the taxpayers' money in 1995 to dye inmates' underwear pink. "If you want to wear Calvin Klein, don't do the crime," the Sheriff gibed.[17]

Sheriff Joe used military surplus tents to create the Tent City Jail outside of Phoenix, where summer temperatures could reach

145 degrees.[18] Arpaio was pleased with the site of the Tent City, between the city dump and an animal crematorium.[19] He also organized chain gangs of minimum-security convicts, including the first woman chain gangs in the country, some of which were assigned to bury indigent citizens.[20]

Arpaio's policies, "innovative" in his view, were accompanied by a cavalcade of publicity. Outside of Arizona, plenty of the attention was negative. Yet Arpaio reveled in controversy, priding himself that Maricopa County was "the most talked about and nationally recognized Sheriff's Office in the country."[21] Reporting for NBC on July 13, 1994, Fred Francis described Arpaio as a "dinosaur." Francis also noted that "this tough-talking crime fighter has a 1990s knack for self-promotion that would rival Madonna."[22] Despite criticism from the outside world, Arizona voters continued to support Arpaio.

Like others awaiting trial or serving time in the county jails, Scott saw Sheriff Arpaio "as the type who would poke a stick at an animal in a cage." But there was an even darker side to the sheriff's vaunted "toughness" than merely making prisoners uncomfortable. In Arpaio's administration, Maricopa county jails quickly acquired a reputation not only for discomfort, but also for brutality. When officers in the intake "fish tank" area subjected a new detainee to life-threatening levels of force, Arpaio supported his staff's violence with such statements as "I'm sure that my officers had a reason to slam him against the cell block."[23]

During that first year of Sheriff Joe's regime, Scott was paged on the overhead speaker and told to pick up the legal phone. Would he mind coming to talk to a media coordinator? When he asked what about, the official voice told him they didn't know. Scott was too curious to refuse. A sergeant quickly escorted him down to an office by the recreation rooms. He recognized the woman inside—a news reporter he'd seen on local TV, a stunning woman. Only that had been some years ago. Now her heavy makeup and blood-red lipstick gave her the look of an aging vampire. She introduced herself as Lisa, or Melissa, Something, the media coordinator for Sheriff Arpaio.

Lisa-Melissa said she'd heard that Scott disagreed with some of Sheriff Arpaio's policies. She'd read some of the lawsuits Scott had filed against the jail, and his intelligence impressed her. She thought that Scott would be an articulate spokesman for the inmates. Would he like to discuss jail policies with Sheriff Arpaio—and a reporter? The Sheriff was willing to discuss his policies on camera, and the discussion would likely be televised. And, Lisa-Melissa made clear, Scott's legal case would not be an issue in the interview.

Scott didn't hesitate. He had plenty to say to Sheriff Joe, and he carefully rehearsed his arguments and criticisms. He knew many voters didn't care about the niceties of "innocent until proven guilty" and didn't see any difference between the offenses of drug use or violent crime. To them, everyone in jail belonged there and deserved to be treated badly. But, Scott let himself believe, surely some would have the empathy to realize that mistreating prisoners—even guilty one—was never going to educate them or improve their behavior; it would more likely harden them for future crimes.

Waiting for the interview was nerve-wracking. Of course, Scott had never been on TV, unless you counted the humiliating perp-walk on the news as they led him into court in shackles to be arraigned. He lay awake, worried that he'd go tongue-tied, that he'd embarrass himself and not do justice to the issues that meant so much to him and the others. He made lists of points to make and questions to ask the Sheriff.

When the time for the debate arrived, everyone on the pod was sent to the cells for lockdown. The officers frisked Scott in his cell, then sent him out, uncuffed and alone, to meet the interviewers in the pod. As Scott walked down the stairs, a camera man recorded his arrival. Waiting for him were also Sheriff Joe Arpaio, a mob of felonious looking bodyguards who could have been linebackers, and a familiar-looking TV reporter in a sports shirt.

Scott had seen clips of Sheriff Arpaio on television, but being in the same room with him was more distasteful than he expected.

It was like having to pass close by a hungry predatory animal in the zoo, with only the glass of his cage protecting you. A huge, ugly snake, maybe. Arpaio was short and pot-bellied, though; his threat definitely wasn't physical. It was more his passionate cruelty; that and his obvious pleasure in having the power to do whatever he wanted. Still, when the Sheriff extended his hand, Scott shook it; he intended to rise above Arpaio's pettiness.

Arpaio didn't make eye contact, but backed off a few feet and cast a sidelong glance at the man in jailhouse stripes. Take away the uniform and the mean disposition, and the Sheriff had the looks of a clown. Black hair was strategically parted at the side to hide the thin spots on a broad, blocky head. A dye-job, no doubt, because the guy had to be well over 60. He wore oversized aviator eyeglasses, maybe to distract attention from his big nose and beady little eyes. With a practiced, aggressive good cheer, Sheriff Joe waited for a signal from the media people. The reporter abruptly asked Scott whether there was anything he'd like to ask the Sheriff. The camera focused on him expectantly.

After Scott's first question about jail conditions, Sheriff Joe began to speak, tilting his head as he spoke and jutting his chin upward. He didn't answer the question at all; he just asked Scott to tell everyone what he was in jail for.

Damn Lisa-Melissa! Scott managed to say that that was not what he'd been invited to discuss. He was a pre-trial detainee, never convicted of any crime.

Like a constrictor clutching a rabbit, Arpaio didn't let go. He countered that it was going to be up to the courts whether Scott was guilty or not. And he was sure Scott wouldn't be there in the first place if he was innocent. With an extra little jab of his chin, Arpaio asked Scott whether he wasn't in here for killing a bunch of women.

Scott's eye's widened in shock.

The sheriff chortled like a twelve-year-old bully.

Scott fought to calm himself. And he kept asking his questions. As Scott tried to get back to the subject of inmates' issues, Sheriff Joe ignored the questions, answering each with his usual lines. Did

Scott think people like himself, who kill women, should live in a resort?

Scott tried at least to make the point that there was a difference between convicted criminals and people like himself in the jail, unable to afford bond while they waited for trial. "Have you ever heard the legal premise of innocent until proven guilty?"

But Arpaio's agenda didn't include a thoughtful debate of jail conditions, let alone of constitutional protections. No matter what Scott tried to discuss, the sheriff responded with another variation on the theme that people in jail don't deserve to be treated with respect. Stabbing the air with his forefinger or hammering with a high, clenched fist, as if cracking an imaginary whip, Arpaio made it clear that prisoners would have no say as long as he was sheriff.

Scott felt as if he'd stepped off into quicksand. Though most of them would never admit it, the guys in Scott's pod had been excited about the upcoming debate, all but the hopelessly psycho ones. But when the debate aired on T.V. that evening, it never presented their concerns. The carefully edited exchange between Sheriff Joe Arpaio and prisoner Scott Lehr was pure P.R. for the sheriff's office. From the 30-minute discussion, the only words of Scott's that were broadcast were those of his weakest moment. "We have a RIGHT to those magazines!" they showed him blurting out. Maricopa County audiences saw only what appeared to be the toughest sheriff in America, coolly weathering the emotional outbursts of a murderer who expected to be coddled in jail.

14: The Temple Murders

1991 - 1994

Any defense lawyer would be wise to avoid taking a client to trial in Maricopa County that year.

Sheriff Joe Arpaio might not have come to power in 1993 if the Maricopa County Sheriff's Office (MCSO) had not been reeling from an embarrassing case known as the temple murders. A human tragedy—and a public relations nightmare—it was the bungled investigation into the temple murders that likely helped Arpaio beat the incumbent sheriff, Tom Agnos, in the Republican primary election.[24]

The Phoenix area boasts a diverse population, and the opening of a Buddhist temple in 1989 drew little attention. A group of Thai, Laotian, Cambodian, and American Buddhists built their temple, Wat Promkunaram, in the desert near Luke Air Force Base. Two years later, Wat Promkunaram would be associated with carnage. On the morning of August 10, 1991, nine people were found shot to death in the temple, lying face down. The victims were six monks, an elderly nun, a visitor, and a 17-year-old acolyte—all but one shot without apparent resistance.[25]

MCSO investigators' assumption was that more than one killer committed the atrocity. Certainly no one could single-handedly subdue and murder nine people, even unusually gentle ones.

Cameras and stereo equipment were missing from the temple, suggesting that the murders were motivated by eliminating witnesses to a burglary. An escalation from apparent robbery to slaughter might have resulted from the panic of amateur criminals. On the other hand, the cold efficiency of the crimes pointed to hardened professionals.

Some observers suspected the involvement of organized crime. Credible rumors circulated that the murder victims might have witnessed a heroin deal. Five weeks earlier, U.S. Drug Enforcement Administration agents in California had confiscated a huge shipment of China White heroin,[26] and additional large amounts of heroin had allegedly been smuggled into the United States around that time. Thirteen years before the temple massacre, a layman who was later on the board of the Wat Promkunaram temple, Lamthong Sudthisa-Ard, had himself been arrested in possession of 10 pounds of heroin in Los Angeles.[27]

Surprisingly, though, Maricopa County detectives did not pursue the possibility of an underworld connection to the killings. Instead, the MCSO task force working under Sheriff Agnos rounded up four young men from Tucson.

The Tucson Four, as the press called them, were arrested in September 1991, on the strength of the confession of one, who implicated the others. Although that man was hospitalized for mental illness at the time, his confession was embraced at face value. Threatened with the death penalty if they refused to cooperate, three others signed confessions as well. In addition to being intimidated and interrogated for hours without food, some of the Tucson Four suspects were improperly questioned after viewing a "prop" room displaying photos and charts that supplied details about the crime scene.[28]

The quick arrests were celebrated by the media. Within a month, however, the triumph of Sheriff Agnos's team had been replaced by humiliation. For the weapon used in the temple murders was traced to a couple of Phoenix-area teenagers, who confessed to the crimes. The jailed Tucson Four were completely innocent.

The temple murder investigation was later found to have involved official incompetence at the very least, if not misconduct. Once the arrest of the Tucson men had been publicized, it would have taken substantial courage and integrity to admit a serious mistake. Apparently falling short in those qualities, some in the sheriff's and county attorney's offices were reluctant to accept the truth.

On September 11, 1991, Detective Rick Sinsabaugh brought in a .22-caliber Marlin rifle confiscated from a teenager who'd been stopped while driving on Luke Air Force Base.[29] In the excitement surrounding the questioning of the Tucson four, the rifle sat behind an office door for nearly a month before it was sent to the Department of Public Safety (DPS) lab for ballistics testing.[30] On October 24 the DPS reported a match: that rifle, taken from 17-year-old Rolando Caratachea, Jr., bought by his mother at Kmart, was the murder weapon used at Wat Promkunaram.[31]

The sheriff's task force first assumed that Caratachea had assisted the Tucson Four with the murders. Investigators could not come up with any link between the teenager and the men from Tucson, however. Instead, they found a completely different group of suspects, teenagers who called themselves the A.M. Posse, named, supposedly, for their after-midnight escapades. The group included Johnathan Doody, and Alessandro "Alex" Garcia.[32] Caratachea told police that on the weekend of the temple murders he'd lent his rifle to Garcia and Doody.

Seventeen-year-old Johnathan Doody had been living at the home of Garcia, a classmate and friend Doody considered "like my big brother."[33] Johnathan's command of English was poor. A quiet, slight young man, Doody was born Veerapol Khan Kew in rural Thailand. After his father died, his mother immigrated to Germany, but Johnathan and a younger brother were left in Thailand with their grandparents. When his mother married Brian Doody, an American Air Force sergeant, the brothers joined the family. Johnathan moved to the Phoenix area as a high school student whose English reading comprehension tested at second grade level.[34] When Johnathan's father was transferred from Luke Air Force Base to Colorado, Johnathan stayed behind to live with Alex's family and attend Agua Fria High School. Although he did poorly in school, Johnathan worked two jobs to buy a used Ford Mustang. He was the leader of the high school ROTC honor guard[35] and aspired to a career as a pilot or an air force search and rescue officer.[36]

At sixteen, Alex Garcia stood a head taller than his friend. Classmates described Garcia as athletic, but shy.[37]

On the evening of October 25, Doody was leading the color guard in a flag ceremony at the Agua Fria High football game. Detective Pat Riley and an FBI agent went to the game to bring the teen in for questioning. Courteous and cooperative, he accompanied them to headquarters in his ROTC uniform. At the same time, undercover officers looked for Alex Garcia and other potential suspects. At the Garcia home, detectives found a 20-gauge pump shotgun as well as cameras and stereos that might have been stolen from the temple. DPS tests confirmed within hours that shells found at the scene of the murders had been discharged by that shotgun.

Johnathan Doody was questioned by detectives without his parents or an attorney present. After repeated questioning, he agreed that on the weekend of the temple murders he borrowed Caratachea's rifle to test silencers that he and Garcia had made of potatoes.[38]

Alex Garcia was brought in to task force headquarters at 2:30 the following morning. Garcia also admitted to borrowing Caratachea's rifle. After detectives told him that the same rifle had been used to murder nine people, Garcia asked for an attorney and invoked his right to remain silent.

Doody was still being questioned in a nearby room. "Trust me, my man," Detective Sinsabaugh repeatedly urged the teen.[39] Around 3:55 a.m., Doody admitted that he'd driven to the temple in his Mustang on August 10. Still, he insisted that he had been outside the building and played no part in the killings. He said that Garcia, Caratachea, and two others were at the scene but that he did not know who pulled the trigger.[40]

After consulting with his father, Alex Garcia told detectives he wanted to set the record straight. According to Garcia, it was Doody who called for "no witnesses" and committed all the murders.[41] Garcia supplied details about the crimes, down to where the murdered nun kept her dentures,[42] that the Tucson Four could never have guessed in their false confessions. When pressed to agree that the Tucson Four were involved in the slayings, Garcia insisted that Doody and he acted alone.[43]

Rather than freeing the Tucson suspects, however, the sheriff's men continued to look for a connection between the Tucson Four and the teens. Staffers who expressed any doubt about this theory were called "imbeciles" by command staff.[44]

Prosecutors and investigators had cooperated in jailing the Tucson Four, but now County Attorney Rick Romley distanced himself from the arrests. Just before Thanksgiving, Romley ordered the Tucson Four released after 2 ½ months in jail. They sued Maricopa County for false arrest, and an out-of-court settlement cost taxpayers $2.8 million.

In dropping charges against the Tucson Four, Romley played down his own role in the fiasco. In fact, his office had filed first-degree murder charges against the Tucson Four without evidence to corroborate their questionable confessions.[45]

Sheriff Agnos lost his job to Joe Arpaio in 1992, but Rick Romley easily won reelection as county attorney. Sheriff-elect Arpaio set up an internal investigation of the temple case, professing a wish to make sure nothing similar ever happened again. Arpaio's inquiry concluded that Sheriff Agnos and his staff wasted money and time. The report described twenty-two "major errors" in the temple investigation, ranging from mismanagement to intimidation and coercion of detectives. Without implicating Romley himself, the report did criticize high-ranking members of Romley's staff, K.C. Scull, then head of the major felony unit, and Myrna Parker, then a top assistant to Romley.[46]

Under an agreement with Romley's office that they would not seek the death penalty, Alex Garcia pleaded guilty to the temple crimes. During the plea negotiations, Garcia also confessed his involvement in an unrelated murder committed on October 18, 1991—two months after the temple massacre. Garcia admitted to being present when his girlfriend, Michelle Hoover, then 14 years old, shot 50-year-old Alice Marie Cameron to death at a Verde

River campground. According to Garcia, after Hoover shot Cameron in the back, she and Garcia waited an hour at the campground as the dying woman begged for help. Once they were sure she was dead, they plundered her belongings for about $1 and a bank card.[47]

When confronted with Garcia's confession, Michelle Hoover told a substantially different story. She admitted to the murder but claimed that Garcia asked her to prove her love for him by killing Cameron.[48]

Alex Garcia's role in the murder of Alice Cameron had previously gone unnoticed because the Maricopa sheriff's office had arrested the wrong man for that crime, George Peterson, a Vietnam veteran with a history of mental problems, and pressured him to make a confession that turned out to be false.[49] If detectives had investigated further, they would have found that an automatic camera at Cameron's bank had taken a picture of Garcia and Hoover attempting to use their victim's ATM card.[50]

When Peterson was released after 14 months in jail, he also sued the county. After initially refusing to negotiate a settlement, Romley broadcast a desire to "do the right thing."[51] $1.1 million[52] was the price taxpayers paid for the negligent investigation of Cameron's murder.

Sheriff Arpaio did not take disciplinary action against the investigators who had extracted a transparently false confession from Peterson and then failed to take into account the more than 180 pieces of evidence that suggested his innocence.[53] While faulting the former sheriff, Sheriff Arpaio blandly characterized the detectives involved as "inexperienced."[54]

Only Johnathan Doody was tried and subject to the death penalty for the Wat Promkunaram murders. Alex Garcia testified against his friend, claiming that Doody killed all nine victims in the temple with the .22-caliber rifle. Garcia stated that he himself shot four of the victims with the shotgun, which wounded but did not kill them.

The jury convicted Doody of nine counts of felony murder, suggesting that they thought he was party to the crimes but not the murderer. Judge Gregory Martin sentenced Doody to nine consecutive life sentences, rather than execution. At a pre-trial hearing, Judge Martin had actually asked K.C. Scull, lead prosecutor for the case, whether the county was sure that Alex Garcia was the defendant they wanted to grant a plea bargain.[55]

Romley had claimed that his office had to strike a deal with Garcia to ensure that Doody would not go free.[56]

Interviewed by Mike Sager after the sentencings, Alex Garcia bragged, ". . . I could write a guidebook about how not to get caught."[57]

Whatever the truth of the temple murders, the implications were serious for Scott Lehr. It was County Attorney Romley's office that would prosecute Scott's case. Even though Scott was charged with the "baby-seat" crimes during Sheriff Agnos's term, Scott had been held in jail long enough that the current sheriff and prosecutor would be discredited if Scott was not convicted. And Romley was so sensitive to political pressure that he'd proclaimed his disappointment in 1994 when Johnathan Doody was not sentenced to death for the temple murders. "If death were ever called for, this case called for it,"[58] Romley said.

1994 was a dangerous time to be charged with murder in Maricopa County. The memory of Sheriff Agnos's fall was still fresh. Yet another high-profile case of false arrest might spell professional disaster for County Attorney Romley as well. He needed a good, solid win. What's more, to convince a conservative public of his effectiveness, Romley's win needed to be not only a conviction, but a death sentence.

15: "Will You Still Be Our Daddy?"

1995

In the Madison Street Jail, three years dragged by while Phil Seplow and the State of Arizona parried with motions and memoranda. The time went by less painfully after Scott learned to occupy his mind. During the day, socializing in the pod could take much of his attention – too much, since he'd discovered that he enjoyed reading. Locked down at night, he had long, dark hours for remembering. He replayed in slow motion a life out under the hot blue sky that had raced by as if he'd lived it on a motorcycle. He wished he'd known enough to treasure his freedom. Instead, he'd agonized over money, doubted his ability to succeed at anything, and feared that Elaine would stop loving him.

It ate at his gut that his time with Elaine was shorter than the years he'd already spent in jail. Now one of his favorite memories was of their last evening together. After the girls were asleep, the couple walked two blocks to a convenience store to buy milk. With so little time alone, the walk was a luxury. They held hands and talked about what their future would be like when they moved to Prescott, where his sister lived. For a few minutes, they felt the sense of adventure they enjoyed after buying their little house, less than a year before. The next morning, their dream of a better life vanished like a mirage when Scott opened the door to Detectives Johnson and Chapman.

But that life had been real, he had to remind himself. It left precious little Melissa, and it left the twins with memories of two parents who'd deeply loved them, and each other. But how could he be a father to them in jail? One voice in his head told him it would be better to just disappear and pretend he didn't care about his children. They could forget him and go on to live normal lives.

But after growing up without his own father, Scott couldn't believe that would be right. How could their father's love be a bad influence? Besides, he was innocent and wouldn't be in Madison Street forever.

So he fought for his kids, as he'd fought for custody of the twins when Trish* split. Now Elaine and Yvonne were allies when it came to keeping him in touch with the girls. For the first two years, Elaine brought Melissa for visits. The last time he saw his daughter, she was a pretty four-year-old, smart, energetic, and headstrong. She still called him Daddy; Elaine had kept the memory of him alive for a child who hadn't seen him at home since she was 20 months old.

He wished he'd known that would be Melissa's last visit. Afterwards, Elaine told him she'd found another man. Scott forced himself to understand. As far as Elaine's feelings were concerned, he'd violated their marriage. The police and her family had persuaded her that he'd committed the crimes he was accused of. She wrote from time to time, but only with news about Melissa. Scott wrote to Melissa every month, and he thought Elaine read her the letters. Elaine said that although she wanted Melissa to know her father, she didn't believe that visiting him in jail was healthy for the little girl. Trust Elaine to be honest.

But Lindsey and Hallie were seven when Scott was arrested, and they remembered him. For better or worse, they'd have to deal with it. After the first few months, when the girls stayed with Trish's* parents in California to protect them from the media, Trish kept them with her and Kurt* in Glendale. At first, Scott could only talk to them on the phone when they visited his mother. Trish—who'd been happy enough to leave the twins with Scott when they were babies, now took the position that Scott should not be allowed any contact with them. She told them to forget Scott; Kurt was now their daddy. Trish even refused to let Yvonne take them for visits to the jail. But his mother did what she thought was right; she brought the girls to see him.

Why had he thought their first visit would make them all feel better? Trying to talk to his kids across the glass of the visitation tank, seeing the confusion on their faces, was torture. They were plucky little girls, but the ugly sights, sounds, and smells of the jail scared them. He'd thought he was ready for their questions, but he was not: Why? When? Will you still be our daddy? Tough questions, when he didn't know the answers himself.

Trish found out about the jail visits and kept Hallie and Lindsey from visiting their grandmother. Scott thought he'd never see his twins again. Not one to walk away from a battle worth fighting, Yvonne hired Phil Seplow to represent her and her son in a custody hearing. The judge had psychologists interview and observe Scott, Trish, and Kurt. Their report concluded that Trish was impatient and domineering; she should take parenting classes in her daughters' best interest. The psychologists reported that Scott had been a loving, patient father who'd provided a positive environment. They added that his daughters loved him very much and wanted to see him often. Before the end of Scott's first year in Madison Street Jail, the custody order gave him visitation rights with the twins and established Yvonne's grandparental rights to frequent visits. And on every weekend when they stayed with her, she brought one of them for visiting hours. Only one child was allowed in with an adult visiting an inmate. It was hard for both the twins and Scott that only one of them could see him at a time.

Catching only brief glimpses of his daughters' childhood, Scott pressured Phil Seplow. Whatever happened to the right to a speedy trial?

Phil reminded him that delaying a trial was to his advantage. New evidence could come to light, or people who were convinced of Scott's guilt might cool down and lose interest. Most criminal cases never go to trial; the accused agrees to plead guilty in return for a lighter sentence than he might get if convicted by a jury.

16: Reeves

1995

Phil Seplow secured funds to have an additional attorney appointed to the case. Mike Reeves was hired to deal solely with DNA evidence. The nationally hyped murder trial of O. J. Simpson made DNA profiling a household word in May 1995, but most Americans didn't understand it. In fact, the public had reason to be wary of DNA evidence. It was still a new field, and protocols for lab analysis were not firmly established.

In contrast to funky Phil, Mike Reeves, a devout Mormon, dressed meticulously in business suits and maintained a formal distance from his clients. His politely skeptical manner suggested that he never believed a word Scott said. On the other hand, Mike often pointed out inconsistencies in the State's case. Scott could understand how bad he might look as a suspect, and he respected Mike's lack of B.S.

Mike also pushed Scott to agree to a plea bargain, and Scott was beginning to trust him. After three years of talking to Phil and doing his own reading, Scott saw that any attorney would tell him plea bargaining was the kindest thing for his family. County Attorney Rick Romley's office had publicly announced they would seek the death penalty for Scott. Among insiders, it was known that a plea bargain to save him from execution might be arranged. But Scott had heard about innocent people who were frightened into signing plea bargains. It was nearly impossible to have their cases overturned.

On the other hand, what chance did he have if he went to trial? Even though the victims had given a wide range of descriptions of their attacker—some of which could not possibly have been Scott—the prosecution claimed that several victims had identified him back at that lineup. And juries tended to believe the victim, no matter how wrong he or she might actually be about an identification. Then, the State claimed to have DNA evidence implicating Scott. He knew that was impossible, but could Reeves persuade the jury that the State's claim of scientific evidence was baseless? And finally, the political climate was against Scott. Many Arizonans bought into a macho, string-him-up, guilty-until-proven-innocent brand of "justice," or they would never have elected Sheriff Joe Arpaio. And the cases had received so much biased publicity that any jurist aware of local events already assumed that Scott Lehr was the "baby-seat" rapist and killer.

As the years dragged on, Scott saw that even Seplow lost confidence in a successful trial. If Scott's own lawyers thought his chances for acquittal were slim, how could he risk his life in a trial? When he considered the alternative of a life sentence, however, Scott wasn't sure that spending the rest of his life in prison was a big improvement over just getting it over with in the death house. But could he subject his family to seeing him executed?

And he wanted the world to know he was innocent. Back when Scott was free, he'd sometimes wasted his time in depression. Now, even though conditions looked hopeless, it was finally possible to believe that where there's life, there's hope. If he was executed, the truth would die with him. He told Phil he'd consider a plea bargain.

There was a condition, Phil said. Scott also had to plead guilty in the Brandy Myers case.

Scott was astonished. Wasn't it enough for the County Attorney's résumé to put Scott away forever for the murders of Margaret Christorf, Michele Morales, and Belinda Cronin, and for the sexual assaults of the other victims?

Among the hundreds of missing persons cases in the Phoenix area, one that had received intense publicity was the disappearance of 13-year-old Brandy Lynn Myers in May 1992. Brandy Myers was an unusually young-looking sixth-grader, weighing only 80 pounds and standing 4 foot 9. The blonde schoolgirl was last seen

around 7 p.m. at a grocery store in the general area of Scott and
Elaine's apartment complex. Brandy had walked to the store to
collect money for a school project. She never came home.
Thousands of fliers bearing Brandy's photo were circulated;
hundreds of volunteers searched for weeks in Valley mountains
and desert areas but found no trace. Although the girl was never
found, police, prosecutors, and the media assumed she was another
victim of the "baby-seat" predator.

In no way did Brandy's disappearance resemble the "baby-
seat" crimes, but both investigators and the media made much of
the fact that she was last spotted at the Smitty's grocery store
where Scott Lehr shopped. "He just lived so close, it's hard not to
think it was . . . him," Brandy's mother said in an *Arizona
Republic* interview after Scott's arrest.[59] No one but Scott seemed
to notice that this was just one more *difference* from the "baby
seat" victims, not one of whom was picked up near Scott's
residence.

Sadly, horrendous crimes against young girls were not
uncommon in Phoenix. Among the volunteers who searched for
Brandy in May 1992, Steven Barton Taylor had himself admitted
to molesting a 14-year-old. Two little girls had managed to survive
heinous abductions in the area that same year, committed by men
who were clearly neither Scott Lehr nor the "baby-seat" suspect.
Two months before Brandy's disappearance, six-year-old Tara
was taken from her bed in North Phoenix. She was assaulted and
left with her throat cut north of Camelback Road. In the following
October, a bearded man with long, matted hair and three tattoos
persuaded a six-year-old west Phoenix girl to walk with him over
three miles before he assaulted her. Although those two cases were
never solved, police somehow felt sure that Brandy had not been
kidnapped by the unknown man who'd tried to kill Tara.

The plea bargain that the County Attorney offered did not strike
Scott as any kind of "bargain." He rejected the offer vehemently.

But Seplow thought the deal was the best Scott could hope for
and hammered home this point over weeks of heated discussion.
Leaning towards bargaining, Scott ran the idea by Yvonne and

Dee Dee on the phone. At first, they couldn't understand it. If he was innocent, he should go to trial. No jury would convict him just because the police *thought* he was guilty. Why accept a compromise that would put him in prison for the rest of his life?

Scott couldn't convince them of what he'd learned from Phil: that the presumption of "innocent until proven guilty" was meaningless to the average citizen. A jury would assume that any suspect brought to trial was almost certainly guilty.

In the end, though, Scott refused the deal. When he phoned his mother with the news that the plea bargain had fallen through, her voice broke with relief. "No jury could possibly go along with the story they've cooked up," Yvonne said.

17: State of Arizona v. Scott Alan Lehr

SEPTEMBER 18, 1996

"All rise."

Between nervous anticipation and the usual chatter echoing through the pod at night, Scott hadn't slept much. He'd been up since 3:30 that morning, and it was now after 10 a.m. But as he pushed himself to his feet, his weariness evaporated.

For the first time in over four years he was in public without bracelets or leg chains. He felt light, almost free. There was, of course, always an armed guard at his shoulder. They might as well have hung a warning sign over Scott's head: "Beware of dangerous criminal!"

His mother had been at the jail before 7:30 to bring him a jacket, pants, and shirt that felt like the fanciest things he'd worn since his wedding. After getting used to being in the courtroom—with what felt like hundreds of people gawking at him—he looked out at the crowd. Yvonne and Dee Dee sat up front behind him, less than seven feet away, without a wall of safety glass separating him from them. They beamed confidence he'd be acquitted. If there wasn't so much else to think about, he would have blubbered.

A dark-robed judge marched in through a side door and took his prominent perch.

"Please be seated," the bailiff pronounced, as if leading a church service.

"Thank you. Good morning." The Honorable Judge Stephen A. Gerst was known as a tough-on-crime kind of judge, but he reminded Scott of Dennis the Menace's father on TV, aged a couple of decades. Gerst's dark hair, suspiciously black for his age, was stretched strategically over the baldest part of his scalp.

Otherwise, he looked the role of a judge. Clean-shaven, with wire-rim glasses, he peered over the bench with a judicious air.

Phil Seplow had tried to have the cases severed into ten separate trials. Even though in each individual case the contradictory facts did not implicate Scott, the County Attorney (echoed by the Phoenix media) argued that the cases "fit a pattern." According to this whole-is-greater-than-sum-of-its-parts theory, a vague detail here and a general resemblance there somehow added up to more certainty about guilt in ten cases than the facts supported in any single case. So Seplow's motion to sever had been denied. Instead, seven cases, including four so-called baby-seat rapes plus the murders of Margaret Christorf, Michelle Morales, and Belinda Cronin, would be tried together over the coming weeks. Three others, assault cases involving Nicole Churchill,* Emily Caldwell,* and Alison Brooks,* would be tried together in the future. Those victims had been hypnotized by police, a method of gathering evidence that was considered suggestive, inadmissible in many courts. By trying those cases together, the prosecution protected its allegations against Scott: if the cases involving hypnosis were overturned on appeal, the State would still have a laundry list of other charges from the first trial. However, Scott had heard that the prosecution also planned to call Alison Brooks and Nicole Churchill as witnesses at this trial, even though their cases weren't being tried here.

A gaggle of dark suits huddled over the prosecution's table. A thin man in his 50s, Bill Clayton was dapper in his dark suit. To the close observer, though, the prosecutor's beard was short enough to betray a weak chin. His eyes were cold and piercing, and he was as intense as if he faced the legendary showdown at the OK Corral.

Scott sat at the defense table with Seplow and Mike Reeves, plus Phil's legal assistant, an easygoing guy who'd been helpful when Yvonne called Phil's office. Then there was the investigator, Colonel Dick Schafer, who reminded Scott of a thinner version of Ernest Hemingway, if Hemingway had been a retired cop. Although Shafer acted friendly, Scott didn't trust Schafer's scrutinizing, faintly superior air of knowing more than he was telling. And, as far as Scott knew, Schafer's "investigations" had turned up zip.

Though Seplow and Reeves discussed everything together before the trial, in the courtroom their labor would be divided. Seplow was Scott's defense attorney, while Reeves would specialize in cross-examining witnesses on topics involving DNA or other physical evidence. Forensic DNA analysis had only recently been introduced in the U.S., and Scott's trial would be one of the earliest in Arizona to involve DNA evidence. The prosecution would try to establish that techniques of DNA analysis had been followed correctly. Well, Scott knew they couldn't have been, primarily because he was innocent, but also because the Department of Public Safety, or DPS, laboratory had a reputation for bias and sloppiness. With over 100 witnesses to testify and 400 exhibits to be displayed in the weeks ahead, Scott could only hope that the facts would emerge so clearly that the jury would not be swayed by the presentation of junk science.

He'd learned from Seplow that rules of evidence were an elaborate game that sometimes prevented acknowledging the truth. They couldn't just ask, straight out, "Did you commit those crimes, Scott?" and let him deny it and present the facts he'd learned from combing through the police reports. Instead, the jury would have to grope through a jungle of procedures to find fragments of truth. And it was the job of both defense and prosecuting counsel to raise objections whenever the other violated the rules of evidence. If an attorney did not object to a statement or line of questioning, he'd lose the chance to object to it in a future appeal.

What the jury would hear was like a censored stage play. The real issues and facts would be discussed more openly between judge and counsel, beyond—or *supposedly* beyond—the jury's hearing. Before the jury entered that first morning, Seplow and Clayton had already argued before Judge Gerst. A lot of it was mere formality: defense and prosecution had to repeat motions and make objections for the record, even though they knew they didn't have a snowball's chance. Some of it went by too fast for Scott to follow, but it sounded as if Seplow renewed his motion to dismiss the case involving Michelle Morales, who was last seen getting into a truck with a man who was clearly NOT Scott. Gerst denied the motion.

Scott wasn't surprised; it had already been decided that the State of Arizona was going for every charge they could possibly pin on him. Even if the prosecution couldn't prove that Scott had committed murder, planting that suspicion in the jurists' minds would make them hesitate to find him not guilty of lesser charges.

Judge Gerst had so far refused to admit evidence of "third parties"—other men more likely to have committed the crimes. There were those known to the victims, some of whom had given vague or inconsistent stories. The police reports were littered with the names of other men who matched the suspects' descriptions. Unlike Scott, some of them had criminal histories. There was Carl Frederick Gardei, in prison after confessing to serial sexual assaults in Phoenix in 1991-92. Gardei had rigged interior doors of his car so that his victims could not escape, which sounded like the situation that Mona Barnett* described: a car without interior door handles.

Stephen Glen Blondel's* hair and blood type matched the rapist in the case of Nancy Caporaso.* There was also David Bowles,* who drove a car similar to that used in some of the attacks. Looking at a photo of Bowles, Caporaso thought that he could possibly have been the attacker described by victims. And Caporaso had spotted Robert T. McGinnis* within a couple of months of the attack. She told police she was "pretty sure" McGinnis had raped her. Why were none of these guys shown to the victims at a lineup? And why were no DNA tests ever done to determine whether Blondel, Bowles, McGinnis, or some other person of interest was guilty?

Also at issue were the crimes against Teresa Martinez* and Carly Sweet*. If there was a pattern to the "baby-seat" attacks, those two cases fit it well. However, both Martinez and Sweet had seen Scott at the lineup and were sure that it was *not* him who attacked them. Would the jury be able to hear from them?

As they waited for the jury, Clayton put on the record that Alison Brooks was present in the courtroom. Witnesses were not supposed to listen to testimony before they took the stand, but crime victims—who might later testify as witnesses—were exempted from that rule and could attend all the sessions. To Scott, that exception was outrageous. If the rule was intended to prevent witnesses from being biased by previous testimony, victims were no less prone to being influenced.

With the jury in place, Judge Gerst lit up. He welcomed them jovially and explained that each one was given a notebook with his or her name, instructions, notepaper, and forms to ask questions to witnesses. Gerst would decide on whether to ask any questions submitted by jurors. That was a new procedure, and it sounded nuts to Scott. If there were strict rules to control what the attorneys asked witnesses, would the jury be allowed to ask the questions they really wanted the answers to? On the other hand, he worried that the jurors' questions could be used against him.

These jurists had all met a "death-penalty qualification." That meant that anyone with ethical objections to the death penalty was not allowed to serve. Not surprisingly, research had shown that death-penalty-qualified juries were more likely to find the defendant guilty. And in their responses to a jury selection questionnaire, ten of the sixteen jurists here claimed to have "a moral conviction that the death penalty is good." Not a sad necessity, but "good"!

Scott had attended the jury selection. To begin with, anyone who stated that the length of this trial—probably a couple of months—would create a hardship was excused. Jurists were paid only $12 a day, so people who couldn't afford to take time off work were excluded. Then, both prosecution and defense were able to strike a number of jurists they guessed would be least sympathetic. As Scott watched people who seemed open-minded and progressive being eliminated from the pool, he thought the process should have been called "jury rejection." Bill Clayton rejected one jurist with long hair, claiming that the man might identify with Seplow on that account. Then Clayton rejected a woman who'd previously served on a jury that found the defendant not guilty of sexual assault.

Maybe it could have been a worse jury: these were steady people in clerical, financial, or manufacturing jobs, for the most part; an older group including several retirees. Conservative people, but basically decent, Scott thought. Though they might be inclined to trust the State's allegations, he hoped they'd be capable of objectivity.

Judge Gerst recited the charges against Scott from the 1992 indictment by the Grand Jurors of Maricopa County. Today's jury would never learn that the foreman of that very grand jury, Richard Donohue,* matched the description of the baby-seat rapist and owned a car and license plate similar to that reported by several of the victims. A man who'd been arrested for violence and drug possession, Donohue himself had been questioned as a person of interest in the crimes he helped charge Scott with!

The list of charges was long: one count for every possible act of violence an assailant might have committed against each victim: the kidnapping and assaults of Mona Barnett, Nancy Caporaso, Margaret Christorf, Michelle Morales, Meredith Porter, and Amy Perry; plus attempted murder of Caporaso and Porter; premeditated murder of Christorf, Morales and Belinda Cronin; and presumed sex crimes against Cronin, although no evidence of such acts existed. Totaling twenty-four counts, it was an inflated list of the worst charges that prosecutors would ordinarily use to scare a suspect into agreeing to plea bargain.

In horrified silence, today's jury heard the charges handed down by the grand jury. Scott wished someone would explain that a grand jury never saw evidence contrary to the County Attorney's case and usually delivered whatever indictments the County Attorney requested. Not to mention that, in this case, the foreman of that grand jury was at least as likely to be guilty of those crimes as Scott.

Gerst added, "to which the defendant has pled not guilty as to each and every count alleged in the Indictment." In a sanctimonious tone, the judge explained, "Every defendant is presumed by law to be innocent. The State must prove the charges beyond a reasonable doubt."

"Hear, hear," Scott thought, though he wondered if it was possible for the average jurist to believe that, seeing him here under armed guard, accused of inhuman cruelty.

18: Clayton v. Seplow

Seplow had warned Scott that Bill Clayton was good with a jury. As Clayton stood to give his opening statement, he pasted on a smile and thanked the jury in advance for their time. His manner deftly indicated that, as responsible, law-abiding citizens, they were naturally on the side of the prosecution.

"The crimes are horrible," Clayton intoned. "They are despicable. . . . I ask for you to look at the evidence as evidence. Look for the exhibits and the testimony as they come together as a whole. Do not judge a book by its cover, in other words."

Scott hoped they would follow the prosecutor's advice.

Clayton told the jury that the main issue "in this case"—*these cases*, Scott thought angrily, *these seven very different cases*— would be identification. Scott agreed heartily. But then Clayton went on to define *modus operandi* as "helping to identify something from someone else." What modus operandi really meant was a perpetrator's method of committing a crime. Clayton's cock-eyed definition seemed designed to confuse the jury into looking for patterns that didn't exist. "You will receive this evidence one piece at a time . . . but nothing is unto itself. Look at it all together."

Damn, no; Scott thought. That was the fallacy these charges were based on.

Beginning with the assault against Mona Barnett, Clayton launched into a vague summary of the crimes. The prosecutor's narrative was one long train of omissions and exaggerations that made the crimes look more similar than they were. The stars of Clayton's story were Maricopa County detectives who "developed" a case that pointed only to Scott Lehr. "The defendant's blood was analyzed. They did what is called DNA, and I will talk about the match later."

Scott held his face impassive. There was no "match," and surely Clayton knew it.

Clayton stressed that the victims were all small women, although they weren't, and that they all got into a strikingly similar car, which they didn't; and that they were all assaulted in a similar area, which was only true if you considered the hundreds of miles of desert around Phoenix "similar." Clayton made it sound as if the assailant did not have vaginal sex with Nancy Caporaso, though he had. Clayton also implied that the attacker tried to kill Nancy Caporaso, which he evidently had not. Clayton made a big deal about the claim that a fragment of a fingerprint left on a McDonald's cup found near the crime scene matched Scott's, though it did not. The prosecutor claimed that Nancy had "awakened" with "a mighty bump on her head," although the doctor who examined Nancy did not note any bump at all. "You'll hear more about pounding someone's head on the ground later," Clayton said darkly.

Scott had a strong urge to vomit.

The prosecutor next described Margaret Christorf as "a person who is older, kind of hung out late at night. She would drink a bit. She would accept rides."

Another lie. Scott remembered a police interview with a friend of Christorf's who said that she would NOT accept rides with strangers, no matter how much she'd been drinking.

Then the prosecutor was describing the crime against 10-year-old Amy Perry. Clayton said that Amy remembered a package of cigarettes in the car. He didn't mention that the cigarettes were Camels, which Scott did not smoke. Worse yet, Clayton actually hinted that the cigarettes Amy saw were Marlboros: "You'll hear about some cigarettes and some Marlboro cigarettes that are common in these cases, these victims. There is this car that keeps appearing, that's a large tan or '80-type Chevrolet, four-door."

That was misleading, since Amy had described a "copper-colored" car. For that matter, not one of the victims had ever described a car like Scott's Chevy Caprice, which was tan with a black top.

Clayton next made the murder of Belinda Cronin sound as if it could have been committed by the man guilty of the so-called "baby-seat" rapes. Clayton said that items found on Belinda Cronin's remains included "a necklace, a Swatch watch, still running, a small ring was on her finger—or was it a bracelet . . ."

Well, Scott knew that no ring could possibly have been found on her finger because her hands were missing, most likely taken by animals. Scott doubted that the man was just sloppy; more likely he was eager to have the jury blur the details of the cases. Scott had started the day believing he'd already buried every illusion he'd had about the legal system. Still, he was shocked by the tactics of the distinguished-looking prosecutor.

"Had a discussion with Elaine Lehr, the defendant's wife. She'll testify in this case," Clayton said, insinuating that Elaine would testify against Scott. ". . . There was one item that she gave to the detectives that she said was given to her after Christmas by Scott . . . . It was a ring, a diamond ring."

Great. So Clayton was going to claim the garage-sale ring that Elaine had handed over to detectives was taken from Cronin. But Scott knew he'd brought it home *before* Christmas, because he remembered the twins fighting over it. If Scott really had committed these crimes and stolen the victims' possessions, it was remarkable that detectives had not been able to find any evidence when they searched his home and car.

"And let's talk about Michelle Morales," Clayton blustered on. The prosecutor spoke as if she was murdered in the very same area as other crimes, "just north of the Caporaso and Belinda Cronin clump of trees."

Scott remembered the police reports all too clearly. Morales' body was found over 5 miles away from the other two crime scenes.

Clayton painted a heart-wrenching picture of the murdered young woman: "She's laying there exposed and she had been there for a couple of weeks. Her body is maggot infested. A single sperm is found . . . . And that one band is present on the DNA autorads . . . It is in the same position as one of Scott's but it is not a match. It's just not an elimination."

Jeez, Louise; Scott thought. So having NO evidence somehow demonstrated that he was guilty? They sure tossed that "presumption of innocence" out the window early in the game!

Clayton turned to the Meredith Porter case. Even amid the barrage of distortions, Scott sat up and took notice when the prosecutor hinted that Porter had not been assaulted on Sunday, February 23—which was the date specified in the police reports— but on the day before, and that she'd wandered disoriented for two days. Clayton must have known damn well that Scott had an airtight alibi on February 23, the twins' birthday party.

Clayton went on to suggest that a positive DNA comparison had been made in the Porter case. Well, of course, they couldn't have a DNA match with Scott because he was home asleep when the girl was assaulted. "Flying DNA," Seplow had joked. But maybe the prosecution's excesses would work in Scott's favor here: If Seplow could show how preposterous it was to accuse Scott of the crimes against Porter, the flimsiness of the other cases would also show through.

If this was the longest opening statement on record, Scott wouldn't have been surprised. Clayton rambled on about ABO testing and enzyme testing and DNA testing although he pretended to be concerned about the jury getting hungry. It sounded as if the prosecution's goal was to pound the jury into sheer confusion. Scott had read that when juries are confused, they convict.

Scowling, Bill Clayton wound down. "At the end of the case, the State is going to ask you to look at each and every one of the charges of the Indictment . . . and I'll ask you to return a verdict of guilty on every one."

Scott hoped the jury *did* look carefully.

While the court broke for lunch, the guards took Scott back to the holding cell behind the courtroom. Between disgust at Clayton's tactics and fear that his life was now in the hands of strangers, he couldn't even try to eat the stale sandwich in his

Ladmo bag. He settled for the dry, bitter orange and the little carton of milk.

With judge and jury reassembled, sleepy and dull after a good lunch, Scott supposed, it was finally Phil Seplow's turn to open the defense's case. Seplow shot a confident smile at Scott before striding before the jury box. At least the attorney left his high-top sneakers and jeans at home. Except for the curly, salt-and-pepper hair cascading down to his collar, Seplow in a jacket and tie was within the ballpark of how an attorney should look.

Seplow formally wished Clayton and Gerst a good afternoon. To Scott it seemed rude not to greet the jury as well. But Seplow was transparently uncomfortable talking to a jury. He tried to be casual, but it came out condescending. "You know," he said, "when I was listening to my learned opponent this morning . . . I was thinking, 'Well, I should just close up the book, walk out the door.' Then I remembered what the attorneys tell you is not evidence. There's been no evidence presented."

True enough, but lukewarm, Scott thought.

Seplow continued. ". . . I can certainly tell you that I believe the evidence will show that when Mona Barnett talks with a police officer, she says that the person who assaults her has blond hair. . ."

He "believes"? Didn't Seplow remember the police reports they'd pored over together?

Then Seplow set out on the risky tightrope walk between discrediting unreliable testimony from victims and coming across as denying those victims justice. "Nobody from this table. . . is saying that these horrible things did not happen to these young girls. What we're saying is you've got the wrong person." Seplow went on to observe that Mona Barnett had been attacked in an American-made blue car, with no inside door handles. But he wasn't allowed to mention that those details might link that crime to others confessed to by Carl Gardei. But Seplow stepped over the line into finding fault with Barnett. "She doesn't even give the officer her full name because there's a warrant out for her arrest."

Scott was relieved when Seplow moved on. "The big point here that the prosecution made . . . is that there is a partial fingerprint on a cup, McDonald's cup. That fingerprint was checked approximately against 38 people, including Mr. Lehr, making it 39, not once, but twice and maybe a third time, as will come out in the evidence, until all of a sudden after interviews and after finding out that the DNA is inconclusive, there's a, quote, enhancement of this partial fingerprint."

Scott hoped the jury followed that. Seplow had coached him not to look at the jury; they might interpret his curiosity as guilt or hostility. Still, he sneaked a peek. They looked half asleep.

Seplow warmed up. "He's like, encased in a shroud. And it becomes the prosecution's job to rip that shroud apart and until you say: Okay. We believe beyond a reasonable doubt."

Scott wished his defense attorney wouldn't for a moment talk in a way that made Scott sound guilty.

"Again, in the Christorf case . . . The last person to see Margaret Christorf was a clerk in a convenience store . . . She had a boyfriend named McFadden. They had an argument. She took off." Seplow brought up the freshly chewed gum found near Christorf's body. "They did a DNA analysis of the gum, and it's inconclusive to Scott Lehr. . ."

Scott wished that Seplow would argue a little harder. The DNA from the gum "wasn't just inconclusive"; it positively eliminated him!

Seplow then told the jury that Amy Perry had identified a "big and fat" assailant with a mid-chest length beard, "a Santa Claus" beard. "That's what this case is about—identification. May be, to some degree a rush to judgment . . . ."

"To some degree"?!

"DNA doesn't identify. It excludes . . . . And what the State will be asking you to do is judge those DNA tests based on the emerging science at the DPS laboratory before it ever really knew what it was doing."

Although everything Seplow said was true, Scott imagined that it would be tough to persuade a conservative jury to look critically at the State's "scientific" evidence.

Turning to the murder of Belinda Cronin, Seplow mentioned that she had been seeing a Dr. Storm. But the lawyer abruptly changed the subject, as if he'd remembered that he probably wouldn't be allowed to introduce the evidence of other men who might have killed her.

Scott wondered why Seplow didn't just go ahead and tell them about Dr. Storm anyway; Clayton had already said things that weren't even true. It all seemed so lopsided and unfair.

"If this is the same perpetrator—and it may be several different people, if the evidence points to that."

Come on, Phil! "It *may* be several different people"? What happened to the confidence in Scott's innocence and the cynicism about the prosecution's case that Seplow had always expressed?

But Seplow did turn up the heat when he got to the murder of Michelle Morales. "She was last seen going into a pickup truck with an older man somewhere between 40 and 50 years old. He had a receding hairline . . . No evidence that it's Scott Lehr. . . . She had multiple hairs on her body. None of those hairs matched Scott Lehr."

Seplow finished with the case of Meredith Porter. "She was battered horribly."

No, Scott thought. The girl had not been beaten—neither according to her own statement nor the medical notes. She was hit once, but most of her injuries were the result of falling as she made her way through the dark.

"But when she first talks to the police officers, she says she was picked up at Central and 19th Avenue by a guy in a newer gray pickup truck, possibly a Nissan. Meredith Porter tells the police that . . .this assailant, had blue-green eyes. It will be pretty easy to see as the trial goes on that Mr. Lehr has dark-brown eyes. . . . She also said that her assailant had large smooth hands. And the reason that's important is because you'll know from the evidence, Mr. Lehr is a tree-trimmer. He's not going to have smooth hands."

Good enough, Scott thought. But Seplow also needed to tell them that Porter said the assailant had large, prominent ears, as Scott did not. Grand juror Richard Donohue—who had also been interviewed during the investigation—did, though.

"The other thing I think is imperative for me to remind you all is that Scott Lehr and his attorneys do not have to present one shred of evidence in this case. He doesn't have to testify. We may not want him to testify, depending on what we know from trial experience from many, many years. But the one thing we do know is that you are not to make any negative or any unseemly, take it as implication, indication in any way whatsoever."

Hm. Scott wondered whether a jury really could believe that a man who was innocent would not speak in his own defense.

After reminding the jury that the cases were ugly, Seplow concluded, "Ladies and gentlemen, two wrongs don't make a right. And at the end of this case we will be asking for you to review the evidence and to see that there is reasonable doubt pursuant to the instructions that His Honor will give you and acquit Mr. Lehr. Thank you."

"There is reasonable doubt"? Scott reminded himself to keep breathing. How about an indignant, "He's innocent of all these charges. There was never sufficient evidence to charge him"? He glanced at the clock. Seplow had talked for about 35 minutes, Clayton for at least an hour and a half.

19: Mona Barnett Tells the Truth

Abruptly, they were swearing in Mona Barnett. The poor woman looked like an aging street person trying to pass for middle-class. Scott supposed the State provided her with the modest slacks and blouse she wore.

Bill Clayton began his direct examination with a courtly, "Good afternoon, ma'am."

Barnett smiled, revealing a jack-o'-lantern gap where her front teeth should have been.

"Okay. Miss Barnett, I'm going to ask you something that's probably taboo. That's how old you are."

She answered without embarrassment that she was 54.

"Okay. Now, Miss Barnett, I'm going to call your attention back to the year of 1991, and ask if you were residing in the Phoenix area?"

"Yes, I was."

"Okay. And, particularly, in the month of February, let me ask you where were you working February of '91?"

"I was not working at the time."

"Not working" was probably a stretch of truth, Scott remembered; Barnett had a record of arrests for prostitution—as well as shoplifting and drug possession. But now all of that was forgotten as she testified for the prosecution.

Step by step, Clayton directed her to re-create the crimes for the jury, beginning as she walked on Van Buren and 27th Avenue. "Do you remember what you were doing there . . . ?"

"I was walking. I was trying to get home. . . . I was offered a ride by a gentleman. And he was supposed to take me home, and, instead he took the freeway. . . . And the next thing I know he reached over, and I think he had taken his hand and put his hand through here somewhere." She indicated her neck. "And I kind of blacked out. . . ."

With a tolerant smile, Clayton backtracked and teased out the details. He asked if Barnett was hitchhiking "with your thumb out or anything"?

No, the woman answered. The man had just offered her a ride. Because it was late, she accepted. Barnett described the car as a smaller, light-blue sedan, messy inside. The man said his name was Dave. When the man grabbed her around the neck, she blacked out, she said. When she came to, she thought the car was turning off to the left, onto a paved road with "desert scenery."

Then Clayton asked Barnett to describe the assault. Calmly, she recalled the man telling her to take her clothes off and to climb into the back seat. He ordered her to have oral sex with him. She did as he said. Clayton prodded her for the man's exact words, but she couldn't remember. Then, "He asked me to—to have sex with him."

Clayton was claiming to have DNA evidence in this case, so if Barnett didn't say that the assailant ejaculated, this one was lost. "When a man ejaculates, do you know what that means?" the prosecutor asked, as if addressing a nun.

Barnett acknowledged that she knew what ejaculation was and that the man had done so. Afterwards, she said, he ordered her out of the car and shoved her into a ravine.

"Did he say anything to you then?"

"I can't remember. I think he said something very degrading, as far as I can remember, but I can't . . . "

Clayton cut her off. "Were you injured?"

"Some, yes."

Clayton showed the jury photos of her with a few abrasions.

Barnett told how she found her way out to get help. The man had driven away with her clothes and purse, so she found a scrap of carpet to wrap herself in.

"Do you recall what that person looks like?"

"I think so."

Seplow had prepared Scott for the dramatic "courtroom identification," in which the prosecutor would lead each victim to point to Scott. The reliability of such identifications was laughable. Even if the person being tried was guilty, in court he or she'd be dressed and groomed differently. Often it would have been years since the crime—in this case, over five years. It would be difficult for most victims to identify a perpetrator under those conditions, but the procedure was rigged. Prosecutors would make sure witnesses knew where the defendant would be sitting. In this trial, some of the victims would already have watched others identify Scott. And even if a victim really did not recognize the accused, she had come to feel that identifying him was her only chance to see justice done. But biased as an in-court identification might be, it made a strong impression on a jury.

Scott steadied himself to show no feeling when this stranger would point to him as the man who raped her, years ago, on the day before he celebrated his first wedding anniversary with Elaine.

"Look around the courtroom," Clayton instructed. The jury froze attentively. Just in case, Clayton gave her an out. "And you said a while ago that you did not have your glasses on. You do not have them on now."

"I can see from a distance," Barnett asserted.

Clayton had no choice but to go on. "The person who picked you up and attacked you, do you see that person here today?"

Barnett nodded. "It looks like him, that gentleman back there."

"Somebody back here?" Clayton's voice was strained.

"That blond," Mona Barnett confirmed.

"That blond in the very back?"

"Yes."

Seplow jumped to his feet. "Would that person please stand up, Your Honor?"

Judge Gerst agreed.

The blond guy seemed amused. Scott guessed he was some kind of cop.

Clayton hustled to keep his show going. "That particular night—and this may be embarrassing, but I'm going to ask you if you had sex that night with any other person?"

Barnett paused. "I can't remember."

Now the prosecutor was sweating. "Okay. And let me ask you if that particular time, February of 1991, you ever remember coming into contact with this gentleman right here?" Clayton pointed to Scott.

"No."

"Okay. Have you ever had sex with that man right there, that you recall?"

"No."

"How is your eyesight?" Clayton asked hopefully.

Scott struggled not to laugh out loud.

"Not real good," Barnett admitted.

Now the prosecutor had a little something to work with. He asked her about the lighting in the car, which she agreed was "kind of dark."

It wasn't yet three o'clock that Wednesday afternoon, but they adjourned until the following Tuesday. Scott was satisfied that the jurors would have five days to mull over the fact that the State's first victim emphatically denied ever seeing him before.

Judge Gerst directed the jurors to leave their notebooks on the chairs. "Camille will pick them up and keep them safe for you."

How convenient, Scott noticed. How easy it would be for the staff to peek into those notebooks and learn how each of those jurors was interpreting the State's case. While the court was supposed to be impartial, judges were kept in office by voters who wanted them to punish the bad guys. A high ratio of guilty verdicts must be as valuable to a judge's resume as it was to those in the County Attorney's office.

But there was no point worrying about it. Seplow and Reeves turned to him, cautiously pleased with the trial's first day. Scott could imagine that he'd walk out of here soon.

Dee Dee and Yvonne smiled and waved before they turned to leave. Now they didn't have to fake their good spirits.

As Scott was led back to the holding cell, Dee Dee's smile lingered in his mind. Before today he hadn't really noticed that his sister was a beautiful young woman. He should have seen that, even though she dressed simply, usually in jeans, and didn't use makeup. What an angry, competitive relationship they'd had as kids. He'd never really gotten to know her as the woman she'd become. Now here she was, interrupting her life for him, keeping faith in his innocence, braving the disgust of ordinary people.

20: "Identification"

SEPTEMBER 24-26, 1996

When the trial resumed, Phil Seplow asked the judge to put on the record that the man that Barnett had identified in court as her attacker was blond, with a receding hairline and a round face. He stood 5'6", with a small-to-medium build. Scott was 6'1", 205 pounds, with a full head of brown hair and brown eyes. Scott's jaw was angular enough that no one would describe his face as round.

The next witnesses Clayton called were a couple of detectives who'd worked on the case of Mona Barnett and the nurse who examined her after the attack. There was excruciatingly long testimony about the process of examining a rape victim and using what was called a "rape kit" to swab samples of physical evidence from her mouth, vagina, and anus.

The prosecutor then called Donita Bueno, the police officer who'd taken custody of Mona Barnett's rape kit. For exhibits of the sexual assault kits and other fragile physical evidence, counsel for both sides had agreed, or stipulated, that photographs could be displayed, rather than bringing the actual evidence to court. That avoided the risk of damaging the evidence, which was supposed to remain frozen. As she looked at the photos, Bueno admitted she did not see her initials on the seal of the rape kit, although they should have been there. Bueno said she would seal test tubes containing evidence with a white tape after drying the swabs, but in the photo Clayton displayed, the tubes were Scotch-taped. To the careful observer, the possibility that someone could have tampered with the rape kit was clear.

It was Mike Reeves who cross-examined Officer Bueno. In response to his questioning, she admitted that she carried the physical evidence around for as long as four hours before taking it to the General Investigations Bureau. She also agreed that the swabs from anal, oral, and vaginal areas were touching, possibly contaminating one another in the police dryer. Bueno admitted that the trays in the dryer were not cleaned after every use. She had not cleaned the trays herself before putting the swabs in the dryer, where air circulated freely.

Scott exhaled with annoyance. If the state was going to produce some claim of "DNA evidence," they would obviously be on shaky ground.

With no announcement to the jury, testimony shifted to the case of Nancy Caporaso. Detective Kenneth Proudfit had investigated the crime scene by flashlight, some three or four hours after the attack on April 4, 1991. He showed photos of rocks "with what appears to be blood on them."

On cross-examination, Seplow prompted Proudfit to admit that he wasn't sure the red substance on the rocks *was* blood. Apparently they had not been tested. Proudfit also said that he'd supervised taking photos of tire tracks at the site, but that he didn't know what became of the photos after he turned them in. Scott's opinion went back and forth on whether Maricopa County was incompetent to conduct a thorough investigation, or worse— deliberately careless.

Finally came the moment the jury had been waiting for. Nancy Caporaso herself approached the stand. She was a very small woman.

After solicitously offering clean cups for drinking water, the prosecutor asked, "And you came to court here today with someone else; would that be correct?"

"Yes."

"And who was that person?" Clayton prompted sweetly.

"My mother."

At 27, Nancy Caporaso was old enough to come to court without her mother, but Clayton seemed to want the jury to mistake her for a child. Caporaso's clothing and manner also played up her youthful appearance. She referred to herself as a "teenager" at the time of the crime, although she'd been 21.

Guided by Clayton's questioning, Caporaso related how a man had given her a ride that afternoon after work and offered her a housekeeping job. He suggested taking her to meet his wife. He said he owned horses, so at first she wasn't surprised when he drove out to the desert on the northwest edge of town. But then he didn't seem to know where he was. The car veered off a side street and hit some barbed wire.

Caporaso recalled that the suspect announced, "This looks like a good place to fuck," and choked her until she agreed to cooperate.

It was late afternoon, and Judge Gerst recessed the court for the day. As the judge wished the jury a "nice evening," Scott thought he might have one, too, or as nice an evening as a cell in the Madison Street jail would allow. Mona Barnett had frankly stated that he was innocent of assaulting her, and the facts of Nancy Caporaso's case would exonerate him as well. So far, so good.

But the following day would teach him otherwise. Scott had gone over the police reports so many times that he noticed every difference between what Nancy Caporaso had told police and what she was testifying now. He didn't want to suspect her of dishonesty, but it sure looked as though the prosecution had coached her to say what would best support their case against Scott.

With a display of concern for the woman's emotional state, Clayton tried to steer her away from statements that made it clear that she had been attacked by a man who could not have been Scott. The prosecutor made a big deal about the man wearing a large gold watch and a red T-back shirt. Caporaso had reported to police that the suspect's watch was square, with no numerals on it, and looked expensive. Now Clayton displayed photos of "evidence" they'd collected from Scott's house after arresting him: a red tank top, which was not a T-back, and a greatly enlarged photo of Scott, wearing a square gold watch on his left arm.

Yes, the young woman agreed, those "did not differ" from the ones the rapist had worn.

But square watches are common, and his tank top was not a T-back, Scott wanted to yell. How could anyone in good conscience agree that his shirt and watch "did not differ" from those of the rapist?

And yet, to her credit, Caporaso continued to insist that the man who attacked her drove a two-door tan car. That didn't correspond to Scott's black-topped four-door. Yet when Clayton showed Caporaso a photo of the interior of Scott's four-door Caprice, she contradicted herself, agreeing that Scott's car looked "the same" as the crime vehicle.

After Clayton elicited from Nancy the details of the rape, she related how, afterwards, the attacker pulled her out of the car by her neck. She said that was the last thing she remembered before waking up a few minutes later with a headache. Clayton also got Nancy to agree that the rapist had not ejaculated; Scott knew that the doctor who examined Nancy did in fact find sperm. DNA analysis of that rape kit had proven Scott innocent, but Clayton apparently intended to hide that fact.

Clayton assumed a stern tone. "Would you look around the courtroom, please, and see if the person who did this to you is here in the courtroom?"

"Yes."

After the fiasco with Mona Barnett, Scott knew Clayton would make sure Nancy Caporaso knew where to find the accused. Wide-eyed, she pointed to Scott.

Clayton trumpeted, "Let the record reflect that she's identified the defendant, please."

Although it was no laughing matter to be accused of rape, Scott almost smiled at Clayton's relief.

When Seplow stepped up to cross-examine, he went out of his way to be pleasant to Nancy Caporaso. Still, it was essential that he expose her mistake in identifying Scott. Seplow began by questioning her about the rapist's height. Several times, as the police interviewed her, she'd described the suspect as between 5'5" and 5'7". But now she claimed to have forgotten her description of the rapist, which made it easy for her to identify

6'1" Scott as the guilty man. Seplow also reminded her that she identified someone other than Scott in a photo lineup in October 1991 as possibly being her attacker, and that seven weeks after the attack she had identified yet another man at a Star Mart. She took down his license and called police, telling them she was "pretty sure" he was the attacker.

"No, I didn't do that," she now insisted.

Well, she had; but here she was, denying it under oath! Scott supposed that Seplow could later get testimony to prove that Caporaso had identified a couple of other men. He wondered, though, whether the jury would remember back to Nancy's erroneous testimony today.

Caporaso also claimed to have forgotten that she'd described the suspect as having a "layered" haircut and a beard at least several days old. Seplow was able to show that Scott at the lineup was clean-shaven, with very short hair, quite different than the composite drawing that Nancy had earlier said resembled the assailant, with a confidence of 9 on a scale of 10. Yet at that lineup, Nancy claimed that Scott had the same face, same hair, and looked the same as the man who assaulted her!

With his re-direct examination, Clayton tried to undo the damage. "Are you tired?" he asked gently.

"Please make him hurry up. I think I'm going to throw up."

As Judge Gerst interrupted to call a brief recess, she muttered, "Oh, God."

When the court reconvened, Caporaso had everyone's sympathy. Clayton asked her whether anything that happened today had made her change her mind about her confidence that Scott was guilty. "No," she said firmly.

The silence in the jury box was painful.

But Seplow had a card up his sleeve. He had overheard the prosecution the day before, actually coaching Nancy to identify Scott. Now Seplow asked Nancy if she remembered speaking with Clayton after the jury had been dismissed.

"You were asked. . . 'Was there anybody in the courtroom that you can identify?'. . . And your answer was: 'I think there is.' Is that correct?"

She admitted that it was.

Clayton jumped in. He reminded Caporaso that his question about "recognizing" Scott had to do with having her glasses on or off. "And do you recall my then asking you . . . if there is somebody or a person in the courtroom you recognized as having done this to you?"

"At this moment, I can barely remember my own name."

Although that also supported Scott's innocence, Clayton responded as if her answer was somehow evidence against Scott. "That's all I have, Your Honor," he concluded, with a stagily sympathetic look at Caporaso. The man was a master of spinning a situation to his advantage.

Clayton's next witness was the Phoenix Police Department Crime Lab's fingerprint expert, Karen Jones. Jones had eliminated Scott on the basis of the latent prints found on the McDonald's cup, but then, a couple years later, Detective Dimodica sent her Scott's prints again. This time, Jones found a way to claim that one of those fingerprints matched Scott's, after all! That questionable fingerprint analysis was the only thing that even arguably linked Scott to the crimes against Caporaso.

A nondescript, middle-aged woman took the witness stand. There was nothing about Jones's appearance to suggest that she was capable of faking evidence.

Clayton asked questions aimed at making Jones sound impeccably competent: first her credentials as latent print examiner in Phoenix for 23 years and then the basic principles involved in fingerprint analysis. Since the 1700s, Jones noted, "no two individuals have ever been found to have the same fingerprints." Then she explained why she'd reversed her opinion to declare, several years after concluding that Scott's fingerprints did NOT match the evidence sample, that one of those prints actually WAS Scott's.

On the surface, her explanation was plausible. She claimed that when Dimodica asked her to compare Scott's prints the second time, better technology was available: the ability to "enhance" the latent print by photographing and enlarging it 8 to 10 times. She indicated 14 "points of similarity" between the partial print on the cup and Scott's thumbprint. That sounded good, to anyone who didn't remember that she said there are 50 to 75 points of identification on any fingerprint. And, for reasons she didn't explain, she'd analyzed xerox copies of Scott's prints, rather than his actual prints.

Mike Reeves's cross-examination was devastating. Within minutes, he got Jones to admit that the partial print on the cup was really only a small area of a thumb. Reeves also asked if she was aware that Detective Dimodica had asked her to compare the print to Scott's for the second time only after DNA tests had ruled Scott out.

She said she was not.

Reeves also jumped in on Jones's claim of a 14-point comparison with one of Scott's prints. She confirmed that, in England, a fingerprint must be matched at least 16 points before being admissible in trial, and in France, at least 20 points.

While studying the police reports, Scott counted over 30 possible suspects in this case who'd slipped through investigators' hands in 1991 and 1992 because their fingerprints didn't appear to match this smudge of a partial print, which might, for that matter, have belonged to a server at McDonald's!

Reeves asked whether Jones had gone back and compared the "enhanced" fingerprint to any of the other suspects.

She had not.

On his re-direct examination, Clayton asked Jones, ". . . are there other experts outside the Phoenix Police Department that could look at these prints and verify or not verify those?"

She agreed that there were.

At that, Seplow asked Judge Gerst for permission to approach the bench. With the jury out of hearing, Seplow made a motion for a mistrial. By asking Jones whether there were other experts who could check the prints, Clayton had attempted to shift the burden of proof onto the defense. The defense had no obligation to produce such experts.

Scott's pulse jumped at the mention of a mistrial, but Gerst flatly denied Seplow's motion. Even though Scott knew this was a game they had to play, it was maddening to hear Seplow denied.

Clayton called Officer Gayle Jarrell to testify. The senior officer at the scene, Jarrell interviewed Caporaso at the hospital and noted her description of the suspect as only five foot-five or five-six, about the same height as Jarrell himself. Seplow asked Jarrell to stand next to Scott, who at six-one stood a head taller.

21: Connections

SEPTEMBER 26-27, 1996

Before the end of the third day at trial, Prosecutor Clayton called a witness for a third case, the murder of Margaret Christorf. The way the testimony jumped abruptly from one case to the next still surprised Scott. Even though his study of the police reports gave him a solid memory of individual cases, the endless procession of witnesses sometimes left even him confused. It seemed as if every witness was testifying about the same case, which was, he supposed, exactly what the prosecution wanted the jury to believe.

When court reconvened on Monday morning, Clayton went back once more to the Caporaso case, calling to the stand a nurse who helped examine Caporaso after the rape. And when good old Reeves cross-examined the nurse, he got her to read from the hospital report, "patient states that she was choked and gives a history of questionable loss of consciousness."

Aha, Scott thought. So Caporaso's blackout had seemed "questionable," even to a sympathetic medical team. So much for the prosecution's insinuation that she'd suffered serious injury, let alone that the attacker had tried to kill her.

The prosecution's next witness was Dr. Larry Shaw, who'd performed autopsies for the Maricopa County Medical Examiner's Office on both Margaret Christorf and Belinda Cronin. Dr. Shaw would testify about both cases today, although the Cronin case would not be discussed for some time.

The jury was shown ghastly photos of the dead Christorf. Scott couldn't see how such "exhibits" served any purpose but to arouse outrage. Outrage was certainly the appropriate response to the murder, but not relevant to the question of *who* killed her. Shaw stated that Christorf had died quickly of massive brain injury caused by crushing blows to the left and right side of her head.

Clayton asked Dr. Shaw what kind of object could have caused the fatal injuries.

"Usually a blunt force," Shaw answered, "a blow to the head with usually some object, and anywhere from a flattened board to a baseball bat to tire iron to anything that will give you a relatively flat or at least broad, round surface and a lot of impression at the time of the impact . . ."

That didn't sound like a rock to Scott, but Clayton got Dr. Shaw to agree that the injuries could possibly have been caused by two rocks found at the scene.

Clayton then questioned Shaw about his autopsy of Belinda Cronin nearly six months after her disappearance. Shaw described Belinda's body as mere "skeletal remains" with "a very small amount of parchment of skin." Her hands and feet were missing, along with the front of her skull. The jury recoiled at photos of what was left of the pretty young woman. As Shaw put it, "There isn't anything to autopsy."

The remains of Belinda Cronin were too decomposed to determine possible other factors in her death, and the only visible injury was an area of five or six fractures at the front of her head plus a small fracture at the top or back of her head. Scott remembered that Shaw had originally said that he believed that a single powerful blow had caused all the fractures, but now the prosecutor was asking if it could have been more than one blow, to make it sound more like the murder of Margaret Christorf, Scott supposed.

The doctor's response was puzzling. "My experience, it would be more than one blow. It could be one blow."

Seplow cross-examined Doctor Shaw about Margaret Christorf first. The doctor confirmed that there were no defensive wounds or other signs that she'd resisted the killer. And apparently neither the police nor Shaw had taken any fingernail clippings from Christorf, which might have provided DNA evidence of the murderer.

Moving on to the doctor's findings on Belinda Cronin, Seplow asked him to look at the photo showing the missing front of the woman's skull, apparently cut off along a straight line. How, Seplow asked, do you get such a straight line?

"When I look at that," Shaw answered, "it comes to mind a sharp instrument, ax, something with a sharp pick."

At Seplow's urging, the Doctor drew a line around Seplow's face, showing where Belinda Cronin's face had been cut away.

The jury murmured at the dramatic effect. Scott couldn't imagine how such an injury could have been caused by a rock.

Clayton's next witness was, Rafe Collins. A recovered alcoholic, Collins testified that he'd tried to help his friend Margaret Christorf stop drinking. She was "not a bit interested" in romance, he said; drinking was her main focus. He agreed that Margaret would have resisted anyone who made sexual advances.

Scott remembered that Collins also told Detective Clayton that no matter how drunk Christorf was, she never accepted rides from strangers. Collins had believed that Christorf knew whoever murdered her.

On cross-examination, Reeves tried to get Collins to tell them about bruises that Margaret suffered at her friend Colonel Mansfield's house. Clayton quickly objected that such information was "hearsay," and Judge Gerst sustained Clayton.

Reeves tried a back door to the same facts, asking Collins if Margaret ever seemed upset when she called from Colonel Mansfield's. Clayton objected again, but this time the judge overruled him. Now, however, Collins said he could not remember Christorf pointing out bruises on her arm, which she'd claimed Mitch Kraus had caused.

Damn, Scott thought. Couldn't remember, or afraid of retribution?

Under Reeves's questioning, Collins did confirm that he'd told Detective Clayton that Margaret liked to party with people her own age or older. That would have been at least a decade older than Scott.

With the jury dismissed, Clayton argued that the defense should not be allowed to bring out evidence of a "third person" who might have killed Christorf.

The Arizona Supreme Court had found in the *Fulminante* case that the defense could offer evidence concerning someone else who might have committed a crime, but only if such evidence inherently connected that third person to the crime. Reeves pointed out that Rafe Collins told police in January 1992 that Mitch Kraus held Margaret Christorf against her will at Colonel Mansfield's house at least once. And police reports suggested that Bill McFadden's sperm was found in Margaret's body, and that he'd contradicted himself twice in his statements to police about when he last had intercourse with her. A neighbor reported that Margaret said McFadden hit her on the back of the head and locked her out, just a few weeks before the murder. And McFadden told police that within a month before Margaret's death, he'd found her on the floor in Mansfield's house, with her top off and her pants pulled partway down.

"Is that as close as you come with connecting any of these individuals to the murder?" Judge Gerst sighed.

Mike Reeves was out of patience. "Having Mr. McFadden's sperm seems pretty close. . . . Yes, the prosecution can't get any closer than that with Mr. Lehr."

Gerst, however, ruled that there was insufficient evidence to suspect any link between Mitch Kraus, Colonel Mansfield, or Bill McFadden and the murder. He would not allow the jury to learn about their relationships with Margaret Christorf.

And since Bill McFadden had died in a traffic accident a couple of months before the trial, the truth might have been buried with him.

22: Memory

After Detective Thomas Clayton was sworn in, Prosecutor Bill Clayton jokingly asked him to clarify that they were not related. The prosecutor asked about the weight of the two rocks that he was trying to establish as murder weapons in the Christorf case. Fifteen pounds and 27 ½ pounds, the detective confirmed.

On cross-examination, Mike Reeves led Detective Clayton to agree that the photographer who assisted him at the crime scene had taken pictures of tire prints, which did not match any vehicles owned by Scott. The detective also admitted that there had been a smear on the victim's thigh and buttock; Scott remembered that it was described in the police report as "some type of hand wipe." For unknown reasons, investigators had never tested that smear for fingerprints or DNA. Or had they—and suppressed evidence that exonerated Scott?

Reeves also questioned Detective Clayton about photographs taken of the partial shoeprints the prosecution was making such a big deal over. The detective agreed the partial shoeprints could not give accurate information about the length or width of the actual shoe presumed to be the murderer's.

Scott remembered that a forensic artist used those fragmentary footprints to reconstruct a sketch of what the complete shoeprints might look like. That investigator then combed area stores to find soles that resembled them: Kmart Trax running shoes.

Detective Clayton had also assisted with the search of Scott's home after the arrest, and Reeves took this opportunity to ask whether investigators had found any Trax shoes belonging to Scott.

Detective Clayton admitted they had not. He also agreed that the piece of gum found near Margaret Christorf's head was fresh. The detective could even smell the mint flavor. Yes, he recalled, the gum was sent out to a crime lab for DNA testing.

Scott knew the DNA evidence did not match either him or the victim. So what happened to that evidence?

The next day, Prosecutor Clayton called Jack Emerson to the stand. Emerson had been one of the last people to see Margaret Christorf alive. On November 8, 1991, he was working at a Circle K store near the apartment Margaret was sharing with Bill McFadden. When she came into the store at around 2:30 that morning, she was drunk, Emerson testified. She tried to buy cigarettes with food stamps. When he refused her illegal request, she left, muttering. He last spotted her talking to a man pumping gas into his truck.

Scott sat up. Wait a minute! Emerson's remarks to Detective Clayton back in 1991 were dramatically different. Emerson had said that a "business-type man" in a white shirt gave Christorf a ride to the Circle K in a vehicle resembling a light-colored Jeep Wagoneer. Emerson had also told Detective Clayton that during that time there was a man who'd been making obscene calls to women on the payphones in front of the store. And on the morning that Christorf was killed, a young man in the store, who looked as though he might have been Indian, took offense at Christorf's appearance, commenting that she was a whore. Apparently, detectives never even tried to locate any of these men.

During Reeves's cross-examination, Emerson claimed not to remember his earlier statements, even though he admitted to having "refreshed his memory" with the police report, just 45 minutes before testifying today!

Next Prosecutor Clayton laboriously questioned John Wintrow, the forensic artist who had imaginatively extended the partial shoeprints found at the crime scene and concluded that they had been made by a Kmart Trax running shoe, somewhere between sizes 8 and 10. Scott was amazed that they were offering the jury this ridiculous shoe "evidence" at all. Wintrow purchased a white

Kmart jogging shoe with gray trim and Velcro straps. Clayton solemnly displayed the shoe to the jury, as if there were some connection between these never-worn shoes and the murderer of Margaret Christorf.

Wintrow mentioned that he'd analyzed the shoeprints after an FBI expert who looked at the prints was unable to give an opinion.

On cross-examination, Reeves got Wintrow to admit that he had studied, at most, an hour in class on the subject of shoeprints. This was no expert whose opinion was better than the FBI's! Also, Wintrow agreed, there were significant differences both between the photographs of the shoeprints and Wintrow's sketch of them, and between Wintrow's sketch and the sole of the shoe he purchased as a supposed match.

Wintrow was apparently the last witness concerning Margaret Christorf. Now they would hear testimony about the crimes against Amy Perry,* who'd been only 10 at the time. Clayton called Officer Michael Gauchat, the Peoria police officer who interviewed Perry at the nursing home where she ran for help after the attack. At least a couple of times Clayton asked Gauchat if he had responded to the nursing home at 2 a.m.

Both times, Gauchat answered that it was about 1 a.m.

Scott supposed Clayton wanted the jury to believe that the crime had lasted longer than it had, or that the girl had been abandoned farther from help than she had been.

On cross-examination, Seplow elicited from Officer Gauchat that Amy described the man who raped her as very fat, with a "Santa Claus" beard, mid-chest length. He was wearing white tennis shoes, she'd said.

Judge Gerst read a question from a juror as to whether the scene of the crime was used as a dumping area. Apparently at least one juror was taking seriously the prosecution's argument that Scott was familiar with all the crime scenes because he dumped tree trimmings there. Plausible, Scott supposed, but untrue. He took his trimmings to the dump and paid the fees, rather than risking a high fine for illegal dumping.

Gauchat denied seeing anything dumped, describing the area as "pristine."

On re-direct, Clayton asked the officer whether he hadn't noticed "things dumped in the area, vegetation-type especially."

Gauchat responded with a vague "some."

But then on recross-examination, Seplow had Gauchat look at an aerial photo of the crime scene. In black and white, there were no dumped tree trimmings.

As Scott waved goodbye to Mom for the weekend recess, both smiled their confidence that the mass of contradictory details would prove the State's case to be transparently false.

On Monday morning, Judge Gerst called Amy Perry to be sworn.

Next to the murders, Scott most hated being falsely accused of raping a little kid. As a teenaged girl walked calmly to the witness stand, it would have been impossible to guess that the 15-year-old had been raped five years before. Interesting, Scott thought, that this most innocent of victims seemed to be living her life with the least psychological damage. He hoped her apparently good mental health would allow her to trust her true memories of the crime.

Clayton elicited from Amy Perry some details about how she'd moved back to Phoenix a month before the assault. The prosecutor's trivial questions seemed calculated to demonstrate that she had a good memory.

Perry related how she'd watched cartoons and news that evening while she waited for her dad to come home. She added that she wasn't concerned that her father was late, because, "I was used to his leaving and then coming back and . . ." Clayton interrupted her with another question.

Perry said she'd finally taken the bus to look for her father around 9:00 that night. When she didn't find him at his friend's place, she started back home. After waiting 5-10 minutes for the bus, she began walking. The lighting from streetlights and businesses was "very good." A man in a car drove out of the Abco Foods parking lot and offered her a ride. She refused and kept walking. But he circled back to her, and when he offered a ride again, she accepted. As she got into his car, "I noticed there were some items, looked like children's things, and I felt fairly secure thinking he was a family man." She added that there was a baby-seat in the car, and when Clayton asked her the color, she answered "blue-gray."

Scott's stomach cramped. That was not what she'd told police. Back then, she said the baby-seat in question was dark blue, with red and green stripes on the pad, an unusual color combination. But now Amy Perry was starting to repeat details that came closer to what victims of other crimes had said. He guessed that she no longer trusted her real memories. The technical term was "witness contamination."

She testified that the man stopped at a Circle K and asked her if she wanted anything. She waited in the car until he returned with a bottle of Dr Pepper for himself and a little plastic bag. They drove on. She told him they were going the wrong way, but he said he knew a shortcut. In the desert, the man said he wanted to go to the bathroom and parked behind a tree. "He came around to the passenger side, opened the door, and lifted me out."

"How did he do that?"

"Like a bride and a groom, when they go over the threshold, like one would carry a person that wasn't small enough to be cradled," Perry answered. The man said something like "You're going to do what I say now."

Perry described her ordeal without exaggeration or self-pity. Still, to Scott it was clear that she tried to say what would be helpful to the prosecution. Scott supposed that if his wife or daughter had been raped, she would respond the same way. But in his position it was hard to accept that the justice system wasn't always worthy of the trust that victims placed in it.

Perry testified that after she put her clothes back on, the man threw one of her shoes out of the car. When she ran to retrieve it, he drove away. She described his car as a like a Cadillac or Buick, a tannish color with seats like velvet.

Scott remembered that she'd told police the car was not tan, but "copper" color.

When Clayton asked her to compare the photo of Scott's car to the one used by her attacker, Perry honestly said that it was a similar shape and size, but that she wasn't sure the colors were the same.

OK, OK; Scott mentally telegraphed to the jury—this was the third victim who did NOT identify his car.

Perry described the assailant as having a beard, but no mustache.

Scott wished that he could stand up and make it clear that he'd never worn a beard without a mustache. It wasn't something that he was terribly self-conscious about, but he had a good-sized mole above the right side of his mouth. He liked having the moustache there to distract from the mole. Not to mention, if he'd committed any of these crimes, surely at least one of the victims would have noticed the mole—on the side of his face a passenger in his car would have had time to notice!

To credibly accuse Scott of the crime, the prosecution needed to talk Perry out of saying that the rapist's beard had been long: Clayton asked her if it was like his own neatly trimmed beard. "It was like as long as yours, only there was more of it," the girl waffled.

Now, apparently trying to establish a link to the murder of Margaret Christorf, Clayton asked Perry whether the Kmart Trax running shoe that Wintrow purchased was "extremely similar" to the one the man who had raped her was wearing.

And she agreed.

Huh?!! Well, Scott supposed it didn't matter, since he himself had not owned Trax shoes.

When Clayton then asked her to recall identifying Scott in the lineup four years before, she said she'd thought it might be one of two of the men there. Scott remembered that the police recorded her saying something like, "I can't be sure."

Clayton also showed her a photo of Scott wearing his wristwatch, which the teen agreed was "pretty much the same shape" as her attacker's, which she said he wore in addition to a wedding ring.

Scott wondered where this wedding ring came from. Neither Perry nor any of the other victims had mentioned one before. For that matter, Scott never wore his wedding ring; it got in his way as he trimmed trees.

When the time came for the courtroom identification, the prosecutor reminded her that "people can change what they look like, hair, beard, clothing." The day before she testified, Seplow had seen the prosecutor bring Perry into the empty courtroom and show her where the defendant would be seated. By eliminating 99 percent of those in the room, Clayton could pump up the odds that she'd identify Scott.[60]

As Clayton led the girl up to the defense table, Scott busied himself with doodling. Seplow told him never to make eye contact with the witnesses. *Not* making eye contact seemed guilty-looking to Scott, but he tried to cooperate with his attorney.

The teen stood in front of Scott. "Could you look me in the eye," she commanded, surprisingly forcefully. Scott looked up. She leaned forward and stared at him.

Clayton had Perry face the jury. "Who is he? Point him out."

She pointed to Scott.

"Could the record reflect that she walked over in front of the defendant and looked him directly in the face?"

The jury murmured, with loathing, Scott thought. He tried not to show his feelings—disbelief, fear, anger. To the jury, his emotion might only confirm his guilt.

But now it was the defense's turn to cross-examine Amy Perry. Phil Seplow asked if she remembered telling Officer Rafferty that her assailant had shoulder-length hair. She said she didn't remember.

Seplow also reminded her that at the lineup she'd said she didn't get a good look at the assailant's nose, which was one of the reasons she hadn't been sure of her identification then. He prompted her to admit that she didn't recall ever seeing the attacker wearing a watch, but only a gold band, which might even have been a bracelet. It was on his right wrist, she said.

Well, Scott always wore his watch on his left wrist, but by the time that fact was brought before the jury, would they remember why it mattered?

Then Seplow asked Perry if she had ever, before today, mentioned that the attacker was wearing a wedding band.

"If I said it today it was probably because I assumed he was wearing a wedding band." The girl explained, "Over the years things begin to change in your mind . . ."

Clayton must have been craving a Pepto Bismol.

And Seplow drove the point home, asking her again about contradictions between the details she'd given police and her testimony. As she summarized it, "There are a lot of things in my report which are inconsistent with my memory. I personally don't know which one is correct. . . . I don't know how good my memory is."

Scott wished he could thank the girl for her honesty there.

Seplow asked her about the attacker's shoes. On two occasions, she'd told police that the shoes had a gray band around the soles, but the prosecution was trying to make that the same as gray trim on the top of those new Trax shoes!

Perry readily admitted that last week Clayton had shown her the Trax shoe that she identified today. When Seplow pointed out that Perry had never before a couple of days ago said the suspect's shoes had Velcro fasteners, she simply answered that she didn't remember.

Seplow also elicited that Perry had attended a hearing with other alleged victims. Surely, Scott thought, those group hearings had encouraged the women to identify with one another, to see themselves as victims of the same criminal. They had come away thinking that to express doubts now would be to betray the others.

Finally, Seplow asked, "Would your memory have been better when you were talking with police officers right after the event than it would be today?"

"Much better," she agreed simply.

Good kid, Scott thought, in an impossible situation.

But Seplow had to push this witness until the jury lost faith in her identification of Scott. Seplow reminded her that at the lineup four years earlier she'd said she wasn't sure that Scott was the attacker. Today she was saying she was sure it was Scott. As Seplow pressed the girl, Clayton interrupted with objections.

But Amy Perry admitted that yes, twice she had said that she wasn't sure it was Scott at the lineup. Her identification of Scott was dissolving before the eyes of the jury.

At that moment, Judge Gerst asked whether the girl needed a break. If Scott had had a shred of doubt that the judge was firmly on the side of the prosecution, he could let go of it now. What a convenient time to take the pressure off her!

But Perry refused to be coddled. "I'm doing fine."

Under Seplow's questioning, she again described the attacker's baby-seat as a bluish gray. Scott was frustrated that Seplow let that contradiction slide without clarifying that she reported to police that the baby-seat was dark blue, with red and green stripes on the pad. Maybe there were just too many holes in her testimony for the attorney to keep track of.

When Clayton tried to do undo the damage with his re-direct examination, Perry made it worse for him by admitting that she'd listened to the testimony of one of the other victims at an earlier hearing.

Judge Gerst asked Perry a question from a jurist. "At the time the composite drawing was created, how close did you think the resemblance was to your attacker . . . ?"

Perry explained, ". . . I thought it was very close. It wasn't until after a short period of time that I began to realize that it was not what my memory was."

Scott sighed in relief. No juror could take this well-meaning teenager's identification of him seriously.

The following day, Detective Frank Dimodica testified again. Clayton showed the jury part of a family photo they had taken from Scott's house. They'd greatly enlarged it to show Scott's gold wristwatch.

Reeves immediately objected to the relevance of the exhibit: neither Nancy Caporaso nor Amy Perry had a clear enough memory to be able to identify the watch worn by her attacker. Also, the photo showed the watch on Scott's left arm, where he wore it. Perry said she saw a watch or bracelet on the rapist's RIGHT arm.

But Judge Gerst overruled the defense's objection.

Undaunted, Reeves caught Dimodica on the fact that the detective's "hot sheet" described the man who raped Amy Perry as having mid-length hair and a week's growth of beard, despite the fact that Amy had described him as having shoulder-length hair and a mid-chest length beard. Even shortly after the crime, Dimodica had described the suspect, not as the victim remembered him, but as the "baby-seat" rapist, based on details selected from several other crimes!

Next to testify was Paul William Brown, a gabby fellow who'd waited on the rapist at a Circle K the night of the assault. Scott knew the guy hadn't identified Scott at the lineup back in 1992. In fact, he very confidently identified someone else! Today Brown told the jury more than they could possibly want to know about his work history; how to read a cash register receipt; his system for making change; his habit of small talk with customers.

Clayton asked solemnly whether he remembered the man who made those purchases in the Circle K well enough to identify him in the courtroom.

Brown asked everyone at the defense table to stand and then pointed to Scott: "The one over here with the khaki-colored shirt and the maroon tie. . . .if I took a few pounds off of his face, I would say that's the person."

"I have no further questions. Thank you."

Even though the guy was an odd duck, Scott worried that the jury might believe him. But on cross-examination, Reeves made that unlikely. Apparently Brown never realized that at the lineup he had not identified Scott. Reeves drew Brown out to babble on about how positive he'd been about his identification at the lineup. It was a "jitteriness in his eyes," Brown remembered, adding it was the same for the suspect at the lineup four years ago and with Scott today.

The guy's identification was already demolished by Reeves's cross-examination, but then Judge Gerst read a jurist's question: "Did the guy at the Circle K have a beard on the night in question?"

Brown hesitated. "I don't think so."

Gerst politely thanked Brown for coming in.

23: Victims

Waiting for testimony to begin, Scott breathed more easily. The jury had seen that the true recollections of the rape victims, Mona Barnett, Nancy Caporaso, and Amy Perry, were hopelessly contaminated. In the murder cases, it would be even easier to prove his innocence. All three women were last seen with other men. The only possible connection to the so-called "baby-seat" rapes was the locations of the crimes, a weak link at best. The body of Margaret Christorf was found over 8 miles from the nearest assault, and Michelle Morales more than 5 miles away from the nearest crime scene. While the body of Belinda Cronin was found near where Nancy Caporaso had been assaulted, extensive publicity over the previous crimes made a copycat predator a likely possibility.

Clayton called to the stand Jeffrey Wayne Smith, who discovered the remains of Belinda Cronin on June 11, 1992, while patrolling the area by truck with another security officer. "We could see the outline of an upper jaw and then we could see fillings in the teeth. At that point, we determined that, you know, we had what was a body partially buried."

Hmm! Scott was glad the jury heard from the start that the body was buried, an important difference from the other two murders.

The following day, Clayton called Joseph M. Kezele, M.D., who examined Amy Perry after the assault. Dr. Kezele had found a 'very small tear in the mucous membrane of the vagina." The doctor confirmed that the child's hymen was intact.

Even though Doctor Kezele had just said the girl's hymen was intact, Bill Clayton asked, as if innocently, "The tear that you saw with Amy Perry's hymen . . . was it sufficient in nature to cause bleeding?"

What a sleazy trick! Scott glanced over at Phil, who nodded reassuringly. And on cross-exam, Seplow asked, "It wasn't the hymen that had the small tear, it was the mucous membrane more toward the opening of the vagina; is that correct?

"That's correct." Doctor Kezele also agreed that there was no bruising or trauma to the rest of Amy's body.

Clayton returned to testimony about the murder of Belinda Cronin, calling Detective Chuck Gregory to the stand. Clayton showed chilling photos of the young woman's body and had Gregory identify a clump of "long brownish hair," the bra and necklace found on her remains, a turquoise sweater hanging six feet above the ground in a tree, and a wristwatch lying on the ground.

Belinda Cronin, Gregory said, was lying face down. Parts of an arm and a leg were collected some yards from the body, apparently scattered by animals. Gregory identified other items collected 30 to 40 feet away—jeans and panties.

While Gregory was on the stand, Clayton asked the detective about "other involvement in this investigation." Scott swallowed his frustration. By "this investigation," Clayton meant the unrelated crimes against other women.

Gregory responded with testimony about his examination of Scott's cream and black Chevy Caprice and gray Sentra after the arrest. Scott knew they'd gone over those cars with a fine-tooth comb and found nothing—no hair, fingerprints, or any other crumb of evidence—to link him to any crime at all. But the prosecutor didn't ask Gregory about the results of that search.

On cross-examination, Seplow led Gregory to confirm that, when luminal was used to search the Cronin crime scene, no trace of blood was found.

"You can't say one way or the other that the death occurred at that spot. Would that be a fair statement?"

Detective Gregory agreed.

Next on the stand was Dr. Walter Birkby, a forensic anthropologist with the University of Arizona. Under Clayton's guidance, Dr. Birkby partially contradicted the previous testimony of Dr. Shaw, who had autopsied Cronin's remains. Scott remembered Shaw testifying that Cronin might have been killed with an ax. Although the lower front of her skull was never found, Dr. Birkby confidently maintained that a massive blow from a blunt object had fractured the skull. Birkby also waffled about his own 1992 report, testifying that the murder weapon was "not necessarily a baseball bat," as he'd then suggested. Birkby generally agreed that an ax handle might have produced the blow that killed Belinda Cronin, or a baseball bat, or a large, smooth rock.

Of course, Scott thought, if Cronin had in fact been killed with a rock where she was found, surely detectives would have found that rock.

Seplow also drew out of Professor Birkby that he was neither a medical doctor nor a medical examiner. That only left for Seplow to drive home the point that Dr. Shaw was the superior authority.

The next day's proceedings began with a conference before the jury was brought in. Seplow objected to a photo exhibit of Scott's license plate, which the State claimed was connected to the case of Nicole Churchill, one of the three cases that were not even being heard at this trial. Seplow argued that there was no point in severing those three cases if the jury would hear testimony regarding them.

Judge Gerst overruled Seplow's objection, with a placating "you may be right."

Next, Clayton asked the judge to hear testimony from Dr. Ben Storm without allowing Seplow to cross-examine Storm on certain issues.

Seplow explained to the judge that both Ben Storm and his brother had reportedly paid Cronin for sex. He added, "I think it's the stepbrother . . . tells one of the officers that Cronin was blackmailing Dr. Storm . . . On the night before Belinda Cronin disappears, I think she goes over to Dr. Storm because he owes her money. And people have been killed for a lot less than that. . . ."

Clayton countered that the issue of blackmail was only "speculation," and Judge Gerst agreed, preventing the jury from learning about Cronin's relationship with Dr. Storm.

When osteopath Ben Storm sat down at the witness stand, his face glistened with sweat. Storm confirmed that Belinda Cronin called him on January 20, 1992, at about 7 p.m., and he returned her call.

"You had a conversation?"

"Yes."

"After that point in time, did you ever hear from Belinda Cronin again?"

"No."

For once, Scott thought, Clayton had a witness who knew enough to keep his mouth shut.

"No further questions, Your Honor."

Gerst offered, "Do you have any questions at this time, Mr. Seplow?"

Although Gerst had severely limited Seplow's cross-examination, Scott expected the defense attorney to at least ask what was said during that "conversation," bringing out that Cronin was last seen on her way to Storm's apartment. But Seplow busied himself with his notes as if the man's testimony was unimportant. "No, your honor."

His pulse pounding in his temple, Scott watched a man who might know how Belinda Cronin died smile and walk briskly out of the courtroom. The jury looked bored.

Next, Detective Chuck Gregory was called back for cross-examination. Seplow asked about details of the site where Belinda Cronin's remains were found. "Now, you also found either—in one part of your report you called a gray and another part a white, a white hair about three feet, nine inches above the body. . . ."

Gregory agreed.

Detective Gregory ended his testimony by answering a couple of questions from the jury. One jurist's question made Scott suppress a hopeful smile. "Is it possible Belinda was killed at another site and driven to this site and buried?"

Gregory deflected the question. "I didn't find any evidence of that. . . there was no indication of her being buried."

Even Clayton asked whether there was a depression in the earth below the body.

The detective's response was bizarre. "It appeared . . . someone had been digging at that location, maybe removing dirt at some point, but as far as it being a grave, no."

Jeez, Scott thought; this charade would have been funny if it did not involve a slaughtered woman and an innocent man threatened with execution.

On re-cross examination, Seplow pursued Gregory on the subject of the gray hair found near Cronin's body. "When you talked to Mr. Clayton you said it was animal hair, but isn't it true in your report you said it was either human or animal hair?"

Gregory claimed he couldn't remember.

The prosecution's next witness was Paulette Dionne,* who'd worked with Belinda Cronin's mother at an insurance office. Dionne testified that Belinda Cronin visited her mother at the office three or four months before her death and showed Dionne a ring she'd found. Dionne had particularly noticed that, although the setting looked antique, Belinda's ring was in excellent condition.

Clayton picked up Exhibit 147, a plastic baggie containing the diamond ring Scott had bought at a garage sale. Before the prosecutor could even remove the ring from the bag, Dionne called out, "That's the ring she had."

Clayton put in a lame, "Do you need to take that out, or can you see that clearly through the plastic?" He passed the ring to the jury, still in its plastic bag.

While the jurists examined the ring, Clayton asked Dionne questions that made her sound like a jewelry expert: "Did you ever see another ring like that?"

She said that she had, adding that that type of mounting of the diamond was common 50 or 60 years ago.

On cross-examination, Mike Reeves revealed that the woman was no expert on jewelry, just someone who enjoyed browsing in jewelry stores a couple of times a year. Dionne had just testified that the ring was in excellent condition, and now, after looking at the ring in evidence, she had to admit that the band on Belinda's ring was not bent and broken like Scott's ring.

As Judge Gerst excused Paulette Dionne, he asked where the ring was.

There were giggles from the jury, who were taking turns trying the ring on.

Scott hoped the jury hadn't been too distracted by the ring itself to pay attention to the testimony. No witness had ever suggested that Cronin was wearing a similar ring the last time she was seen. Jewelry she had been wearing when she died had not been stolen, but was found with her remains. Investigators had never confirmed whether Scott's ring was the same size as other rings Cronin had, or even whether Cronin's ring had been left at home among her belongings.

Next on the stand was Belinda Cronin's mother, Brenda Atchison. Clayton asked her to identify a photo of the 21-year-old, while the jury sat at hushed attention. Atchison said she had bought most of Belinda's clothing. She recalled going to the police department, six months after her daughter disappeared, to identify items found with the remains: a boot, a necklace, a watch, underwear, and a sweater. At the memory of identifying Belinda's boot, Mrs. Atchison broke down crying. "All of her shoes are worn down that way."

However, she could not identify the jeans and the turquoise sweater found at the scene.

Mrs. Atchison also testified that Belinda had been separated or divorced for approximately 8 months before her disappearance.

Another lost lead. What was her relationship with her ex-husband? As far as Scott knew, investigators hadn't bothered to interview him.

On cross-examination, Reeves brought out that Belinda's roommates reported that she was last seen wearing a red or pink sweater and a black leather jacket.

Scott hoped the jury was puzzling over why Belinda was found near different clothes than she was last seen in. Had she changed clothes somewhere—maybe at Doctor Storm's? Or, did her roommates, for some reason, give an inaccurate description?

After Gerst dismissed the jury for Columbus Day weekend, Seplow asked again to introduce testimony about men in Belinda Cronin's life who had motive and opportunity to kill her. In addition to Dr. Storm, there was Belinda's stepbrother, Matt Baker. Matt had admitted to investigators that Belinda argued with him on the last night she was seen alive. Apparently there had been warrants out for his arrest for aggravated assault. Mrs. Atchison had earlier told Detective Gregory that Matt and Belinda fought repeatedly and Belinda feared that Matt would hurt her. By the time the case came to trial, though, Mrs. Atchison denied saying such a thing and declared that the conflict between Belinda and Matt was normal sibling friction.

Judge Gerst breezily ruled that suspicions that any other man might somehow be involved in her death were all based merely on hearsay or speculation.

Scott thought that his stomach would be riddled with ulcers by the time he got through this. After all, only "speculation" linked *him* to the crime.

24: Amnesia

After a long weekend, the trial detoured back to the case of Nancy Caporaso. The prosecution called Alvin Webster, M.D., who examined Nancy on April 4, 1991. Dr. Webster testified that Nancy's injuries included contusions on both sides of her neck, abrasions and contusions on her knees, abrasions on her back, and "a small abrasion on the back of her head." In other words, Scott concluded, the woman had been choked, but she had not been beaten, nor had her head been substantially injured. The only similarity between that assault and any of the murders was that Cronin's body had been buried in the same area.

Another interesting fact that came out in the doctor's testimony was that sperm were found in a laboratory test of Caporaso's urine. That was significant, since Nancy had testified that the assailant had not ejaculated. Scott knew that the DPS lab had run DNA tests in this case that exonerated him.

Here Clayton tried another ploy: Dr. Webster had also examined Alison Brooks after she was assaulted on October 24, 1991, and Clayton began to question him about that examination.

Seplow objected. The case of Alison Brooks had been severed and was not relevant to this jury's deliberations. Regardless, Judge Gerst allowed Clayton to continue.

Dr. Webster described Alison Brooks's hematoma and abrasions. Surely the jury now confused the Alison Brooks case with the crimes actually being tried.

The trial focused once more on Belinda Cronin's murder with the testimony of Mitchell Teeman, who'd been a jeweler for over 40 years. Under Clayton's questioning, Teeman stated that Scott and Elaine's garage-sale ring had been manufactured after World War II, but that such rings were no longer made today.

In cross-examination, Reeves asked him how many of the rings were made during the 1950s.

"Lord, could be thousands," Teeman acknowledged.

OK, Scott smiled. It was a common sort of ring. So much for the claim that Scott's ring could *only* have been stolen from the dead woman.

Clayton then called Belinda Cronin's boyfriend, Paul Garces, who testified that when he last saw Cronin, "She had called Dr. Storm a couple hours before then and asked if she could come over and borrow some money, and around 10:15 she left."

But Seplow was not allowed to ask Garces questions that would lead to the revelation that Storm was paying Cronin for sex, or that Cronin had a cocaine habit, both behaviors likely to put her in contact with violent people.

Garces was the last witness to testify about the murder of Belinda Cronin.

Clayton called Detective Joseph Petrosino, Phoenix Police. On February 19, 1992, Petrosino investigated the desert site where the body of Michelle Morales was discovered. It was an unusually wet February, and he found shoe impressions around the body. Petrosino believed the impressions had been left by boots. He recalled that cigarette ash was found in the impression of a boot heel. The detective believed that the ash hadn't been in the location long. He offered the opinion that the men who found the body had left the heel print and the ash, even though they denied smoking and stated that they never dismounted from their horses.

Scott wondered how Michelle Morales had died. The evidence at the scene was puzzling. Petrosino testified that he had not initially taken as evidence a 10-pound rock, which was later thought to be the murder weapon. That rock was found 25 feet from Morales's body, next to a pool of blood six or seven inches deep. But Petrosino noted that Morales had no mud on her bare feet and legs; so she had neither walked nor been dragged to where she was found. She lay face down, wearing a turquoise turtleneck top pushed up to her neck. Her scalp was torn open and her head, anus, and vagina infested with maggots. The young woman was wearing a silver bracelet and a ring in an Indian design. A pair of black stretch pants lay nearly 50 feet away.

It was Mike Reeves who cross-examined. Petrosino said that as far as he knew, no one had taken comparison shoe prints from the men who discovered Morales's body. The detective simply *assumed* that the boot prints—which looked like cowboy boots to him—and cigarette ash had nothing to do with the crime.

Scott couldn't imagine being so casual about investigating a murder. In Maricopa County, it was nothing like the C.S.I. shows.

However, Petrosino was sure photos were taken of the boot prints, although they were not produced as evidence. Investigators had also taken photos of tire tracks at the scene, which also were not considered evidence.

Reeves stepped closer to the detective. "So the tire prints didn't help you, and the footprints didn't help you?"

"My opinion, they didn't, that's correct."

Reeves allowed his voice to betray disbelief. "What is there at this crime scene that seems to help you in your investigation?"

"Well, I suspect that the rock is the implement of death."

Scott suppressed a chuckle. Never mind clues to *who* killed the woman, as long as detectives suspect that they have "the implement of death."

On the following day, Clayton called Craig Jenkins, Michelle Morales's boyfriend. Craig had known "Shelly" since seventh grade in California, and they'd lived together, along with his brother and two other classmates from the Universal Technical Institute in Phoenix.

On cross examination, Reeves probed, "Did the police ever question you about your knowledge of an older gentleman she'd been seen with?"

Clayton objected to the relevance of the question, and Judge Gerst sustained him. Scott had an impulse to pound his head into the table over the investigation's baffling indifference to the men murder victims Morales, Cronin, and Christorf were last seen with.

Next to testify was Craig's brother, Scott Jenkins. Clayton asked Jenkins about the whereabouts of the other roommates on the day they claimed to have last seen Michelle, February 7, 1992.

On cross-examination, Reeves asked Scott Jenkins whether Michelle's lack of money was sometimes a source of conflict. The young man agreed that her lack of money created conflict with all the roommates.

Reeves took the opportunity to ask whether anyone in the household wore cowboy boots. Jenkins volunteered that two roommates, Philip Stockman and Mark Ketcham,* both had cowboy boots.

Clayton then called to the stand Philip Stockman, who would have been the last roommate to see Morales alive, if the young men's accounts were accurate. Stockman's testimony was consistent with what he had told police.

Reeves's cross-examination got to another point. "Were you a hard-partying group. . . ?"

"We drank beer on the weekend."

"Neighbors ever come over and complain about the loudness of the music, screaming . . ?"

Stockman said he didn't think so.

Scott knew that was contrary to what one neighbor had said—that she'd called the police six times in two months about the young people's late-night parties.

Reeves also asked if police ever asked Stockman to identify the clothing found with Michelle. Stockman said they hadn't asked him.

The casual omissions ate at Scott. The jury would also hear nothing about Benjamin Cassell, the neighbor who left Phoenix at the very time of Michelle's disappearance and whose route north on I-17 would have taken him within 300 yards of where her body was found!

The next witness was Mahesh Patel, a criminalist for the City of Phoenix Crime Laboratory, who had analyzed potential biological evidence on the Morales case. Patel explained that blood on the ground at the Morales crime scene was too degraded to yield a conclusive result. However, Patel found that liquid blood from the hole in the ground and the blood on the rock appeared to be the same type, and that both were consistent with the known blood of Michelle Morales. No big surprise there. But Patel also confirmed that there was no blood or semen on the turtleneck found on Michelle's body.

No blood on the turtleneck? That was odd, Scott thought; if the young woman had been bludgeoned on the head with a 10-pound rock, as the prosecution suggested, surely some blood would have stained her sweater. For that matter, none of the witnesses had identified the turtleneck as belonging to Michelle. It might be important, because if she had changed clothes somewhere after she was last seen by roommates, she might have spent her last hours in the company of a person or persons she knew. It struck him that both Cronin and Morales were found dead with turquoise-colored sweaters unfamiliar to their friends and families. Maybe it was just a weird coincidence.

Patel testified that his acid phosphatase testing had indicated semen only on the swab of the victim's anal area. He added, though, that when he tried to duplicate the results of that test, the results were negative. The conflicting results suggested to Patel that the sample was degraded or the quantity of semen was low. There was a maggot on the swab, the criminalist added, one indication that the sample was degraded.

Clayton also questioned Patel on the subject of hair analysis. Patel had received 11 hair samples from the body of Michelle Morales and the crime scene. Patel confirmed that one hair found lying on Michelle's body at the autopsy did not match hers.

On cross-examination, Reeves asked, whether that unknown hair sample matched Scott Lehr's head or body hair,

It was not similar, Patel admitted.

Reeves also cast doubt on the objectivity of crime lab tests. Patel readily admitted that sometimes, when a detective sent a supposedly "unknown" sample for analysis, the criminalist was well aware of the suspect in question. It was clear to Scott that, whether consciously or not, an analyst would feel pressure to produce the results that crime investigators were hoping for to solve the case.

That day's parade of witnesses for the prosecution ended with Michael Johnson, one of the detectives who'd brought Scott downtown for questioning four and a half years ago. Now retired, Johnson began his testimony with a summary of his exemplary 22-year career.

On cross-examination, Seplow had Johnson confirm that he routinely would have ordered photographs taken of footprints and tire prints where a murder victim was found, although the detective—who had also claimed to have seen palm fronds at the crime scenes—could not now remember any prints or whether they had been photographed.

Seplow then asked if Johnson was involved in the search of Scott Lehr's home, which would have included looking for shoes, such as cowboy boots. Of course, they had found no such thing.

Again, the detective drew a blank. "I was there. I can't say that I was actually totally involved."

Seplow asked about conflicting reports as to the date of Morales's disappearance.

Once more, the detective claimed to have no memory.

Michelle Morales's sister, Melinda, was also called to testify. She said she'd last talked to Michelle on the phone on Thursday, February 6, 1992, and had a "very typical phone conversation." But when Michelle hadn't called by the following Saturday, Melinda began to worry.

The woman's testimony shed no light on the murder; Clayton's main purpose in calling Melinda as a witness seemed to have been to elicit more sympathy from the jury. When Seplow stepped up to cross-examine Melinda, he made a sensitive situation worse. "You say that you had contact with your sister Belinda by telephone . . . almost every day for a year; is that correct?"

"Her name was not Belinda," the stricken woman said.

And a few minutes later, Seplow blundered again! "Was one of the reasons you were trying to get Melinda the job . . . because your father didn't want to send her any more money?"

"Excuse me. It's not Melinda. It's Michelle."
Someone in the jury gasped.

25: "He Could Change His Eye Color"

The trial had dragged on for nearly a month before testimony turned to the crimes against Meredith Porter. In this case, not only had the girl's original statements identified someone who could not have been Scott Lehr, but Scott also had an airtight alibi—his twin daughters' birthday party.

This flimsy case was the keystone of the prosecution's theory of a single baby-seat rapist and murderer. Police had focused on Scott as a suspect in all of these crimes only because a review of license records turned him up as the owner of both a Nissan and a General Motors car. Porter was the only victim who claimed—but only after her story had changed several times—that the suspect drove a car that could possibly be a Nissan. Without this case, the prosecution lost their two-car "identification" of Scott.

The next witness was the young truck driver who stopped to help Porter in the Lake Pleasant area on the morning of February 24, 1992. He said he knew the dirt roads and horse trails around the area well. He'd worked there often, driving truckloads of rock blasted out of pits, and he'd also explored the area on four-wheelers.

Several of the "baby-seat" crimes shared that characteristic: the attacks were committed in areas well-known to truck drivers and four-wheelers. Investigators had never pursued that lead, however.

The witness noted that, when he stopped his truck that morning, Porter quickly opened the door and climbed in unassisted and that she talked to him about her friends and family as she waited for the police. The victim's alertness was particularly significant since at that time she'd described to police a suspect who did not look like Scott Lehr. The more that time passed and investigators had questioned her, the more her story had changed to resemble their presumed "baby-seat" cases.

Taking the witness stand next was Antone Jacobs, the second patrolman to speak to Meredith Porter after the crime. Jacobs testified that the girl was in a state of shock, although the truck driver had just said she was chatting with him, and that the teen "was beaten very heavily about the face area," another falsehood.

Identifying photos taken at the hospital, Jacobs claimed, "She was in a lot worse state than the pictures are showing."

According to Jacobs, Porter stated she was picked up between 19th Avenue and Central by a guy in a new gray pickup truck, possibly a Nissan. She described the attacker as white, aged 20 to 30, six foot one, with a light brown mustache and reddish-brown hair and beard, full on the chin like a goatee but without hair on his cheeks.

Officer Jacobs's testimony omitted the features of that description that exonerated Scott. Unlike Lehr, the man who raped Meredith Porter had green-blue eyes, protuberant ears, and large, smooth hands with little hair on them.

Mike Reeves began the cross-examination with a pointed, "Would you grab your report there and finish reading the rest of that description. I think you left out the part about the eyes."

Jacobs succeeded in sounding matter-of-fact as he admitted that Porter had said the guy had blue-green eyes.

When Meredith Porter Blake took the stand, her manner was anxious, but self-righteous. She was now 19 years old.

Prosecutor Clayton gently asked her where she was going to school in February 1992.

"I wasn't . . . I had just dropped out."

"Okay. Let's see . . . how old would you have been?"

"I was 14."

Clayton moved her along briskly, asking if anything "unusual" had happened to her during that weekend of February 22 and 23.

"Yes. I was offered a ride, and I took a ride, and I was raped and beaten, left for dead."

According to the original reports of first responders, Porter could not have been described as "left for dead."

In what would prove to be a landmine for the defense, Porter testified in passing that she wasn't sure whether she was assaulted on Saturday or Sunday. There was no doubt in the police reports about the date. The teen was assaulted on Sunday night, when Scott was home with his family for the twins' party. The facts showed that she had not wandered in the desert for two nights, and it would be up to Phil Seplow to clarify the date on cross-examination.

Porter remembered only that it was dark and she was walking on Indian School Road toward 19th Avenue. A gentleman offered her a ride, and she got in. Lured by an invitation to ride horses, although it was night-time, she agreed to drive with him.

Clayton interrupted to ask whether anyone else had given her a ride.

Porter answered that, at some earlier date she wasn't sure of, two men had taken her out to South Mountain and abandoned her to walk home alone, and that these men were driving a pickup truck.

That was a twist to the story that was not mentioned in the police reports.

Clayton's kindly mask betraying tension, he asked whether Porter recalled telling Detectives Bruen and Bates that the car used in the assault was a gray four-door compact.

She did not.

Clayton asked whether she remembered a detective taking her to see a gray car.

She remembered going "a couple of weeks" later, though she wasn't certain.

In fact, it was at least four months after the crime when Porter was asked to "identify" Scott's Sentra, after they'd already arrested him.

Under Clayton's prompting, Porter said she'd remembered the car because it had "no knobs on the stereo." She also testified that there was a baby seat in the back of the car during the crime.

The relieved Clayton quickly showed her photos of Scott's Sentra and she agreed that the interior looked familiar.

Clayton did not ask if anything about the Sentra, such as the badly dented passenger-side, looked *unfamiliar.*

As Clayton walked her through the crimes, Porter recalled driving with the man for over 45 minutes. Once they stopped, he asked her to give him oral sex. "And then that wasn't satisfying him, so he started to recline my seat back." She said he stopped to move the baby-seat in the back passenger seat. The baby-seat was blue, she said, with metal parts.

The baby-seat Scott and Elaine had for Melissa at the time was maroon.

Then the man had intercourse with her. Porter testified that she didn't believe the suspect ejaculated, a fact that further supported Scott's innocence, since the prosecution claimed to have DNA evidence from the man's sperm.

Porter said the man demanded that she go for a walk. She refused at first for fear he would leave her in the desert. At that, she said, he pulled her out of the car by the arm and they walked down into a gully. Again he demanded oral sex and promised to take her back to town.

Afterwards, she said, they started walking back up towards the car by moonlight and the light provided by the rapist's flashlight.

When Clayton asked Porter about cigarettes, she said the man was smoking Marlboro Reds.

The jury would never hear that both the man and Meredith Porter had smoked marijuana in the gully, another fact that made this different from any of the other crimes.

Then, Porter testified, she dropped her cardigan sweater and felt "somebody or something" hit her head. Although at first Porter said that she didn't remember how many times she was hit, she finally agreed with the prosecutor that it was more than once.

Clayton prodded her for more memories.

"I remember seeing the stretcher and hearing the helicopter. And I woke up three days later in the hospital."

This testimony contradicted two witnesses who had already testified that Porter was quite conscious and verbally responsive the morning after the assault.

Porter went on to claim " . . . I suffered a severe concussion. . . I was in shock, delirious. So I wasn't really in any state of mind to recollect exactly what I was saying or doing."

That was also false. Covered with cactus spines, she had four teeth broken off and must have been in terrible pain. However, the attending doctors had never diagnosed either a concussion—not even a mild one—or shock.

Next, as a prelude to another courtroom "identification," Clayton asked her about the lineup.

Her statements brought up some doubts about that lineup. Because seven victims were brought in to view the lineup in rapid succession, it seemed likely that Porter herself might have overheard the statements of earlier witnesses. She admitted that it was in the hallway outside the viewing room where she told investigators that she recognized "number 3" as the guilty one. As she cried out that the guilty man was number 3, other witnesses being led into the lineup room might have heard her and been influenced to name Scott, number 3, when it was their turn to view the lineup.

Porter testified that investigators "told me that he could change his eye color or gain weight or lose weight . . ."

For detectives to tell an impressionable victim that a blue-eyed rapist might have changed his eye color was surely stepping over the line into leading her to identify the man they believed was guilty, brown-eyed Scott Lehr.

Clayton then asked Porter to point out the man who did this to her.

"The gentleman in the blue tie."

Since all four men at the defense table were wearing blue ties, Clayton had her walk over and point to Scott.

Scott held himself impassive. He had to leave it to Seplow's cross-examination to expose how false this "identification" was.

And Seplow quickly focused on the car Meredith Porter had supposedly identified.

She agreed that she had opened the passenger door herself to get in.

He asked her if there was anything unusual about the handle or how the door opened.

"No, that it was a normal door handle . . ."

But the dented passenger-side door on Scott's Sentra was hard to open. Seplow wasn't allowed to clarify the discrepancy for the jury now; it would have to wait weeks for his closing statement.

Seplow narrowed in on the first account Porter had given of the attack. "Do you recall saying that you were picked up by a newer gray pickup truck, probably a Nissan?"

She didn't remember.

Seplow asked if she'd told Officer Jacobs that the rapist had "reddish-brown hair a little past his shoulders."

She said she could have.

So far, so good. Scott assumed that Seplow would later play the videotape of the twins' party, showing Scott on that very evening with short hair.

Seplow questioned Porter about the photo arrays, including two pictures of Scott, that police had shown her only two days before the lineup. Seeing photos of Scott months after the crime and shortly before the lineup could have made him look familiar to her, contaminating her memory of the actual perpetrator.

Judge Gerst broke in with a timely distraction. "Excuse me a minute. Are you doing okay? Do you need a break?"

Seplow offered Porter some water, but she refused. She said she did remember being shown three photo arrays in June 1992 and saying that the rapist "sort of looks like number 3, but not really."

Just as Seplow was zeroing in on the conflicting facts in Porter's supposed identification, Judge Gerst dismissed the jury for lunch. And the judge advised counsel that after lunch they'd interrupt Porter's cross-examination even further, hearing another of Clayton's witnesses instead.

Scott Lehr with his twin daughters. Victim Emily Caldwell described her attacker's calves as exceptionally muscular, while Lehr's were not.

This photo was taken by the author in January 2003 in the area of two of the crime scenes. Note the palm fronds in the foreground. Witnesses for the prosecution claimed that palm fronds were found near several crime scenes (although crime scene photos showed no fronds). The suggestion was that Scott Lehr, who worked as a tree trimmer, may have dumped the fronds in 1991-1992. The fronds shown here are clearly less than ten years old, demonstrating that others, who may or may not have committed the crimes, have continued to use the area as a dump site.

Scott Lehr's Nissan Sentra. Victim Meredith Porter, who initially reported being raped by a man driving a pickup truck, later agreed that Lehr's car was "similar" to the one used in the crime. This was despite the fact that she'd never described the suspect's truck or car as being damaged on the passenger side.

Note the dented front door and the maroon baby-seat in the front seat (reproduced in color on the back cover). Meredith Porter recalled a blue baby-seat.

26: Evidence

After lunch, Bill Clayton called Philip Keen, M.D., Chief Medical Examiner for Maricopa County, who'd performed the autopsy on Michelle Morales. Keen described a "fairly routine" examination but noted "advanced decomposition of the head and neck when the body had been secondary invaded by maggots or fly larvae." The jury was shown a photo of the young woman's head opened for the autopsy.

Clayton asked whether Keen had had found a hair on the body after it had been washed.

Keen paged through his notes. "I don't have my evidence log, so I can't tell you specifically whether I retrieved a hair or not . . . "

Why Keen's evidence log was not presented as evidence was not explained.

Clayton asked his witness if a hair had been found on the victim's chest, where it might have come from.

"It could have been there all along," Keen replied. "Could have been from the decedent. Could have been from someone else . . ."

The only possibility Keen declined to mention was that the hair could have come from the murderer.

Keen summarized his external findings as "injuries to the head and scalp, skull fracture, evidences of bruising to the left arm area in a patterned distribution and evidence of bruising of the introitus consistent with a sexual assault," in addition to some superficial scrapes on the body.

Clayton whipped out the hospital photographs of some scrapes on the back of assault victim Nancy Caporaso, and asked Keen to make comparisons that were surely irrelevant to the murder of Michelle Morales.

Dr. Keen gamely described cuts and abrasions on both victims and concluded, "Somewhat similar. Somewhat different."

Clayton asked Keen for other observations about Morales's body.

In addition to a fracture of the frontal lobe, Keen pointed out a V-shaped laceration of the scalp over the frontal scalp.

Clayton asked what the V-shape of the laceration indicated.

In Keen's explanation, the injury was a tearing of the skin that just happened to be V-shaped. He emphasized that the injury was made by a blunt instrument, rather than a sharp one. Keen's answer was one explanation for the apparent scalping of the murdered woman. However, Keen also testified that V-shaped tear or cut on the scalp was not overlying the skull fractures, but rather in front of them.

When Clayton questioned him on evidence of possible sexual assault, Dr. Keen described his procedure for swabbing the body for evidence. He mentioned that he sometimes used a speculum for better access to the vagina, but "We didn't have one at the morgue on that particular day. . . "

Why the doctor would not have had basic equipment for an autopsy when sexual assault was in question was unclear.

Clayton asked whether sperm had been found on Morales's body.

Keen waffled. "After about 24 hours, to recognize a sperm . . . you really are looking for either serological evidence or DNA evidence or chemical evidence that there was really semen there . . ."

When he cross-examined Keen, Mike Reeves asked pointedly how long it would take for DNA to decompose.

Keen admitted that "in the case of Miss Morales . . . yes, you would expect the DNA to be rather badly decomposing."

Judge Gerst immediately played down the importance of this revelation with a joke. "Why do I have a feeling we're going to have quite a bit of discussion on this subject matter before this case is over?"

The jury chuckled appreciatively.

Reeves asked whether Keen had combed the victim's pubic hair, standard procedure in assault cases.

"No . . . the assault kit didn't have a comb available that day . . ."

Reeves kept his poker face. "Okay. So if a detective had said earlier that there had been pubic hair combings on this particular case, he probably was incorrect?"

Keen responded with "I doubt if we had a comb . . ."

The missing combings from the victim's pubic hair left open the question of whether evidence that might have exonerated Scott Lehr had been destroyed.

Finally, Phil Seplow was allowed to resume his cross-examination of Meredith Porter. She claimed not to remember her interview with Detective Bates, during which she had looked at pictures of different automobile makes.

Seplow made the best of her answer, questioning her about memory loss. "Do you recall ever telling any police officer prior to actually seeing the vehicle . . . that the knobs on the radio were missing?"

"Yes, I do."

Seplow countered, "Well, on that day that you were looking at the photographs, Officer Bates says that the only information you could remember was that the back seat was dirty and that the suspect had kids."

Porter said she didn't remember any of that.

Seplow moved on to the contrast between Porter's description of the attacker and her identification of Scott in the lineup four months later. As he questioned Porter about the height of the man who attacked her, it was clear that she'd been an unusually large 14-year-old: five foot eight or nine and around 205 pounds. That mattered because the prosecution claimed that a key similarity among the crimes was that all the victims were small women.

Seplow circled back, asking whether, after being released from the hospital, she had a photographic image of the attacker.

She said that she had not.

During that cross-examination, Seplow did not ask Porter questions about the date of the assault that could have clarified that Scott had been home with his family at the time.

On his re-direct examination, Clayton asked what it was that made her identify Scott at the lineup.

Porter answered quickly, "Just a flashback. . . . It's a face I'll never forget."

Meredith Porter seemed certain. Some members of the jury looked puzzled. It would be up to them to decide whether the blue-eyed, large-eared man Porter first described to police could possibly have been Scott Lehr.

For the next morning's testimony, Clayton called William Heath, who'd helped administer that lineup. Heath now worked as an investigator for the County Attorney's office, of which Bill Clayton was second in command.

Heath described how persons other than suspects, sometimes fellow officers or inmates who volunteered, were used to fill lineups.

The prosecution showed a brief video, in which the camera panned across the six men in their places at the lineup. They seemed to have been arranged in order to make Scott Lehr look conspicuous. He had chosen position 3. The man in position 4 next to him was a blond with a pock-marked face. The man in position 5 was a detention officer, and he looked like one. The man in position 6, in jail for some offense, was only 18, though the suspects in these cases had been described as in their late twenties or early thirties. Going back to the beginning of the line, the man in position 1 had blue eyes. Only Meredith Porter said the attacker had blue eyes. The man in position 2 was unusually tall—6 foot 4. The witnesses called to this lineup could have quickly ruled out all the other men. In addition, Scott's blue jail uniform—a much darker shade than the others wore—called attention to him. Lineups were supposed to present only people who met the description of the suspect in question. This lineup had done the opposite.

In one more puzzling omission, the witnesses' actual responses at the lineup were not recorded on the official videotape. Instead, police had written brief notes.

That afternoon Clayton also called Detective Randy Chapman, Phoenix Police Department. Chapman described how he participated in surveillance of Scott "as a possible lead" back on June 24, 1992. Chapman was also involved with the live lineup, and Clayton had him describe how the witnesses had been seated in separate rooms in the area before being asked to view the lineup. Chapman admitted that "They were all brought down rather timely within one another, maybe five minutes apart or so . . . . "

Chapman's testimony left open the question of whether the victims could have overheard and been influenced by each other's responses at the lineup.

Speaking of Paul William Brown, the Circle-K clerk in the case of Amy Perry, Chapman simply said, "He positively identified participant No. 2."

In other words, Brown was sure the assailant was not Scott. It was one of many key facts dropped so casually that the jury might not have picked up on the difference between "participant No. 2" and Scott, in position number 3.

As he cross-examined Detective Chapman, Mike Reeves's questions emphasized the conflicting details given by the victims as to height, hairstyle, hair color, eye color, ear shape, and beard.

Reeves summed it up, "I'm just asking you if you were using their descriptions."

"We were using a compilation of all of those descriptions and a composite artist drawing."

Reeves said, "So let me get this straight then. You're looking for a guy who is 20 to 40, right?. . . A guy who is five-six to six-four?"

Astonishingly, Chapman answered that the size and build of the suspect didn't matter.

"So you were just looking for a white guy, weren't you?"

At that, Clayton objected that Reeves was "argumentative," and Judge Gerst agreed.

Chapman had also testified about assembling photo arrays presented to victims for possible identification.

"Before you take a victim to see an in-person lineup, do you normally show them a photographic lineup beforehand?"

"No," Chapman growled, his answer confirming that showing Meredith Porter photos of Scott just two days before the lineup had violated procedures designed to prevent false identifications.

Reeves brought the questioning back around to Scott's car, asking whether during Chapman's surveillance of the Lehrs' apartment he had seen a car-seat in the Nissan.

Chapman had.

"What color was the car-seat?

Referring to his report, Chapman read that "it was red-colored."

Scott inhaled deeply. His car-seat had been maroon, but Meredith Porter had testified to seeing a blue car-seat, among the other holes in her testimony.

27: Omissions

To Scott's disgust, the prosecution was calling Nicole Churchill to testify, even though her case had been severed and was not being heard at this trial. Apparently unconcerned about biasing the jury with irrelevant allegations, Judge Gerst assured them, "You may consider evidence of other acts that the State alleges that the defendant has been involved with."

Nicole Churchill looked both sickly and mentally unstable. A 34 year old who could pass for 40, she was dressed neatly in clothes that might have come off the Salvation Army racks.

Clayton questioned the woman at length about the afternoon of March 23, 1991, when she accepted a ride from a man who drove her north on Interstate 17 to 12th Street and Joy Ranch Road. Out in the dirt roads beyond, he raped her. The car she described as being used in the crime was not Scott's. "It was a light brown in color. It had lighter color top on it. . ." she said. Scott's tan Caprice had a black top. However, the car that belonged to Richard Donohue matched Churchill's description, and Donohue himself resembled her description of the suspect. This was the same man who, in a coincidence that reeked of conflict of interest, had served as foreman of the grand jury that voted to charge Scott Lehr with the crimes.

Churchill testified that after the suspect had vaginal intercourse with her, he wiped his penis on her clothes.

There had never been any DNA analysis of that evidence—at least none that the defense was allowed to know about.

The man released her from his car near a residential area, saying, "This is close enough to civilization; get out."

Clayton asked her about the assailant's license plate.

Churchill admitted that she couldn't clearly see the number on the license plate because of the dust billowing up behind the car, but that she believed the letters were ADW or AOW.

The plate on Scott's Caprice had begun with ADW, as had thousands of other plates, including Richard Donohue's.

On his cross-examination of Nicole Churchill, Seplow had her confirm that she was currently in custody for felony possession of narcotics and that she'd previously been convicted of both trafficking in stolen property and theft.

Under Seplow's questioning, she admitted that she'd injected heroin eight or nine hours before getting in the car with the suspect. She agreed that she would have been sick from craving heroin at the time of the attack.

Churchill also confirmed that the perpetrator did not strike her, nor did he injure her in any way that left bruises on her.

When Clayton was allowed to re-direct his witness, he asked her what effect heroin had on her.

Her answer was not reassuring. "The effect on me for heroin would be the same as if I would take codeine, Darvon, Percocet, or any other type of narcotic drug as a pain reliever."

But Clayton didn't give up. "Your memory, is it affected by the heroin use?"

She claimed it was not.

Clayton's next witness was Sergeant Lawrence Lee Luginbuhl, Maricopa County Sheriff's Office, who'd taken Churchill to the hospital after the assault.

On cross-examination, Seplow asked Luginbuhl about the photo lineup he'd shown Nicole Churchill a couple of months after the assault.

Luginbuhl confirmed that Churchill had picked out photos one and five, neither of which was of Scott. And Luginbuhl confirmed that photo number five was of Richard Donohue. Luginbuhl acknowledged that he'd shown Churchill Polaroid photos of Donohue's car. "She said the color and the top were right, but the interior is in much better condition and this is not the car."

Still, Donohue's car was much more like Churchill's description of the crime vehicle than was Scott's.

Next Clayton called Detective Wayne Charles Scoville, Maricopa County Sheriff's Office. Scoville had been interviewed in the *Arizona Republic* as a hero for the "breakthrough" that focused the "baby-seat rapist" investigation on Scott.

Scoville testified that he'd run a computer search on all owners of both a full-sized General Motors car with an Arizona plate beginning ADW and a Nissan sedan.

No Nissan sedan was used in these assaults, however. Only Meredith Porter had reported a similar vehicle, and she identified a Chevy Spectrum—after she'd changed her story from reporting that her assailant drove a Nissan pickup.

Scoville concluded, "There is only one individual subject who owns both . . ."

"And what was the name?" Clayton pursued.

"Scott Alan Lehr," Scoville pronounced gravely.

"The license number of the GM full-size product with the ADW number was what?"

"ADW015."

Scott was betting that they weren't going to mention the plate number that a victim really had identified, ADW519. According to police reports, the license plate Emily Caldwell identified, ADW519, was stolen from a wrecking yard between February 11 and March 7, 1991, right when these crimes started.

Scott might have been the only individual who had owned both a General Motors car and a Nissan at the time of Scoville's search, but Scoville testified that "a number of" businesses owned both combinations of vehicles, including State Farm insurance and some wrecking yards.

If the jury was paying attention, Reeves's cross-examination was deadly. He asked Scoville how many of the companies owning both combinations of cars he had driven by, or checked for employees matching the descriptions of the rapist.

Scoville admitted that the investigation had not checked any.

The following day, Clayton called Alison Brooks to the stand. Like the case involving Nicole Churchill, the crimes against Brooks were not being tried here. Yet amid the hundreds of hours of testimony they'd hear, Scott doubted that the jury would remember that distinction.

Although only 13 at the time of the assault, Brooks had been an unusually experienced girl who was apparently cutting school that day. Now 18, she was visibly pregnant.

She testified that on the morning of October 24, 1991, she'd fought with her mother, gone to her boyfriend's for half an hour or so, and then started walking to her aunt's house. A man stopped his beige, four-door car and asked directions to an employment agency. When the man offered her a job cleaning his house, she got in his car. She saw a blue baby-seat in the back. The man drove to her aunt's house. After Brooks discovered that her aunt wasn't home, she got back in the man's car and agreed to go with him to meet his wife and children. In the desert near Deer Valley Road, he pulled into a circle of trees and parked. "And then he put his arm around me and . . . said: 'Now, you and me are going to have sex.' " When she tried to escape, he choked her into submission. He told her to get in the backseat. There, he performed oral sex on her. Afterwards he tried to penetrate her vaginally. When she told him it hurt, he changed positions. Brooks said he was "sitting in the middle of the car in the back seat . . . And I just kept asking him to stop. And he said to me: 'Would you rather give me head?' . . . And I said: 'Yes.' So he sat down on the passenger's side in the back . . ."

Scott wondered what happened to that baby-seat she'd mentioned. Didn't most people who buckled a baby-seat in the backseat put it on the passenger side?

After raping her, he "put his hands around my neck and . . . picked me up off the ground . . . and started beating my head against the ground."

She said she lost consciousness. When she woke up, he started choking her again. "I blacked out again . . . I don't have any idea what happened, if he stopped or what. . . ."

But Scott remembered. Twice she'd told police that she asked the man to stop choking her, and he did.

Brooks said that, after she regained her strength, "I took my one sock off. I don't know why. . ." She walked through the desert to the Granatelli Race Building, less than a half-mile from the crime scene.

Brooks described the attacker as "probably in his early 30s," but she couldn't recall his height and weight. He was barefoot, and wearing aqua shorts. She said he had brown hair with red highlights in it and a few days' growth of facial hair. She described a drink caddy in the front seat of the car.

When Seplow stepped forward to cross-examine Alison Brooks, he asked her the color of that car caddy.

She said it was beige.

Good, thought Scott. The caddy in his Caprice had been maroon.

Seplow continued, "Do you recall if the car that you traveled in was a two-tone car or a one-tone car?"

"I believe it was a one-tone."

"You didn't see a black top in it?"

"No."

Alright! Not Scott's maroon caddy, not his black-topped car.

Seplow also elicited from the teen that she had not been sure whether the rapist ejaculated and that she'd had unprotected sex with her boyfriend the night before the crimes.

And then Seplow went to the heart of the problem with this witness. She admitted that, when she was nine or ten years old, after an argument with her mother, she had lied to Child Protective Services, falsely accusing her mother's boyfriend of molesting her.

Prosecutor Clayton sat stone-faced as his fiction of an innocent little girl dissolved.

Seplow questioned Brooks about other troubling facts. She agreed that she had first told officers that the attacker had grabbed her on the street and pulled her into the car, when in fact she had entered willingly.

Finally, Seplow asked about her claim that the man had hit her head against the ground, although there had been no evidence even of superficial head injuries.

"I don't know . . . I blacked out."

She claimed that her head was bleeding, although when Seplow showed her photos taken at the hospital, she couldn't show any blood.

Seplow asked if she had reported that the man had "a few weeks' growth of beard," but now she insisted that it was a few days. She added, "No. A lot of things in that, in Officer Sweeney's report, are incorrect."

Scott hoped the jury would realize how much more likely it was that Brooks's memory had been thoroughly contaminated than that the officer's report was grossly inaccurate.

Clayton's next witness was Dave Szenyes, one of the officers who followed Scott's truck around on his last day of freedom back in 1992. Scott was curious about the methods of the surveillance team.

"We use different vehicles that tend to blend in with other cars on the road. . . . And we try to change positions as often as we can," Szenyes explained. He said that the officers kept a handwritten log.

Clayton asked about the locations they'd followed Scott to.

". . . one sticks out in my mind. . .We followed him to the Skunk Creek Landfill." Afterwards Szenyes had taken pictures of the trash Scott dumped.

Clayton melodramatically showed photos of some pine branches and a little household garbage.

Scott hoped that the jury saw that, having disposed of his tree-trimmings legally, he was not the prosecution's palm-fronds-dumping culprit.

Next Clayton questioned Detective Frank Roberts, who'd done surveillance of Scott that night. Roberts told how he'd followed Scott to Kinko's, where Scott copied his little tree-trimming business fliers, then back home, and then out again at about 10:45

pm in an old yellow Ford pickup. Roberts rattled off the roads Scott traveled for an hour and fifteen minutes.

Scott remembered vividly how, in his fear at being followed, he'd turned continually, trying to shake whoever was behind him.

On cross-examination, Reeves did all that he could to overcome the image the prosecution was trying to create of a predator out hunting for victims. "You don't know why Mr. Lehr was out driving around that night, do you?"

Roberts acknowledged that he didn't.

"You don't know if anywhere in your report that Scott Lehr pulled over and talked to anyone?

"No."

Again Clayton called Detective Dimodica to the stand. Clayton asked him about some photos taken as evidence from Scott and Elaine's apartment. The pictures showed Scott with different hairstyles and facial hair over the years.

On cross-examination, Reeves questioned the detective about a long list of incriminating evidence that investigators had *not* found.

Dimodica grudgingly admitted that his search team found no Kmart brand tennis shoes, no tan-colored car caddy, no Camel cigarettes, no marijuana, no hair samples to match any of the victims, and no tires matching tracks from any of the crime scenes.

With the jury dismissed for the weekend, the attorneys and Dimodica conferred with Judge Gerst. Seplow and Reeves wanted to present evidence about the assault on Teresa Martinez by a man driving a small, gray pickup truck, about a month after Meredith Porter was raped. Martinez's experience resembled some of the "baby-seat" assaults, but she was a level-headed woman who'd viewed the lineup and was sure that Scott was NOT the man who attacked her.

Gerst looked uneasy. "But the jury, of course, at this point knows nothing about a Teresa Martinez—is that her name?" He asked whether the Martinez case had been resolved.

Dimodica hemmed and hawed, "Well, I found the subject that is mentioned with the pickup truck and interviewed him, and I don't believe any charges came of that."

Why not?! Scott wanted to scream. Police had their hands on a guy who'd raped a woman. She believed the only reason he hadn't killed her was that she jumped out of his moving truck. Michelle Morales was last seen with a guy in a truck, and Belinda Cronin's body was found within a mile of the assault against Martinez. And Dimodica just let this dude GO?!

As if his hands were tied, the judge sighed that the Martinez case would be simply "a lot of hearsay."

Lying on his bunk that night, Scott felt as if he was drowning in the sea of the prosecution's omissions and distortions. Judge Gerst let the jury hear allegations from victims whose cases were not being tried here, but he blocked testimony about the very similar case of Teresa Martinez because he knew damn well that Scott was innocent there.

When court reconvened, Clayton called Ed Lukasik, a forensic serologist with the DPS Crime Lab in Phoenix. Lukasik testified that his tests confirmed semen stains on Margaret Christorf's warm-up jacket. Lukasik also testified about a couple of vaginal swabs from Christorf. He said that he used clean paper on his countertop to prevent cross-contamination, and he washed his equipment between samples with "soap and water and scrubbing . . . And lots of rinsing."

Scott was no biologist, but soap and water didn't really seem adequate to protect minute DNA samples from contamination.

At the end of a mind-numbing series of questions, Lukasik testified that he was unable to eliminate Bill McFadden, Margaret's boyfriend, as the sperm donor.

It was another maddening instance when a crucial revelation flew by the jury in a flood of trivial detail.

Clayton's next witness was Randy L. Leister, a criminalist for the City of Phoenix Crime Laboratory. In the case of Nancy Caporaso, Leister examined swab evidence that yielded a blood PGM subtype of one plus, two plus. This was consistent with

Caporaso herself and with Steven Glen Blondel, whose name had come up in the police reports. Leister's tests ruled out Scott, whose subtype was one plus, one minus.

For damage control, Scott supposed, Clayton called Detective Michael Johnson, Old Bugeyes, back to the stand. Clayton asked whether there was a pattern in the assaults and murders Johnson was investigating in 1992.

The most the detective could claim was that the victims "were mainly picked up in the metropolitan Phoenix area and that the locations where all of the incidents occurred . . .were in secluded areas, either in north Phoenix or northwest Phoenix. . . ."

That could be said of many violent crimes in the Phoenix area.

Clayton asked Johnson about an exhibit map marked with colored dots indicating the locations of various crimes. Scott was not at all surprised that the scale of the map made the crime scenes appear much closer to one another than they really had been.

Then Clayton showed a videotape of some of the crime scenes, photographed from a helicopter. Johnson repeated that the crimes were committed in "secluded areas." Even then, Johnson had to admit that Margaret Christorf's body had been found in "kind of a residential area." As Johnson pointed out where Michelle Morales was found, he noted that "vendors" were selling things there, but quickly added that "they weren't there on the day that this incident occurred."

Since the date of the murder was unknown, Johnson could not have been sure of that.

Then Johnson testified that he made "mental notes" that there were palm tree trimmings in the general areas of the crime scenes.

"Mental notes" hardly seemed worthy of testimony under oath, since there was nothing about palm fronds in any of the police reports, and not a one was visible on the videotape the prosecution had just shown.

28: Elaine Lehr, Witness for the Prosecution

OCTOBER 29, 1996

When he first learned that Bill Clayton was calling Elaine as a witness for the prosecution, Scott was numb with disbelief. But Seplow convinced him not to take it personally. It didn't matter which side called her to testify. Her testimony could only work in Scott's favor.

Now Elaine sat at the stand, very nervous, astonishingly beautiful. Scott hadn't even talked to her on the phone in months; they knew it was best not to communicate during the trial. Tears welled in his eyes. He wondered how life had been for her and Melissa.

Clayton loomed over her. She confirmed that she was Elaine Lehr, aged 32. She and Scott married in 1990 and had a daughter, now 6 years old. Clayton had her point to Scott, and an affectionate smile flickered across her face.

"May the record reflect that she has identified the defendant, Your Honor?" the prosecutor called out, as if recognizing her husband somehow implied that he was guilty.

Clayton asked where the family lived in 1990 and 1991.

Hesitantly, she testified that they'd lived at 3334 West Devonshire, followed by the townhouse at 25th Ave., off Northern, and finally the apartment at 8th Street and Townley.

When Clayton asked for the dates of the moves, she could only remember it would have been December 1991 when they moved to 8th and Townley.

In his most suggestive tone, Clayton asked why they'd moved. As she answered his questions, Scott saw that Elaine's patience with the prosecutor was wearing thin.

Then Clayton asked her about cars they had owned.

" . . . We had a brown car, it was sort of a tan color. . . "

Weird, Scott thought. Maybe she was just overwhelmed by being on display as the wife of an accused rapist-murderer. Whatever the reason, honest-to-a-fault Elaine came out sounding devious. And why didn't she mention the black top? That was the key fact.

Clayton asked when they "got rid of" the tan Chevrolet, as if to suggest an ulterior motive.

Elaine told how she'd wrecked the Caprice in December 1991 and they sold it because it was undriveable, totaled by the insurance company. They'd parked it on a busy street in their neighborhood with a "FOR SALE" sign until they found a buyer.

Hardly the behavior of a guilty man trying to "get rid of" a car, Scott chuckled.

She described the battered Nissan Sentra as a gray two-door, with a gray interior and a radio.

"What happened to those knobs?"

Someone had broken into the car one night and taken them, she testified; she couldn't remember exactly when.

Scott tried to relax, tried not to make Elaine more nervous. But as Clayton asked about the baby-seats they'd had, she grew increasingly flustered. She said the car-seat that was stolen was maroon, although that wasn't right, Scott remembered clearly. It was the other way around. The car seat they had in the Sentra at the time Scott was arrested was maroon, and police had a record of that. The one that was stolen—almost a year earlier—was blue. Maybe she couldn't remember—it had been five years—or maybe she was in some unconscious way trying to help him—only it was backfiring.

Clayton asked if she remembered telling Detective Chapman that there used to be a gray-blue car seat, but that the car seat had been stolen out of that vehicle.

"If that's what I said, then I must have."

Elaine looked positively disgusted by the prosecutor. And now, between her anger and her nerves, she sounded unsure of anything.

Clayton showed her the ring he was trying to link to Belinda Cronin and asked when and "from whom" she'd got it.

"I got it from Scott. . . . he had taken it down to see if he could pawn it and get some money for it, along with a couple of my rings, and it wasn't a very good offer so he brought them back. . . ."

Clayton asked her when she first saw the ring.

She found her footing and answered that it was before Christmas.

"Let me ask you," Clayton began melodramatically, "whether or not you told Detective Chapman that it was after Christmas of 1991?"

She replied crisply that she didn't remember. Establishing that Scott had brought home the ring before Christmas 1991 was crucial to prevent Clayton from claiming Scott had taken it from Belinda Cronin, who was last seen on January 20, 1992.

Responding to Clayton's questioning, Elaine testified that Scott would deliver his advertising fliers to mailboxes in the evenings or mornings, and that he only used his truck. ". . . He wouldn't leave me without the car. I didn't drive the truck."

Scott hoped Seplow could bring the jury's attention to that fact. He was not in the habit of driving the cars the prosecution was trying to tie to the crimes.

Clayton showed Elaine photos of Scott and asked her to describe Scott's facial hair in 1991 and 1992.

She said she thought that it was just a mustache, and that he didn't let his beard grow.

But then Clayton showed a picture of Scott with a beard and asked sharply, "In 1991 and 1992, would he have had a beard like this at any time?"

She had to admit it was possible.

Clayton displayed a series of photos of Scott with different hairstyles and facial hair. Miserably, she identified them all as Scott.

"Thank you," Clayton finished airily.

Elaine looked devastated. Seplow positioned himself near her. "Good afternoon, Elaine." His voice was firm and kind. "The beige car. . . how would you describe the top of that car?"

"That car has a black top."

Seplow showed her a photo of their Nissan, registered to them on February 7, 1992. She agreed that it had been a couple of months later that the car was broken into and the radio knobs taken.

"Certainly well after February 23, then?" Seplow emphasized.

"Yes."

Scott hoped to heaven the jury was keeping their dates straight. If Meredith Porter had been assaulted in a car with missing stereo knobs, it was not Scott's car.

Then Seplow asked her to explain why she couldn't remember Scott's facial hair style at any given time.

"You know, he'd let it grow out and then he'd get sick of it . . . Most of the time, he had a beard," she said.

Well, that was true, Scott knew, but it contradicted what she'd testified earlier.

Seplow asked her about the ring.

She described how Lindsey and Hallie had fought over the ring when Scott first brought it home, prompting her and Scott to get the twins rings for Christmas.

Seplow next focused on the girls' birthday party, Scott's alibi on the night of the Meredith Porter assault.

Elaine confirmed that the twins' party had been the evening of Sunday, February 23, 1992, at their apartment. She estimated that the children would have been in bed by nine because the next day was a school day. She recalled that Scott had gone to bed while she and Donna sat up and talked until three in the morning.

"If Scott had left the house that night," Seplow asked, "would you have known it?"

"Yes."

"Did he leave the house?"

"No." She described the layout of the apartment. It would have been impossible for Scott to leave without the women seeing him.

Then it was Seplow's turn to show photos, sweet family snapshots including Scott playing with the kids.

Finally, Seplow asked Elaine about her meeting with Detective Chapman after Scott was arrested, while her home was being searched.

"Would it be fair to say that you were in a panic . . . ?"

She agreed.

Scott relaxed back into his seat. Seplow had turned this around.

Then Clayton had his turn for redirect-examination. He tried to make it sound as if the twins' party had been on February 24.

Elaine didn't blink. "24th was their birthday. We had the birthday party the night before."

But Clayton had one more dig. "Do you recall telling me that you had looked at some of the things that had been written down before to refresh your memory?"

"Yes."

"And did you tell me that they were notes that Scott had written up . . . ?"

"Yes."

"And you still haven't shown those to me, have you?"

"No," Elaine said, a bit sharply.

"No further questions, Your Honor."

Anger choked Scott. Elaine's "notes" were just the dates of the crimes. She and Mom had tried to figure out what Scott had actually been doing during the times in question.

As Elaine walked down from the witness stand, she smiled at him, apologetically. He wondered whether the jury perceived her quiet decency and realized it said something about him that she was his wife.

On the following morning, Clayton called Detective Michael Johnson for additional testimony.

On cross-examination, Seplow asked him whether any of the victims described a tan car with a black top.

"I have them describing it as a four-door tan."

Seplow displayed the photo of Scott's Caprice with its black top. "Did any information that you have . . . give you this description shown in Exhibit 55?"

"I'd have to say yes," the detective answered.

Scott almost laughed out loud.

Phil Seplow pushed back. "Did anybody tell you that the car . . . had a black top?"

Johnson finally admitted that no witness ever had.

Seplow then asked Johnson a series of questions that established that nothing at all was known about any vehicles involved in the murders of Christorf or Cronin, and that Morales was last seen in a black pickup truck.

The judge dismissed Detective Johnson. He was needed to assist in the police escort for visiting President Clinton and Vice President Gore.

29: DNA

OCTOBER 30-NOVEMBER 4, 1996

So far, the jury had heard a morass of vague and contradictory testimony. Scott resisted the impulse to be optimistic, for he uneasily anticipated Bill Clayton's presentation of DNA evidence. Although Scott knew that DNA evidence, accurately tested, would exonerate him, he was also aware that forensic DNA analysis was still in its infancy. It would be tempting—for a prosecution with no qualms about losing hair and DNA samples and describing imaginary heaps of palm fronds—to fudge lab evidence as well.

Bill Clayton called witness Susan Narveson, supervising criminalist for the Arizona Department of Public Safety (DPS) Crime Lab. The middle-aged woman radiated trustworthy professionalism in her gray suit and cropped blond hair. Narveson smiled warmly and addressed the jury as a circle of friends. She explained that she had established Arizona's forensic DNA analysis program and was responsible for monitoring and assigning casework.

She inspired confidence, Scott admitted, as she discoursed about "guidelines for quality operation" and "highly discriminatory" testing. She stressed that only the cells of identical twins would show the same DNA profile. To generate DNA profiles, her staff looked at five or six particular genetic locations, which varied highly among individuals. These locations were identified with such numbers as D1-S7, shorthand for chromosome number one, at the seventh sequence identified on that chromosome. Narveson explained how a "restriction enzyme" could be used to cut the long DNA molecules at a specific site into smaller fragments of DNA. In a process called electrophoresis, the cut-up DNA is put into one end of a gel. When an electrical current is applied across the gel, the

DNA fragments separate out by size, with the largest at the top and the smallest at the bottom. Analysts next transfer the DNA to a more durable nylon membrane. Then, to make the pattern on the membrane visible, it is "probed" with a radioactively tagged piece of DNA designed to locate specific DNA sequences. After the excess probe is washed off the membrane, a photographic image is made. The resulting autoradiograph, or "autorad," reveals patterns of bands from the chromosome probed.

Narveson noted that several different DNA samples, such as blood or semen, would be shown for comparison on every autorad. Also visible on the autorads would be molecular weight markers, DNA fragments of known sizes, used as a guide to help measure the samples being analyzed. A separate lane with a standardized "control" would also be shown, as a check on whether the procedure had been completed correctly. "Compare the patterns and determine for yourself whether or not these two patterns match."

"Determine for yourself"? That sounded way too simple. Scott bet that the Devil was in the details. The jury, far from being fascinated by the wonders of science, looked stupefied.

The same process, Narveson said, would be repeated four more times at different genetic sites to establish a profile for each sample.

Narveson defined the protocol used by her lab as "like a recipe book," which would be followed for every test. If a remainder of a tested sample was analyzed using the same protocol, the analyst would get the same results. She also claimed that photographs were first taken of every evidence sample to demonstrate the amount of DNA available and whether it was in good enough condition for analysis.

The method of DNA analysis used by Narveson's laboratory was Restriction Fragment Length Polymorphism, or RFLP. Scott knew there was a better method, known as PCR, which was more sensitive and better suited to analyzing small samples of DNA.

Clayton asked what the minimum necessary amount of DNA would be for the RFLP method.

She testified that, with samples in good condition, slightly less than one drop of blood or half that quantity of semen would be adequate.

Hmm. That wasn't what Scott had read, which was that at least a dime-sized blood sample was needed for RFLP analysis.

Finally, Clayton asked about the DNA samples Narveson had analyzed in the case of Margaret Christorf. Narveson explained, "I chose a bloodstain from the victim and the suspect . . . excuse me, not the suspect at that point in time, because we didn't have a suspect, but there was an individual who had a prior sexual act with the victim, so we had a known blood sample from the victim and consensual partner . . ."

Scott wished Judge Gerst had not prevented the jury from hearing more about that partner, Bill McFadden.

The autorads were shown on two monitors at the front of the courtroom. Scott found the autorads hard to see; surely the jury had the same problem. The jurists also had xeroxes of the autorads in their notebooks, but Scott wondered how they could possibly scrutinize them and listen closely to the testimony at the same time.

Narveson said that from the vaginal swab from Margaret Christorf "I was able to obtain typeable DNA information at five genetic locations" and from a semen stain on Christorf's jacket she found DNA at four genetic locations. She displayed an autorad with fourteen vertical lanes, each loaded with a different DNA sample or molecular weight size marker. The bands themselves were shadowy.

Narveson testified that she would tell her computer program the size of the standard markers, and then "the computer actually compares how far the other bands have moved in relationship to the marker bands on either side of it." But, she added, ". . . these are size estimates, they are not exact sizes."

"Not exact"? Scott was skeptical. Was this technology reliable, or a crapshoot?

Narveson explained that the DPS used a computerized "image analysis system" supplied by the FBI. "In general, we require that if we're going to confirm a visual match, that all of the sizes of our controls and our matching patterns must agree within a plus or minus two-and-a half percent." She added that in the upper region of the lanes this allowable variability in size was actually "slightly greater," plus or minus 3.8 percent. The first step in declaring or ruling out a match, Narveson said, was "visual identification by the analyst." The second step would be to "compare the size values generated by the computer for patterns that you have declared a match."

To Scott, that sounded fine, in theory—*if* the analyst was objective and if the computer program gave accurate results.

Narveson mentioned that she was not displaying the actual autorads, but Mylar copies.

After dismissing the jury that afternoon, Judge Gerst examined those Mylars with the attorneys and Narveson.

Clayton claimed they were "basically exact duplicates," But Mike Reeves countered that some of the Mylar copies were not as clear as the original autorads. Even Narveson agreed with him. Reeves had previously written four letters requesting that only the original autorads be shown to the jury, with clear lane identifications.

But Judge Gerst blandly responded that the originals would be available for consultation during the trial but that "we're relying upon the opinion of experts . . . whether there is a match or isn't a match."

Scott swallowed his frustration. The jury was being led to trust an "expert" who worked in league with the prosecution. And, so far, the prosecution had confused the jury, not helped them understand the facts.

The next day, Narveson claimed the unknown semen sample analyzed in the Christorf case did not match Bill McFadden's DNA.

Scott shook his head. He remembered the lab report showing that McFadden was a secretor with type A blood. A few days ago, Ed Lukasik had testified that his tests did not eliminate Bill McFadden as the sperm donor. At any rate, *some* man with type A blood was the semen donor, who could not be Scott, a type O nonsecretor.

Narveson admitted that she'd used the entire semen sample from Christorf's jacket, which turned out to be too much DNA. The results were invalid, but the test could not be repeated since Narveson had used up the sample. All the same, Narveson continued to testify about the results of the jacket sample as if they were valid.

How convenient! Scott thought that if DPS had sincerely wanted accurate DNA testing, they could have sent their samples out to an independent lab.

As Narveson showed her blurry exhibits of a swab from Christorf's vagina, she then pronounced that Scott's blood sample matched the unknown male fraction of the DNA. She also claimed that the semen sample from Christorf's jacket matched Scott.

Listening to her claim to have evidence of his semen from a murdered woman he'd never even seen, Scott held his face motionless.

In further testimony, Narveson admitted that it was possible to have an "incomplete washing" of hybridization solution, which would create extra bands on the results. Another potential problem with the results in her tests was "partial digestion," she noted.

Scott let out his breath slowly. In other words, cloaked in hours of technical terminology, plenty of room for fudging.

Then Clayton asked Narveson about the statistical probabilities of a DNA "fingerprint" matching more than one individual.

Reeves objected that she was not qualified as an expert in statistics.

Gerst promptly overruled Reeves's objection, so Clayton led Narveson up to announcing that Scott's DNA profile "matched" the suspect's at five genetic loci, "a frequency of approximately 1 in 11 million individuals."

A murmur rippled through the jury box. At that moment, Gerst adjourned. After two mind-numbing days of testimony, the jury would have the weekend to mull over Narveson's unfounded suggestion that Scott's DNA was a "1 in 11 million" match to Margaret Christorf's killer.

Scott left the courtroom feeling as if he'd been run through a wringer, but by Monday he'd talked himself back into cautious optimism. Surely Mike Reeves's cross-examination of Susan Narveson would demolish the state's claims for its DNA analysis.

And Reeves soon elicited from Narveson that the DPS lab had only begun doing DNA case work in 1991, the year she was promoted to supervisor. Reeves's questions also established that no one working with DNA analysis at the DPS lab had a Ph.D. Narveson, who established the protocol for the laboratory, had a bachelor's of science in chemistry, plus four months of study at the FBI lab. She said she'd set up the DPS lab using a protocol "essentially compiled by the FBI," but she admitted to making changes to the FBI protocol.

Bill Clayton jumped up to object that the DPS protocol and procedures had been ruled admissible by Judge Reinstein in the Frye hearing preceding this trial.

That was not the only possible interpretation of Reinstein's ruling, but Gerst sustained Clayton. The defense would not be allowed to question weaknesses or inconsistencies in DPS's lab methods.

Scott knew Reeves also wanted to reveal weaknesses in the DPS's databases and the problems in their validation studies, which failed to test the reliability of their own work.

Choking back his anger, Reeves made a motion to stay the proceedings.

Gerst serenely denied the motion.

Reeves took a deep breath and turned back to Narveson. "If you look at your protocol from 1991 and compared that with your protocol in 1994, you'd find a number of changes; correct?"

Narveson admitted the possibility of "slight modifications" to the FBI protocol.

"In fact," Reeves said, "I think there is 31 or 32 different modifications?"

Narveson suggested that it "depends on how you're counting them."

But Reeves was back in the game. He asked whether the RFLP method offered an exact analysis of very small segments of DNA, out of the three-billion-pair sequences that every individual has.

Narveson squirmed. "We were not able then, nor are we right now, to say to a certainty that we have identity."

OK, thought Scott. Ladies and gentlemen of the jury, DPS cannot claim to identify an individual through DNA analysis.

Methodically, Reeves went on to question other problem areas in Narveson's testimony. She conceded that within the match range she had given, plus or minus 2.5 percent, a 5 percent total range between any two samples, there could be a 50 base-pair difference.

Scott knew this fact meant that, using Narveson's methods, the DNA of different individuals could be declared a match. But did the jury catch that?

And when Reeves questioned her about the accuracy of her computer measurements. Narveson admitted that it was not the computer, but the analyst who took numbers assigned by the computer and declared a match.

Reeves continued, "And the analyst needs to tell the computer either to find all the bands or to find a certain number of bands?

Scott was shocked by Narveson's answer: "The computer will then mark as many bands as the analyst asks it to mark."

So, Scott thought, Narveson's "computer check" was substantially controlled by the analyst.

Reeves questioned Narveson about the K562 bands on one autorad.

She explained that the K562 bands were a national control that helped assess the accuracy of the process.

"And if these two bands appear in the wrong place, you wouldn't use these autorads?

She agreed that she would not.

Reeves had Narveson look at another blurry autorad.

"It's blown out," she commented. ". . . it's either too long of an exposure or too much DNA was loaded." She explained that in such a situation the analyst "will have to look at where they're placed and either designate a manual override and place them in the correct location . . ."

And how exactly would the analyst know "the correct location" for a band in DNA evidence, unless he or she was trying to match a particular suspect? Scott wondered.

Reeves showed Narveson an autorad including the control K562 in lane 3. "We see three bands, right?"

"No, she answered, "I see two bands. . . ."

"Okay. And the third mark that we see in that lane?"

Narveson's voice dipped. "This does not appear to be a band. . . . It's some kind of an anomaly . . ." She said she would not size that band.

"Now, that isn't what your protocol says to do, though, is it?"

"Yes, it is," she answered sharply.

Reeves asked Narveson to read from her protocol. "If the K562 bands and the MBE control bands are not found in a visually expected position, the autorad cannot be assessed further." He paused half a beat and asked if the protocol said she could decide where the bands should be.

Narveson sidestepped. "I have to decide which of those are bands."

Next Reeves showed a copy of another autorad and asked whether she'd told the computer to score four bands.

She confirmed that she had, including a faint band at the bottom of the lane.

Responding to Reeves's questioning, she agreed that she could not determine whether all four bands came from a single person, and that the lane might show bands from two different people.

Reeves asked whether two of the bands matched up with any other person.

Narveson admitted that "those bands did not match any of the individuals that were tested in regard to this particular case analysis."

Whoa, Scott thought. Whose DNA was being ignored here?

Reeves had Narveson find her original autorad and thermal print for D2-S44. She confirmed that she had noted five bands in the control lane, and that three of those bands were not in the expected position for the control.

"And your protocol says that if the . . . control bands are not found in a visually expected position, the autorad cannot be assessed further, correct?"

She had to agree.

Scott hoped the jury noticed that Narveson just admitted to violating her own protocol.

Reeves then asked her about a 1992 report from the National Research Council (NRC) of the National Academy of Sciences concerning forensic DNA applications. Reading from the NRC report, he asked whether she agreed. "Presentations that suggest to a judge or jury that DNA typing is infallible are rarely justified and should be avoided."

Narveson dodged, "What do you mean by infallible?"

Reeves tried a new tack. "Does your laboratory have an established error rate?"

"No . . . I think most of the community will agree that it's virtually impossible to establish an error rate in the area of DNA testing."

Scott exhaled angrily at Narveson's bold defense of her lab's low standards.

Reeves then asked Narveson about the work of true experts in DNA. "In 1991 Professor Lewontin and Hartl stated the DNA profile of an individual as determined by current procedures . . . has far less information content than a fingerprint. Would you agree . . . ?"

"It's my understanding that they focused primarily on genetics in the application of statistics."

"Do you recognize them as experts in the general field of DNA?"

" . . . I'd have to say that, even though they have wonderful academic credentials, I personally do not agree with many of their opinions."

Scott chuckled to hear the State's DNA "expert" present her bias as a virtue.

With the jury dismissed for the day, Reeves objected that the DPS laboratory had actually doctored some autorads with pencil marks and had the computers score the pencil marks as if they were bands!

Gerst dismissed Reeves's objections. "I'm limiting the testimony in this case to attacks on lab analysis error, individual case matching, lab slop, and things of that nature. . . . And that's a subject which obviously I could be wrong on . . . and the appellate court can tell me if I am."

"I could be wrong"? Scott was stunned by the judge's laziness—or was it something worse?

30: Teresa Martinez

NOVEMBER 5, 1996

Judge Gerst had finally allowed Phil Seplow to question Detective Michael Johnson about the assault of Teresa Martinez in March 1992. In a case very like the ones Scott was accused of, this woman's attacker had been identified, but for some reason never prosecuted or investigated in connection with the other cases.

On the stand, Johnson stonewalled. He claimed he hadn't reviewed his file and didn't have a copy.

Seplow asked how Johnson got involved in the case of Teresa Martinez.

"She was the victim of a sexual assault and it happened to occur in the area where Scott Lehr had been assaulting his victims," Johnson answered.

And Seplow made no objection! Scott covered his mouth in shock. Was he getting a fair trial when a supposedly objective police witness was allowed to assert off-handedly that Scott was guilty?

During lunch recess the lawyers and Johnson conferred with Judge Gerst. Prosecutor Clayton suddenly recalled that there had in fact been DNA evidence in the Martinez case—and that it excluded Scott.

Johnson played down the crimes against Martinez. "She wasn't of that manner for being a sexual assault victim . . . Her lifestyle would not be the same as a person who's never been exposed to violent activity . . ."

"Are you saying that she's been raped before?" Seplow asked.

"I'm saying that she was a prostitute, she was a drug addict, she was hanging out on Van Buren Street where you have a high vicinity of crime and drugs and violence."

But Scott remembered that it was not Van Buren, but Buckeye Street where Martinez accepted a ride from the rapist. Buckeye Street was also where Dr. Storm first met Belinda Cronin.

Johnson claimed that Martinez admitted "she was picked up in order to perform sex as a prostitute."

Scott knew that was wrong. Martinez told police she'd accepted a ride home, just as Mona Barnett, Nancy Caporaso, and Amy Perry had.

Seplow pointed out that Martinez had to be taken to the hospital on a backboard, possibly injured worse that any of the victims who had testified.

With the jury re-seated, Seplow had to drag testimony out of the hostile detective. "This Teresa Martinez gave you and Detective Dimodica a description of a white male 40 years of age; is that correct?"

"Correct."

"He said something to the effect like, 'I'd rather rape you now and get what I can before I have to do a lot of time in prison.' Is that correct?"

Johnson agreed. Slowly, the details of the crime emerged as Johnson grudgingly confirmed the facts stated in the police reports. The rapist sounded like the man Michelle Morales was last seen with: dark hair with some gray in it; a mustache and a couple of day's growth of beard. His truck was a small, dark gray Nissan-type, like the one Meredith Porter first described. And as in the Porter and Brooks cases, the man told Martinez he had horses. He exited from I-17 at Happy Valley Road and drove out to within a mile of where Nancy Caporaso was assaulted and Belinda Cronin's body was found. The man licked Martinez's vagina and made her suck his penis. He penetrated her vaginally, then anally. When another vehicle passed, he told her, "We're going to go somewhere else so we can finish this."

Seplow asked, "While they were approaching the ramp to go north on the freeway, there was something about the way he was driving that made her feel that he was going to get back on the freeway and go north; is that correct?"

"Yes."

Yes, Scott thought, up the freeway to the next exit, where the same bastard probably murdered Michele Morales.

Casually, Johnson agreed that the man had choked Martinez, and that she'd been so afraid he'd kill her that she jumped out of his moving truck.

"During the investigation," Seplow continued, ". . . you were able to locate a vehicle that matched the description that Teresa Martinez gave; is that correct?"

"Detective Dimodica did, yes."

"And the person who owned and operated that vehicle was not Scott Lehr; is that correct?"

"That's correct."

"Do you know whether or not that person admitted having sex with Teresa Martin?"

Clayton jumped to his feet. "Your Honor, this is hearsay . . ."

Gerst agreed, and Seplow was forced to drop the question.

Had the jury heard enough to connect the dots?

31: "You Just Don't Know"

NOVEMBER 5-6, 1996

Bill Clayton's next witness was David Duplissa, a DNA analyst for the Arizona DPS Crime Laboratory. Duplissa's testimony for the Meredith Porter case suggested that he might have conveniently ignored results that the State preferred not to consider. Scott noticed that faint bands counted as evidence when the DPS wanted to claim a match, but were discounted when they didn't suit the prosecution's needs.

Duplissa actually said, "Most of the times faint bands can be explained away. It's quite clear as to where they're from."

Looking at the autorads for the Porter case, Duplissa dismissed DNA evidence he didn't want to take into account. "There appear to be another set of . . . very faint bands, right here . . . And that can be explained as being incomplete stripping from the previous probe." Looking at another lane, Duplissa dismissively noted "other evidence of even fainter bands, you know, at the different probes that I cannot attribute to previous probing . . . And, in instances like that, you just have to speculate as to what they may be. Could be a second source of semen. You just don't know."

How coolly the guy let that drop! So Scott's life was in the hands of "experts" who speculated on the source of DNA.

Duplissa also pooh-poohed the significance of finding unexplained bands in the control lanes. DPS wrote the vendor about the problems, he said. ". . . That ended up making us change vendors."

And so, looking at DNA analyses in which control DNA samples had indicated that the test was not valid, and in which extra bands might represent the DNA of an unknown assailant, Duplissa confidently claimed resemblance between Scott's DNA and that of the man who assaulted Meredith Porter on the night Scott was home at his twin daughter's birthday party.

Clayton trumpeted, "With that, Your Honor, shall we quit for the day?"

Gerst genially sent the jury home. "Have a nice evening. And . . . make sure you vote and watch the election returns tonight."

The following morning, Scott was incredulous when he learned that Duplissa would also testify about the case of Nicole Churchill. Even though the crimes against Churchill and Alison Brooks were to be tried separately, the jury had already heard them testify. Now Clayton was apparently going to introduce what he claimed was DNA evidence in the Churchill case.

In what had become a predictable pattern, Clayton led Duplissa through a shifty claim of a DNA match in the case of Nicole Churchill. "The only thing that would stand out would be, again, the low band for Scott Lehr below the 30th size standards. . . .that's just the way those low bands are, they are faint and weak." A few minutes later, Duplissa admitted that he hadn't sized the low band in 1992. However, "In 1995, when we were revisiting this for the Frye hearing, I did go back and size that lower band for the comparison. . ."

I'll bet you did, Scott thought. You "sized" it to make it look like my profile.

When Clayton began questioning Duplissa about the case of Michelle Morales, curiosity overcame Scott's anger. There had already been testimony suggesting that any DNA recovered would have been badly degraded.

Duplissa admitted that the victim's blood stain "had a rancid odor to it." He also acknowledged "with the anal swab and the vaginal swab that was tested, there wasn't enough DNA there . . ."

Nonetheless, the prosecution displayed autorads representing the compromised samples.

Duplissa was honest in remarking that "That there wasn't much—if any, DNA at all present in most of these samples," and noted "the tremendous smearing" on the autorad. "This is a sign of degradation. . ."

Once the jury was out for lunch, Reeves objected that the autorads in the Morales case had no value as evidence but would serve only to prejudice the jury.

Looking at a photocopy of an autorad showing only a single band, even Judge Gerst described it as "a faint discoloration." Still, Gerst permitted the autorads to be shown, granting to the defense only that the term "match" should not be used in the Morales case.

On cross-examination, Reeves asked whether, according to the DPS's own protocol, extra bands in the control lanes indicated that the probe could not be considered valid.

Duplissa conceded, "If you don't see those two expected number of bands . . . you would end up calling the entire autorad inconclusive."

Going back to the autorads for the Meredith Porter Case, Reeves also cornered Duplissa on the fact that there were bands in a "mixed" male and female sample that could not be accounted for by comparisons to the victim or to Scott. "And you made a notation that says, 'second semen source—husband'?"

Duplissa agreed.

So, Scott thought bitterly. They might be looking at the DNA profile of the actual rapist, but the State was explaining away that evidence.

Summing it up, Reeves asked, "What does the word 'contamination' mean as it relates to DNA?"

"Well, that you would introduce something that normally wouldn't be there . . . sometimes the laboratory could introduce it," Duplissa admitted.

Reeves's poker face betrayed a glimmer of satisfaction.

32: The Defense

It wasn't until after six weeks of testimony accusing Scott that the defense would finally be able to present its first witness. Seplow and Reeves had invested great confidence—and a good share of their budget—in bringing in Dr. Aimee Hayes Bakken, a real expert on DNA analysis. Bakken's résumé was distinguished. She testified that she was an Associate Professor of Zoology at the University of Washington who was doing genetic research. She had worked in "the first laboratory to do human chromosome analyses" and had taken the first pictures of human genes using an electron microscope. Bakken had studied with Dr. Edwin Southern, who developed the Southern Blot test that was a key part of RFLP DNA testing. She should be the perfect witness to debunk the prosecution's shaky claim of DNA evidence.

Responding to Reeves's questions, Bakken pinpointed three major differences between forensic DNA analysis and her own research: that forensic DNA often had only limited samples to work with, while she usually had adequate samples. She always repeated her DNA tests five or six times to check for accuracy, while forensic DNA tests were often done only once. Second, Bakken tried to collect a sterile DNA sample, whereas forensic samples were sometimes degraded and usually contaminated. The crucial, third difference was that RFLP testing was developed to compare samples for the purpose of exclusion, as in paternity testing. "Because RFLP DNA testing cannot tell you, simply looking at a DNA sample, if it's exactly the same as another DNA sample. . ."

It was as if this smart lady had just switched on a lamp over the confusion the prosecution had created.

Reeves asked Bakken why, if she didn't do forensic analysis herself, she was qualified to testify about it.

Bakken answered that DNA testing methods had been developed for basic research and that she had used them since 1981. She'd reviewed the prosecution's autorads and visited the DPS lab several times. She'd also examined their protocol and reviewed 2,000 to 3,000 other cases over the last six years.

Then Reeves asked what *bias* means.

That brought Clayton to his feet, but this time Gerst overruled his objection.

Dr. Bakken explained how she numbered the test tubes that she put samples in, so that she didn't know what was in each tube. ". . . You try to avoid the potential for bias, which is potential to unconsciously affect how you read the result."

The opposite, Scott thought, of how the DPS crime lab worked.

Reeves asked her about the importance of controls.

She said that controls were an essential part of every experiment, because they would indicate if something was wrong in the testing.

With respect to the DPS analyses, she testified, there was "a recurring problem with flaws or extra bands appearing in the controls, which would . . . make you stop the experiment and redo it . . ."

Reeves summed it up, "So. . . we can't place confidence in this, is that what you're saying?"

She agreed.

Reeves asked how autorads were digitized for computer analysis.

Bakken explained how the computer allowed the human analyst to move the cursors to indicate bands wherever he or she thought they should be.

Displaying an autorad, Reeves asked, "Is this where the analyst put the band?"

Bakken couldn't say, since the DPS lab gave no record of where the analyst had intervened to identify bands.

Scott peeked at the jury. Most of them seemed distracted, unaware that Bakken had just indicated that DPS could manipulate their DNA "results" at will.

Dr. Bakken saw an additional problem with an autorad for the Christorf case, where she saw marks that indicated latent radioactivity. Here "a residual image, maybe from another case," looked like bands pertaining to this case. She confirmed that such leftover images were easy to check for. However, there was no evidence that the DPS had checked.

Wow, Scott thought. A superimposed image from the previous testing could easily falsify the results appearing on an autorad. So much for the State's DNA "evidence" in the murder of Margaret Christorf.

Again, Reeves questioned Bakken about bias, and she began to speak about the head of a forensic laboratory in Virginia. Scott thought he knew who she was talking about.—the notorious Fred Zain, who for 15 years deliberately falsified blood and DNA analyses for prosecutors—presumably without those prosecutors' knowledge—in hundreds of murder and rape cases in ten states.

Clayton ran up to the bench with an objection, and Judge Gerst sent the jury out.

Reeves also wanted to question Bakken about the Tsosi case. The prosecution's previous witness, David Duplissa, was involved in that very case, having identified a double band as a single band. In doing this, Duplissa had declared a match between an evidentiary sample and the DNA sample of a defendant who later turned out to be innocent.

Again, Judge Gerst sided with the prosecution. The jury would not hear about Duplissa's history of biased DNA analysis.

With the jury seated again, Reeves displayed a xerox from the lab file for the Morales case. On it was a post-it note.

Reeves read it to the jury. "Dave . . . this is another case that may be associated with Scott Lehr. I'd like to have it ready for probing by December 3rd. SDN."

Scott knew that "Dave" and "SDN" would be David Duplissa and Susan D. Narveson.

Bakken expressed concern that the lab director explicitly told the analyst that the sample might be related to a specific suspect. It was, Scott thought, a perfect example of bias.

Turning to the Meredith Porter case, Reeves asked Dr. Bakken whether she noticed "anything peculiar" with the autorads.

Above the bands that Duplissa had measured, Bakken pointed out three other sets of bands that were ignored. She added, "And in this case I would disagree with his having called these blemishes down here real bands to the exclusion of measuring these other things above it."

For the Christorf murder case, Bakken again noted extra faint bands in the suspect's sample that the analyst had not scored. They did not match the profiles of Scott, nor did they match Christorf herself, nor William McFadden.

Analyzed objectively, the DNA evidence in the Porter and Christorf cases excluded Scott. He hoped that the jury could pick up on that truth despite the overwhelming mass of technical details and misleading statements they'd heard.

After dismissing the jury for the day, Judge Gerst considered the relevancy of the next area that Bakken would testify on—the autorads in the case of Mona Barnett. Bakken explained that she would not rely upon the DPS's results because the lab had not demonstrated its accuracy and reliability through validation studies. Also, Bakken observed, there were questions about the validity of the DPS's database; the continued appearance of unexplained extra bands in their results; flawed controls; doubts about the precision of their match window, because their studies went contrary to what every other lab had found; and inability of the lab staff to load consistent amounts of DNA. Consistent loading was important, she added, because varying amounts of DNA could result in false comparisons. Bakken concluded, ". . .and then, they go ahead and analyze the results anyway without stopping to find out why the results are flawed."

Gerst asked whether she would say that the autorads were wrong.

Dr. Bakken answered that it wasn't a matter of right or wrong, but of the reliability of the results.

Scott thought the Bakken's logic was on the money, but Gerst ruled to exclude her testimony on the reliability of DPS lab results, because, he said, "we're into an area of speculation."

Reeves's voice betrayed outrage. "Well, Your Honor, I believe . . . that's the whole nature of an expert witness's testimony. . . ."

Gerst concluded that Bakken's perspective "would be extremely confusing to the jury" and dismissed them.

Scott felt as if he'd been punched in the gut. That was the end of his star witness's testimony. In the morning Bill Clayton would try to undermine what little Bakken had been allowed to say. Scott would bet money that Clayton had accurately pegged her for a scientist of high integrity and wouldn't hesitate to take advantage of her honesty.

As he cross-examined Dr. Bakken the next day, Clayton displayed autorads analyzing the DNA of the blood sample Scott had willingly given when he was arrested. Bakken agreed that they looked "clean," with no extra bands.

Then Clayton had her look at an autorad from the Mona Barnett case, and asked whether the male sample looked similar to Scott's known DNA.

She agreed that they did.

Clayton asked whether by looking at the autorads she had reason to believe that the analyst had manually moved the base pair size from what the computer had scored.

Bakken continued to answer frankly. "I don't have any basis to judge. . ."

Like a cat leering over a goldfish bowl, Clayton asked sharply, "Have you agreed with every position by those people who write about forensic DNA?"

In response to his absurdly general question, Bakken answered that she had not.

Clayton pounced. "Then would the contra be true, that those that write in the forensic articles don't always agree with you, either . . .?"

"I suspect so. I have never had one actually tell me that, I don't think, but . . ."

Clayton cut her short. "Thank you very much."

Scott wondered whether the jury could see through what the prosecutor had done. Because they hadn't heard why Bakken mistrusted the DPS evidence, Clayton made her skepticism sound academic.

Before Bakken was dismissed, Judge Gerst asked her questions submitted by the jury. One of them asked Bakken whether she had any "explanation as to why the defendant's DNA matched the male fraction on a vast majority of the autorads."

Scott shuddered. "The vast majority of autorads"? Didn't they listen to the testimony?

"I think the question is, 'Do I know,' " Bakken answered. "And, no, I don't, because I don't have any good, clean DNA tests in front of me to give you a solid answer. It may be that they matched because, in fact, the evidence samples did come from Scott Lehr. But that may not necessarily be true . . ."

Scott knew Bakken was only speaking objectively, hypothetically, but what would the jury think when the defense's witness didn't clearly say that the DNA evidence did not implicate him?

The jury took a break. When the door had closed on them, counsel and judge conferred again on the issue of validation studies of the DPS's work.

Gerst's response was revealing. "What's run here is not a research lab . . . that's just not the standard we use."

"We"? Scott thought.

Through his anger, Reeves stayed focused. "I don't understand why we're allowed to put on a defense then if I can't say their work is sloppy and why their work is sloppy . . ."

"All right," Judge Gerst concluded. "I believe we should not be going into the protocols that's been used by the DPS lab for the last six years."

Amazing, Scott thought. Judge Gerst wouldn't mind convicting one more innocent man as long as the DPS's years of shady work were not criticized.

The next day, Clayton called one more criminalist with the Department of Public Safety crime lab—Terry Hogan.

Clayton asked Hogan about his DNA analyses for the Brooks and Caporaso cases.

This was going to be interesting, Scott thought. An honest analysis of DNA evidence in the case of Alison Brooks would likely reflect the fact that she had unprotected intercourse with her boyfriend the night before the incident. And in the Caporaso case, the State had already admitted that their DNA evidence did not match Scott.

Reeves called out his continuing objection, that, like the Churchill case, the Brooks case was supposed to have been severed from this trial.

Clayton asked Hogan to put the autoradiograph on the viewer.

Hogan stated that "the vaginal swab female fraction does match the reference sample from the victim." No other samples on the autorad matched.

Clayton pressured him, "Anything in there that you would say is excluded as a match? For instance, the sock versus the male fraction?"

Hogan said, "We do have a male fraction from the vaginal swab which has a different pattern than the male fraction from the sock."

Scott knew that the prosecution was hoping to persuade the jury that the semen on the sock found near the crime scene, which clearly excluded Scott, had nothing to do with the assault, even though Brooks had told detectives she'd deliberately left her sock at the scene.

Finally Clayton displayed Mylars including Scott's known samples. Clayton elicited from Hogan a claim to have made a "visual match" between Scott's DNA and the male portion of the vaginal swab, presumably the man who assaulted Alison Brooks. But as he explained how he had made the "match" Hogan sounded so fishy that Scott couldn't believe anyone was buying this. Hogan claimed to have used a computerized "image analysis system" to help make his visual match. He testified that he'd made a five-probe match between the suspect DNA in the Brooks case and Scott's, although he had really only counted four of those probes because in the fifth "we could not get the lower band to develop." Hogan then claimed to have used the "modified ceiling principle" to calculate the statistical likelihood of such a match. The frequency of such a match, according to Hogan, would be 1 in 800,000.

Reeves objected that Hogan's numerical calculations were invalid, since the autorads showed extra bands indicating that the tests were not accurate.

Gerst overruled Reeves's objection.

Then Clayton questioned Hogan about the DNA evidence for the Caporaso case. Here, although the police reports referred to a semen sample, the DPS wasn't claiming to have a DNA sample for the suspect. To Scott it seemed outrageous for the prosecution to be showing the jury autorads, as if somehow even an absence of evidence implicated him! It was the same game they'd played with the Morales case.

Clayton displayed the probings of the Caporaso "evidence" and led Hogan through a long discussion about matching Caporaso's known reference sample of DNA from her blood to samples of her own DNA from the rape kit. The problem was, Hogan had also analyzed a sample of Scott's blood on the Caporaso autorads, although the State claimed not to have a suspect sample to compare it with! But Hogan referred to the samples only by lane number. The prosecution's manner of presenting the samples might confuse the average, sleepy juror into thinking that Scott's DNA matched that of the assailant!

On cross-examination, Reeves asked why no suspect's DNA could be found on the Caporaso case.

Hogan explained that the man might have had a vasectomy or not produced sperm because of a childhood disease.

But the rules of evidence did not allow anyone to make it clear to the jurors that Scott was not that man.

As they marched Scott back to his cell that night, it gnawed at him that Dr. Bakken's testimony had been cut short. The days ahead would be his last chance to tell the jury the truth, and he'd chosen to testify in his own defense. Seplow warned him it was always risky for a defendant to testify, but Scott felt he had to. He would have to trust that, seeing him as he really was, the jury would believe him.

33: Taking the Stand

NOVEMBER 19, 1996

Bill Clayton read a brief stipulation that Cathy Holmes, if called as a witness, would testify that on February 7, 1992, she had seen Michelle Morales at the Circle K at 3434 West Peoria between 2 and 4 p.m. Holmes had told investigators that Morales paid for cigarettes and a bag of ice. Holmes saw her leave the Circle K with a white man with a receding hairline, appearing 40-50 years old, who drove a full-size black truck.

Scott wondered why Seplow hadn't brought Holmes herself to testify, to impress upon the jury that the last time Morales had been seen alive she was with another man. Surely seeing her in person would have helped them remember that point.

But quickly Seplow announced, "Call Scott Lehr," and Scott was on his feet, striding toward the witness stand. Walking without shackles! He'd been looking forward to this moment for so long. Now, it felt like a dream.

As he took his seat, Scott glanced out at the jury. Immediately, he looked away. Their faces showed curiosity—without a trace of sympathy. It was a "what makes this monster tick?" kind of curiosity. He tried to put it out of his head.

The bailiff led him in the oath he'd heard so many witnesses repeat. Somebody reached in front of him to adjust the microphone. Shyness seized him. Scott had never spoken in front of such a large audience, let alone a group that by now seemed to hate him.

But then he heard Seplow's reassuring, "Sorry about that interruption, Scott." And that shadow of Bill Clayton in the background, mad as a Rottweiler on a chain, was more effective than a bucket of cold water in his face. Scott pulled himself together.

"Tell the jury your name."

High-pitched, cracking from disuse, his voice broke out. "I think everybody knows my name; Scott Lehr." It was a nervous, dumb attempt at humor, but people gasped, as if he was some vicious thug, bragging about his celebrity. Seplow had warned him not to joke on the stand, but it was just too ingrained in Scott's personality.

Seplow asked a few background questions and then showed the photo of Scott's car. Scott described his 1979 Caprice Classic Chevrolet—a four-door, with a tan body and black vinyl top, always a black top, from the time he bought it to the day he sold it after Elaine's accident.

With both of them warmed up, Seplow got to the heart of it. "Outside of sitting in the courtroom learning about the case over the past several days of what you've been accused, have you ever had any dealings with Mona Barnett?"

"Not to my knowledge." Scott thought that sounded tentative. He only meant to be utterly honest.

"How about Nicole Churchill?"

"No." Now his voice was clear.

"Never saw her?"

"Only in court."

Seplow repeated the question for Nancy Caporaso, Alison Brooks, Margaret Christorf, Amy Perry, Meredith Porter, Belinda Cronin, Michelle Morales, and Teresa Martinez.

No, Scott said he'd never seen them before he was shown their photos or heard them testify in court. After two months of having to sit in silence while they accused him, it was sweet to say it.

Seplow asked whether Scott knew where he'd been on the dates of all the crimes.

"No. No. No, it was—it was too—" He took a deep breath. "At the time that I was arrested and questioned on these cases, some of the cases had happened like 18 months before that. And I'm like most people; I have a hard time remembering what I had for breakfast last Wednesday, so I could not remember where I was at certain times. . . . I work for myself, so I couldn't account for a lot of my time."

Seplow was subtly frowning. Scott was supposed to answer with a simple "yes" or "no."

In response to Phil's questions, Scott told about the twin's birthday party on the night of the crimes against Meredith Porter. As Elaine had testified, he said he'd gone to sleep early that night, while Elaine sat up late, talking to Donna.

Seplow moved on to a photo of the interior of Scott's 1985 Sentra. Scott explained how the stereo knobs were taken on March 18, 1992. He could pinpoint the date because whoever tore out the knobs had taken Scott's wallet, too, and he'd needed to apply for a new license.

Phil asked him about his tree-trimming business. Scott described how he taped fliers to mailboxes in nicer neighborhoods, to interest new customers.

When Phil asked about the ring that Clayton was trying to tie to Belinda Cronin, Scott explained how he used to shop at auctions and garage sales and sometimes resell his finds. He'd bought that ring at a garage sale in late 1991. Short of money as Christmas approached, he decided to pawn it, as well as some tools and Elaine's rings from her first marriage. But when the pawnbroker offered only $5 for the ring, Scott kept it.

Then Phil brought up the subject of Scott's changing hairstyles, displaying photos from 1990 to 1992. He could have shown a lifetime of family snapshots that would have made the same point: even as a boy, Scott changed his haircut often. He couldn't remember a time when he didn't experiment with different styles. The family album would show him clean shaven, mustachioed, stubbly, or sporting a closely-trimmed beard, with hair cut very short, medium length, or sometimes long enough to cover his ears. He parted it left, right, or not at all. And he wished he could point out to the jury that he had a large mole on his right cheek, a feature that no victim had ever reported of the man who attacked her.

Displaying another of the photos, Phil had Scott confirm that he always wore his watch as the photo showed, on his left wrist. Amy Perry testified the man who attacked her wore a watch on his right arm.

Finally, Phil asked Scott how long he worked in his tree-trimming business, which was 8 years.

"So would it be a fair statement to say that you're pretty familiar with the general roads of Arizona?"

Scott agreed, though he wondered why Seplow asked him that, since it was something Clayton could probably twist to use against him. But that was Seplow's last question. Scott couldn't resist a relieved smile. They'd given the jury a glimpse of the normal life he'd lived.

Bill Clayton stalked forward for cross-examination. Without the polite "Good morning," he'd given other witnesses, he began insinuatingly, "Mr. Lehr, you have a sister that lives in Prescott; is that correct?"

"That's correct."

"And you came here from Wisconsin; is that correct?"

"No, I came here from Kansas City in 1973."

"All right. And that was your mother . . ."

"Yes."

"—you, and your sister?"

"That's correct."

"Your father come with you?"

Asshole! Clayton knew Scott didn't have a father. But Scott wasn't going to let Clayton get to him. "No."

Clayton's questions then dredged through the different addresses where Scott lived with Elaine from 1990 through 1992. The prosecutor never asked why the family moved, but feigned astonishment that they made five moves over three years. Apparently, the lawyer had never been short enough of money to understand how hard it was to find affordable housing in neighborhoods safe for children. When Scott mentioned that they chose the Chateau Village complex because it had playgrounds and many children living there, the prosecutor echoed darkly, "A lot of children and playgrounds?" as if that were evidence that Scott preyed upon children.

Then Clayton grilled Scott about how many times he'd painted the cab of his old flatbed truck, implying that he'd also changed the color of his Chevy Caprice. But police had examined the Caprice. Clayton had to know that Scott had never changed its color.

Clayton asked about the gray and blue baby-seat that Scott and Elaine had owned. Scott bought it second-hand early in 1991, and it was stolen from the car the same summer. Clayton reacted as if a gray-blue baby-seat was a unique thing, rather than the most common color for baby-seats made at that time. Then he acted as if it was highly suspicious that Scott would not file a police report over a stolen baby-seat.

After lunch, Clayton came back with a new ploy. Now he had a map of the city and asked Scott to place stickpins in the locations of his family's various homes. Resolved to treat the man like a bratty child, Scott obeyed calmly.

Clayton asked Scott if he was familiar with the 7th Street area, where the crimes against Mona Barnett were committed.

Scott answered that in high school he was involved in kegger parties in the area. He was not afraid to answer truthfully.

Clayton pursued "Could you have made the statement on March 21 of 1996, that you had been in the desert area of 7th Street and Happy Valley Road?"

Phil Seplow approached the bench to object. As Seplow and Clayton talked to Gerst, the judge turned and snapped at Scott, "Don't watch me."

"Oh, I'm sorry." Scott thought he covered his feelings OK, but the judge's hostile admonition shook him more than anything Clayton had done that day. Where was the presumption of innocence when the judge acted as if he had reason to despise the defendant?

Gerst sustained Phil's objection to that particular question, so Clayton had Scott put a stickpin on the map to mark a landfill that he had sometimes used in south Phoenix, a location that had nothing to do with any of the crimes.

Then, holding up a photo of Mona Barnett, Clayton dove in for the kill. "Now, if you never saw this woman before, is there any explanation of why your DNA would end up in this sexual assault kit?"

Well, Scott knew it hadn't. "No" he said evenly, but shouldn't Seplow object to this kind of question?

Clayton showed a photo of Nicole Churchill, and pronounced, stern as the voice of God, "And is there any reason why your DNA would show up in that sexual assault kit?"

"Not that I can think of." Scott yearned to add, "And it was not!"

After making a big deal of the fact that Scott had smoked Marlboro Lights until Marlboro Reds Mediums came out on the market, Clayton asked Scott what his favorite soft drink was in 1991.

"It was and always will be Dr Pepper." Scott remembered that the rapist in one of the cases had drunk a Dr Pepper, but surely no jurist would consider drinking Dr Pepper incriminating. If it were, how many of them could be found guilty themselves?

The prosecutor went back to his silly map and asked Scott where he was living on April 4, 1991, the date of the assault against Nancy Caporaso. It was the Chateau Village Apartments at 2020 West Glendale Avenue.

"And if you would, where is 19th Avenue and Union Hills?"

Scott found it for him. He noticed that the scale of the prosecutor's map distorted the distances. The apartment was at least 12 miles south of the place where Nancy Caporaso was picked up, but Scott wasn't allowed to say so.

Then Clayton asked him if he had ever met Caporaso before court.

"No, I did not."

"Do you know of any reason why she would point you out?"

What could he say? Because you have her convinced that I'm guilty, even though I'm a head taller than the guy who did it? "I can only speculate," he answered curtly. An offended cry escaped from the jury box.

"Where were you living on October 24, 1991?"

That was the house near 58th Avenue and Thomas Road, and Clayton was asking about the date of the Alison Brooks assault. Clayton was probably hoping that the jury would never remember that Brooks accepted a ride near the same spot where Caporaso did. By October, Scott had moved even further from that scene; it had to be at least 20 miles. Clayton's insinuations about Scott living near the locations where the victims accepted rides or were assaulted were really worthless.

Again, Clayton sneered, "You said you had never met Alison Brooks before that date; is that correct?"

"Correct."

Seplow objected; that case was not being heard at this trial. But Gerst allowed the questioning about Alison Brooks to continue.

Clayton pounced as if he'd caught Scott with his hand in the cookie jar: "Since you had never met on that date or before, there is no reason for your DNA to be in this sexual assault kit; is that correct?"

"That's correct."

Clayton displayed the photo of the late Margaret Christorf. "Since you said you never met Margaret Christorf before . . . is there any reason you can think of why your DNA would be in the sexual assault kit?"

"No, it should not have been," Scott answered.

" 'Should not have been'?" the prosecutor jeered.

In the case of Amy Perry, the prosecution couldn't even pretend they had DNA evidence, so Clayton focused on dramatizing how the girl had claimed to recognize Scott in court. Clayton was running a little low on steam when Judge Gerst called a recess. It had been a tough day, but Scott knew he could last as long as the prosecutor.

When they reconvened, Clayton held up the ring taken from Scott's house and asked melodramatically whether Scott had seen it before.

Scott answered that he had purchased it at a garage sale. He surmised that it was the same ring his wife had given police and it had a little break on the bottom of the band. He was glad he got that fact in, since Belinda Cronin's ring had reportedly been in good condition.

Then Clayton went back to his blasted map, insinuating that it was highly significant that Scott and Elaine's apartment had been somewhere between Cronin's apartment and the apartment of Dr. Storm, where she'd said she was going before being murdered.

But Clayton was smart enough to drop that case quickly. Accusingly he waved a photo of Meredith Porter's biological evidence and asked why Scott's DNA should appear in the sexual examination kit.

Scott couldn't keep himself from saying, "I don't believe it was."

"Let me ask you about why you moved from these locations. Were you trying to stay away from the areas where these sexual assaults were reported?"

"No."

". . . Did you keep changing your facial hair so that you wouldn't be recognized from those composites?"

"No."

"When . . . Amy Perry walked over to you, did you look down and away from her so she couldn't be able to recognize you?"

"No."

"Is there a way that we can tell when you're lying or not?" the prosecutor brayed.

Seplow objected, and for once the judge had to sustain him.

"I have no further questions," Clayton pronounced smugly.

Scott ordered his muscles to relax. If Bill Clayton's goal was to bait Scott into showing anger, Scott had won.

On redirect-examination, Seplow tried to help the jury get the facts straight, but the list was long. Scott testified that he'd never died his hair blond, never looked like the man who attacked Mona Barnett, and never owned a car like the one she'd described. He'd never had a car resembling the two-door Chevy Nova Nancy

Caporaso remembered. His cream-and-black Chevy Caprice never resembled the beige car described by Nicole Churchill, Alison Brooks, or Amy Perry.

Then came a couple of jury questions. One asked why Scott was out so late the night before he was arrested if he didn't place any fliers on mailboxes.

"That's a good question," Scott began, but stopped himself. Seplow once said that no one would believe Scott thought he was being followed, so he said he didn't quite remember why, but that he was checking on the state of palm trees at managed property he knew of. If the palms hadn't been trimmed, he'd give the property owners a call. It was true; the area was right on Scottsdale Road and lit-up at night.

But the questions from the jurists had given Clayton the right to re-cross-examine Scott. "Six-twenty-four, that evening that you went to pass out fliers, you stated to your wife you were going to pass out fliers; is that correct?"

"That's correct."

"And you did not?"

"No, I did not."

"Nothing else, Your Honor," Clayton sniffed.

And Seplow concluded, "Your Honor, at this point, the defense would rest, Your Honor."

And that was it? It looked bad, Scott knew, that the defense didn't offer more. Seplow could have called Donna to confirm that Scott was at home, asleep on the night of the Meredith Porter crime, or Elaine's dad, who could show the video of the birthday party that night, clearly demonstrating that Scott didn't look like the attacker Porter described. Scott didn't know why Seplow didn't call them, or other witnesses who could tell the jury that Scott wasn't a violent person. The idea of additional witnesses for the defense had quietly died—as if Seplow was just worn out and ready to move on.

After the jury left, Reeves objected to Clayton's questioning during the cross-examination, when he'd asked again and again why Scott's DNA would be in the victims' assault evidence. The science wasn't precise enough to say that it was a particular person's DNA, Reeves reminded the judge.

But Gerst replied that "in cross-examination, you can use leading and suggestive questions, which may not be factually correct. But we'll get into argument and we may be in a different area."

Huh? Scott wondered what the hell that meant. He knew for sure there would be nothing to stop Clayton from lying up and down in his closing arguments tomorrow.

34: Closing Arguments

NOVEMBER 20, 1996

Before prosecution and defense made their final arguments, Judge Gerst solemnly read his instructions to the jury. "It's your duty to follow the law, whether you agree with it or not. It's also your duty to determine the facts. . . ." He instructed them to consider each witness's credibility, possible prejudices, and inconsistent statements. The defendant is presumed innocent, Gerst explained, and the State must prove guilt beyond a reasonable doubt. He added that every charge should be deliberated separately, as if the defendant were being tried on that count alone.

Excellent, Scott thought. If the jury followed these instructions, they would acquit him.

Gerst also instructed the jury that they should not consider the possible punishment, which would be decided by the judge.

Scott was thankful that this jury could not possibly find him guilty of murder. Gerst could be counted on to sentence him to death.

After Gerst's solemn instructions, the courtroom was hushed as a church. Bill Clayton faced the jury, wearing his impression of a humble smile. He proceeded to apologize for not having been friendly enough to the jury. "Not being able to speak to you all of this time has sometimes led to some awkward situations . . ."

Scott resisted rolling his eyes. Spare us!

Clayton asked the jury to think back to his opening statement. "And if I happen to misquote one little thing or something . . . just go with what it is that you remember . . ."

Again, Scott noticed, the prosecutor claimed in advance that his sloppiness with the facts would be innocent oversight.

"I told you," Clayton said, "this was a horrible and despicable crime . . ."

Scott was grimly impressed with how Clayton encouraged the jury to forget that this was not one "crime" but nine different crimes — even though minutes ago the judge instructed them to consider each charge separately.

Clayton asked the jury to remember the evil and violence the victims had suffered. "What is it that could put these children that were here before you in that car . . .?"

Even Clayton seemed to realize the ridiculousness of describing the victims as "children" because when he continued they were simply "young women."

Clayton referred the jury to the case of Mona Barnett. "Her attacker . . . had this large American car she thought was blue . . ."

No, Scott, recalled. She'd testified that the car was mid-sized, and if she "thought" it was blue, it probably was! And how was Clayton going to get around the fact that Barnett stood up in court and confidently stated that she'd never seen Scott before?

Clayton quickly answered that question, asserting that Scott Lehr had ejaculated and not used a condom. "So this sexual assault kit is an unbiased kit sitting somewhere in the archives property room of DPS and Phoenix Police Department."

Bullshit, Scott thought. The sexual assault kit itself might be "unbiased," but the DPS analysis of it was certainly not.

Clayton moved on to the case of Nicole Churchill, which was supposedly not being tried. Again, he glossed over the inconsistent testimony of the victim, who'd used heroin on the day of the crime, and focused on the State's claim of having DNA evidence.

"Caporaso, Clayton continued, "if there was going to be bias in this case, that was the case that they had been looking to place in his lap and they didn't. . . . "

Scott was startled. That was a warped way for Clayton to admit that even the DPS could not stretch their evidence in the Caporaso case far enough to claim a DNA match.

Here, Clayton claimed, the perpetrator was getting more violent. ". . . He is now pounding her head on that rock that's out there. . . "

Scott stuffed his anger down his throat. The medical exam noted no bumps or abrasions on Caporaso's head. And there was no "rock."

Clayton then speculated that Scott had seen stories about the serial rapist on television and moved his family to keep neighbors from recognizing him.

It seemed to Scott that moving, appearing as a newcomer, would draw *more* attention to someone, wouldn't it?

"And the detectives, now . . ." Clayton scoffed. " . . . I mean are they going to try to frame somebody just to solve a crime?"

Funny how Clayton kept defending himself.

"Looking for anybody, a scapegoat. . . . " Clayton barked contemptuously. "Some people once invented this saying called a red herring. I never understood that . . ."

Oh, brother, Scott thought. Nobody understood red herrings better!

Clayton proceeded to muddle whatever understanding of DNA testing the jury might have acquired. He vaguely claimed that "DNA is not new" and that the evidence offered by the prosecution's witnesses was "very powerful" in telling one person from another.

Reeves jumped up to object that Clayton's statement was "beyond the scope of the evidence."

Scott was surprised to find out that the defense was allowed to object, since Clayton's argument had misrepresented the evidence left and right, but Seplow hadn't objected to anything else so far today.

Judge Gerst avoided the issue and advised the jury to use their own memories.

Clayton took advantage of Gerst's permissiveness, claiming "the figures on the DNA were one in a million."

Clayton continued to undermine the Judge's instructions to determine innocence or guilt on each of the charges separately.

"We're trying to identify the next ones that will come in relationship to what happened in the first ones, identity, where you see it coming together, forming this circle that points to the defendant."

"We'll break now, Your Honor," Clayton announced, and the judge complied.

After lunch, Clayton continued, "as the defendant agreed with you, he has no explanation for his blood to be found or his semen to be found, his DNA to be found in those sexual assault kits."

Scott sat up. "For his blood to be found . . ."! Was Clayton inadvertently revealing that the DPS had gone so far as to switch Scott's blood sample with the real evidence?

"Well, ladies and gentlemen . . . that's because he's guilty."

Going back to the Caporaso case, since the DNA testing exonerated Scott, Clayton reminded the jury about the murky partial fingerprint taken from a McDonald's cup.

Clayton claimed, falsely, that the perpetrator had banged Caporaso's head with a rock, and, when Caporaso didn't die, used a larger rock to murder Margaret Christorf. At that, he triumphantly showed the jury photos of Christorf on the ground with her head crushed. He whipped out another photograph and shouted, ". . . remember the tree of Nancy Caporaso with the litter. . . Same tree. Same MO."

Scott couldn't believe the prosecutor could lie so boldly. "Same tree"? The crime scenes were nearly 9 miles apart! "Same MO"? All that was known about Christorf's death was that she was last seen disheveled and apparently drunk, after a "business-type man" in a white shirt gave her a ride to the Circle K in a vehicle resembling a Jeep Wagoneer.

Clayton launched off into the case of Belinda Cronin. He did not mention that her body had been buried, or that she was allegedly last seen on her way to visit Dr. Storm. He asserted that "this is a sexual assault, just like the others."

Never mind that no evidence of sexual assault was recovered.

Now Clayton preyed on the jury's sympathy for Amy Perry, inventing the ugliest image he could, which was in neither her testimony nor the police reports, ". . . He puts it in her mouth and climaxes, you've got to do it until the juice comes out, and she gags."

Clayton looked sternly at Scott. "And someone can sit here on the stand and say: I know a short cut, I'm a family man, trust me. Don't get in, don't get in the car of trust. . . ."

In spite of his anger, Scott was almost amused by Clayton's phony theatrics.

Clayton proceeded to make baffling statements about evidence. "People can lie to you; the physical evidence will not lie to you." In addition to DNA, which really was physical evidence, Clayton gave examples of witnesses' testimony and their impressions at the lineup.

The stale sandwich Scott had for lunch was getting to him. Physical evidence included blood, semen, fingerprints — objects or physical traces of a crime. Physical evidence did NOT include victims' sketchy recollections of license numbers or lineup identifications. Clayton was either incompetent about fundamental legal concepts or feigning incompetence to mislead the jury.

The prosecutor took a weighty breath. He warned the jury that they shouldn't expect to see the defendant's nose grow, like Pinocchio, when he lies. ". . . And you can see the fingerprint and you can see the DNA, and you can say no, not me . . . Look at the hard evidence here, the real stuff, the circumstantial evidence. Circumstances don't lie. People do."

Scott was stunned. Now Clayton was misrepresenting the concept of circumstantial evidence, which meant "inferential." It did not include fingerprints or DNA. Circumstantial evidence could be interpreted in more ways than one, so it was considered weaker than physical evidence.

When he came to the murder of Michelle Morales, Clayton claimed, "there was a sperm head," in the degraded DNA, which not even the DPS's witnesses had claimed. Clayton made much of the single, smudgy band on the DNA profile that David Duplissa had obligingly testified "does not eliminate Scott Lehr."

Nor, Scott knew, did it eliminate anyone else in the world. His chest tight, Scott told himself that no sensible jury could be fooled by Clayton's manipulation of the facts.

Clayton seemed to be ramping up for a melodramatic finish, claiming that only Scott Lehr could have committed all these crimes.

Bitterly, Scott wished the defense had been allowed to tell the jury about the real suspects, the violent men in the murdered women's lives.

Clayton blustered on that "that man over there is guilty of sexual assault, he's guilty of kidnapping . . . It's when you get to the DNA you know he's guilty of the murders . . ."

Scott thought the prosecutor was finally going to shut up, but Clayton was again misinterpreting the jury instructions, claiming, "I don't have mine with me." According to Clayton, the jury instructions were "simple." Even in the case of Mona Barnett, who testified that Scott was innocent, Clayton advised them, "You have the evidence beyond a reasonable doubt."

Scott closed his eyes. He heard the prosecutor growl, "You've been real patient. Thank you."

Silence. Scott hadn't known how sweet it could be.

Judge Gerst called a break. It was 3:40 that afternoon when Phil Seplow began his crucial closing argument, after Bill Clayton had harangued the weary jury for most of the day.

And Seplow looked tired. "Your Honor," he began. "Detective Dimodica, Mr. Clayton, co-counsel. The evidence is in."

Weird. Why couldn't Phil acknowledge the jury?

"Perhaps, the book has been written," Phil began mildly. "At this point, there's a lot to say . . . it all comes down in the final crunch to making the prosecutor prove each case and each count beyond a reasonable doubt."

True, Scott thought, but tepid.

"During my closing you're going to hear the words "reasonable doubt" quite a bit. It's not a smoke screen . . . . "

Scott fought off annoyance. Couldn't Phil state his case positively?

Seplow sounded as if he was battling a bad cold. He cleared his throat. "There are a ton of charges in this case . . . But each and every one of those charges leveled against Mr. Scott Lehr has to be proven . . . beyond a reasonable doubt, to your satisfaction, to where this presumption of innocence, this shield of the sacred shroud is actually peeled away element by element. . . ."

Scott wondered why Seplow even suggested taking *away* the presumption of innocence. Why not focus on all the inconsistencies, fallacies, and falsehoods in the prosecution's argument?

As if talking to himself, Seplow mused, "If I were allowed to take each case in a vacuum, I don't think there would be too much problem on anything, but the law also allows the prosecution to use this, quote, other act . . ."

Scott stifled a rising panic. Get to the point, Phil!

Again, Seplow faced the delicate task of pointing out holes in the victims' testimony without seeming to deprecate the women themselves. He enumerated the cases, expressing sympathy for each victim. He seemed to be warming up now. "But there's one other nightmare that has to be discussed, and that's . . . the nightmare of a man being accused of a multiplicity of crimes that the State can't show that he committed."

"Can't show"? Scott's face burned. Put some confidence in it, Phil!

Phil focused on the case of Michelle Morales, reminding the jury that she'd last been seen with a man who wasn't Scott, that there was effectively no DNA evidence, and that boot prints had been found near her body.

Yes, Scott thought, and now let the jury know that I haven't owned cowboy boots since I was a kid.

But Seplow didn't mention that. He pointed out that there was jewelry left on her body, and a hair that was not Scott's. "Now, that particular case there is nothing that even comes close to convicting, let alone accusing a man of that particular crime."

Damn right!

Seplow emphasized that the prosecution seemed to be claiming that the rapist-murder robbed the victims, yet Margaret Christorf's body was found with food stamps. After offering evidence that more than one man committed the crimes, Seplow undercut his own point with a lame "And some of these crimes haven't been solved or all of the crimes haven't been solved."

Rallying, Seplow reminded the jury that Amy Perry described a rapist with a Santa Claus beard, and the prosecution couldn't claim that Scott had ever worn his beard long. "Right away that puts you on notice that something is amiss," he added.

No shit! Scott nodded.

Seplow finally brought out that Scott's Chevy had a black top and that there was no evidence that he'd ever changed the color. Again, though, Seplow torpedoed the point he'd just made. "And how many victims talk about a light-tan car with a black top? I don't recall any. . . . Maybe I'm wrong . . ."

Seplow wasn't *sure* that not a one of the victims mentioned a black-topped car? From the first time he'd sat down with Scott and discussed the police reports, that fact had been clear.

Seplow repeated that the defense doesn't have to prove anything, that the burden is on the prosecution. He urged the jury to think of themselves as "independent Columbos, Kojaks, or something like that" and to allow themselves to agree with the defense. He reminded them that Belinda Cronin was found with a crystal necklace and a working watch, and that, since her hands were missing, there was no way of knowing whether her ring was still out in the desert, if she had even been wearing it when she was killed.

Scott hoped the jury wasn't too groggy to catch that point.

Seplow also reminded the jury that Meredith Porter hadn't mentioned knobs missing from a car radio until police showed her Scott's car.

Yes, Scott agreed, and why didn't Seplow go on and point out that Scott's Nissan, from the time he had bought it, was badly damaged on the passenger side? Porter never described that at all!

Finally, Seplow was showing some conviction. He jumped back to the case of Amy Perry and reminding the jury that the Trax shoes the prosecution made such a fuss over identifying had no connection whatsoever to Scott.

He moved on to the case of Mona Barnett. "Now, I'm not even going to talk about the in-court identification," he said.

Scott wished Seplow *would* take a minute more to remind the jury that Barnett had confidently identified a blond-haired man and said she'd never seen Scott in her life.

Seplow added, "She said that the vehicle she was in was light blue, it was an American-made car with no inside door handles."

Let's see Clayton get around that one, Scott thought.

Seplow circled back to the case of Belinda Cronin, pointing out differences from any of the other crimes. The State's own witnesses had testified that an ax might have been used to murder the woman, that she was dumped in the desert after being killed, that she might have been buried in a shallow grave, and that a green sweater was found at the scene, unlike the red sweater she had been reported as wearing.

Scott stole a glance at the jury. Far from being illuminated by all the contradictions Seplow was revealing, they just looked worn out.

Fully engaged now, Seplow reminded them about the "reincarnation" of a fingerprint in the Caporaso case. In July 1992, Karen Jones had compared the print on a discarded McDonald's cup to Scott Lehr's prints and ruled him out. In May 1994, however, Jones compared the prints again and claimed to match the print to Scott's. Phil displayed Scott's actual thumb print on the overhead, remarking, "A real good print." He showed them the indistinct partial print from the cup, adding "some people would say it's a shot of the moon." Seplow snorted, "Is this what a jury of his peers is going to decide a case on?"

Scott had to smile. At least the Caporaso case was a home run for the defense.

For good measure, Seplow reminded the jury that, even though Caporaso had identified Scott in court, she had "partially" identified a different person from a photo lineup and yet another man that she'd seen in person at Star Mart.

Scott was relieved to hear Seplow bring up Teresa Martinez, tying the resemblances in the crimes against her to what was known about the Cronin and Morales murders.

"Maybe we'll start with that in the morning," Judge Gerst interrupted.

35: Mountains of Doubt

NOVEMBER 21, 1996

In the morning Phil Seplow seemed well rested. As he resumed his closing argument, he pointed out the strong resemblances between the Teresa Martinez case and the MO of the other rapes. He reminded the jury that investigators had first considered the crimes against Martinez as one in their series of similar assaults.

OK. Scott relaxed. It looked as if the old Seplow was back today.

But then Seplow concluded, "This is a woman who apparently doesn't pick out Scott Lehr from the lineup."

"Apparently"? Scott's stomach did a flip. Martinez *definitely* did not identify him! And the detectives apparently interviewed the man who *had* raped her.

Seplow petered out, rambling about Scott being a non-secretor and finally calling Mike Reeves to discuss the DNA evidence.

Reeves addressed the jury with energy and charm. "You know, I love law. I've been a lawyer now for 13, 14 years."

Clayton cried out that Reeves was "self-vouching."

This time, Judge Gerst overruled the prosecutor.

Reeves continued, joking about the popular perception of lawyers as "conniving" manipulators of words. In addition to law, he said he liked the precision of science. Statistics, on the other hand, could "muddy the waters." He pointed out that DNA analysis was meaningless if the analyst couldn't provide scientifically valid probability for any match between samples.

Reeves went into a technical, probably brilliant, explanation that Scott sort-of followed about VNTRs, variable numbers of tandem repeats, which varied from person to person. The gist of it was that DPS used a huge match window, according to which different individuals could erroneously be called a match. Scott glanced at the jury. A couple of them seemed to realize that Reeves might be on to something.

Reeves summarized Dr. Bakken's testimony about the necessity of analyzing DNA samples independently and without bias. He quoted from the NRC report: "It is not permissible to decide which features of an evidence sample count and which to discount." And he reminded them that the controls had failed in the DPS analysis. "What does that tell you about the reliability of the results? . . . That is reasonable doubt. . . ."

Go, Reeves!

He recalled for the jury how TWGDAM recommended that forensic laboratories conduct blind proficiency tests of their own accuracy at least annually, which, according to David Duplissa's testimony, DPS did not do. Susan Narveson and her group, Reeves continued, "admit they don't do what she preaches . . . Now, how does that carry over in her laboratory? It's loose. The laboratory is loose. . ."

Reeves turned to the DPS's protocol, which conveniently allowed analysts to make a "visual evaluation" of autorads that both the NRC and the FBI would declare invalid. "It's the old saying, garbage in, garbage out," Reeves summed it up. He reminded the jury of the term "inconclusive," and that David Duplissa testified that the DNA evidence for Michelle Morales was inconclusive. "More than reasonable doubt. He wasn't willing to make any calling, yet the State would have you make a call . . ."

Reeves also pointed out that, although DPS had claimed to exclude William McFadden's DNA, previous serology tests had matched McFadden's pattern, which was different from that of Margaret Christorf and Scott. "Interesting," Reeves mused stagily.

Yeah, "interesting" was one word for it!

Reeves made a final appeal to the jury that was both logical and impassioned. "You're being asked to convict somebody of first-degree murder, based upon a single test that is flawed . . . You don't convict someone of first degree murder based upon something you know is flawed. Thank you."

Scott was close to tears. If the jury understood the truth today, he would have Reeves to thank. As Seplow took Reeves's place before the jury, Scott was painfully aware that this was the last word for the defense. In one more advantage for the prosecution, Bill Clayton would get to present a rebuttal to Seplow's argument. Scott hoped Seplow would drive home the point that, except for that sketchy DNA analysis, the State had no evidence to accuse Scott of the murders, and only questionable identifications to link him to the assaults.

Seplow made a last-ditch effort to remind the jury that they must find Scott not guilty unless they were unanimously convinced beyond a reasonable doubt of his guilt. He repeated that, although the DPS claimed to match Scott's DNA to Barnett's rapist, she had described a blond man and identified another man in court. He wondered out loud whether science could really be taken to say that our human memories are worthless.

Seplow predicted that Clayton would exhort the jury not to forget the victims and to "send a message." At that, Seplow lost his focus. He seemed to be saying that the jury wouldn't want to send the message of convicting an innocent man, but he spoke unclearly. He digressed to talk about premeditation, the difference between first- and second-degree murder. He anticipated that Clayton would argue that "premeditation can occur in a snap of a finger, very short period of time. But if that were the case, every murder would be premeditated, wouldn't it?"

Undeniably, Scott thought.

Once more, Seplow emphasized that Scott Lehr was presumed innocent. At last, Seplow came up with a spark of conviction. "That man who took the witness stand, who got up here when he didn't have to and told you all, to the best of his ability . . . Now, juxtapose . . . the twins' birthday party to what we've just discussed about Meredith Porter . . . and, ladies and gentlemen, there is doubt . . . There are mountains of doubt."

He went on to urge that Scott be acquitted on every count. "And you know what, it's maybe even because he told you the truth when he got up there, that he's not guilty."

"Maybe"? Scott shuddered.

But Seplow made it even worse. "Nancy Caporaso, reasonable doubt. We stood Mr. Lehr up against the police officer with whom she spoke, the size difference was incredible. She was outside the car with Mr. Lehr."

"With Mr. Lehr"? Good God!

Seplow scrambled to undo his blunder. "It wasn't just — not Mr. Lehr, but the assailant. . . ."

Flustered, Seplow rushed on about Porter's identification of a suspect with blue-green eyes, when Scott's eyes were brown; about Barnett's pointing out another man in the back of the courtroom; about four unidentified hairs found on Margaret Christorf's body and about the fact that she had had intercourse with McFadden. "So yeah, there is people out there committing murders . . . out there committing rapes . . . the State wants you to think that they are all him. None of them are him. At least they haven't proven to you beyond a reasonable doubt with evidence on each particular case that it's Scott Lehr."

Damn Seplow's "at least"! He was self-destructing.

"Ladies and gentlemen, I'm closing, I'm done. . . ." Once more, he urged the jury to live up to the oath they had taken, to "examine the evidence and if there is a real possibility . . . give him that reasonable doubt, give him the benefit of it, and to say 'not guilty.' Thank you."

Scott was damp with sweat, though the room was cool. As the courtroom emptied for lunch, he looked back at Mom. Reeves had nailed it on the DNA, but was Phil's scattered, half-hearted summary of three months of complex testimony good enough? Mom was smiling as if she thought so. Scott wasn't so sure.

After the break, Judge Gerst announced genially, "Mr. Clayton, you may proceed with what we call your closing closing."

Clayton radiated confidence, a steel-trap poised for the next unwary stray foot. He told the jury he wouldn't "waste your time by going back over each piece of evidence." Instead, he suggested they doubt Scott's credibility as a witness.

"And don't get on board if he's talking about his children and he's talking about his wife . . . Because that is what the perpetrator of these offenses told the women, the girls, the young girl, the young children in this case, get on board, little children. . . . I ask you to consider who has the greatest motive for lying to you, whose testimony is unsupported by fact."

Scott thought bitterly that an innocent defendant had no "motive for lying" at all.

Clayton then discounted the testimony of the Circle K clerk who had not identified Scott in the case of Amy Perry.

Scott had read that it was bystanders who often provided better descriptions of those guilty of crimes. Such witnesses were more likely to remember facts objectively than the traumatized victims. And surely Clayton knew that.

But Clayton argued the opposite. "These women who went through what they experienced . . . they don't forget . . . That's not to say they won't make mistakes. . . ."

Make up your mind, Scott thought. Are the victims' memories good, or bad? Or is it that the victims' memories were suggestible, easily led to agree with people who promised them "justice" and closure?

Clayton feigned exasperation. "And how many times can they argue that because she didn't see or remember the black landau top, that this is not the car. . ."

Scott wanted to scream his outrage, but he only had to get through one more barrage of Clayton's posturing.

Then Clayton defended the smudgy partial fingerprint on the McDonald's cup, the State's only claim of physical evidence in the Caporaso assault. He claimed that Detective Dimodica didn't realize that the print had already excluded Scott.

Scott knew that was a lie. In 1994, two years after Karen Jones had first ruled out Scott, Dimodica's directions to reconsider Scott's print read, in plain English, "Disregard previous comparison results." But it was too late for the defense to clarify that fact.

Clayton explained away the many points at which the witnesses' memories were inconsistent with the State's case. He speculated that Mona Barnett was wrong about the car in which she was assaulted not having an interior door handle.

Scott thought Clayton must know damn well that Carl Gardei, a blue-eyed blond matching the description of Barnett's assailant, went to prison for assault cases in which he'd rigged the inside passenger door handle so his victims could not escape. And Gardei had confessed to committing two of those attacks on March 15, 1991, and February 5, 1992, during the time period of the State's so-called "baby-seat" crimes.

Clayton blustered on, urging the jury to ignore all the troubling inconsistencies in the testimony. He turned back to the case of Meredith Porter. "The night of the 22nd of February, she says that she started to walk home about 11:00 o'clock at night. In your indictment, it says February 23, 1992. But her testimony, you remember, was a Saturday night, Saturday night, not Sunday night . . ."

Damn. Scott had noticed when Porter testified that she claimed not to be sure what night she'd been assaulted. Now, when it was too late for the defense to set the record straight, Clayton pretended that the crime had not been committed on the night when Scott had an airtight alibi.

Clayton scoffed that the defense had taken so much time "to try to point out every little difference possible in this case," though Scott knew Seplow and Reeves had only been able to scratch the surface after two months of testimony concerning seven cases, plus two cases that were supposedly not even being tried.

Instead of worrying about all those conflicting details, Clayton urged the jury to "just use your common sense. . ." and to check their own notes.

Scott thought Clayton must be banking on the exhausted jurists' not having either accurate notes or the patience to track down the facts. When a jury is confused, it convicts.

"Ladies and gentlemen," Clayton continued, "you don't throw out that evidence and the testimony in this particular case about the faint bands being inappropriate from Dr. Aimee Bakken, who received $90,000 over the last five years for testimony. . ."

Well, that was low, Scott thought, hinting that Bakken's $18,000 a year in consulting fees came only from this case, rather than from cases all over the country!

Clayton changed tacks. "I just want to make sure that if there is anything that was said in closing argument by the defense that you felt was important and that I didn't address it, then you don't hold that against the victims in the case. . . ."

"Hold it against the victims," Scott thought sadly. As if finding an innocent man guilty was the way to do right by victims!

Clayton sanctimoniously added, "There is some personal insinuations perhaps. . . how the prosecutor refused to believe Mona Barnett. . . . Some insinuation that perhaps I am biased or prejudiced. I don't answer those kinds of charges."

Scott had to smile.

Then Clayton huffed that "it's improper for me to tell you what I personally believe about Scott Lehr in this case . . . I cannot, I will not . . ."

In other words, Scott thought, Clayton is hinting that he knows more about the cases than he's saying. One more cheap trick.

Exactly as Seplow had predicted, Clayton obscured the distinction between first- and second-degree murder. "And the jury instruction will tell you that premeditation can be as quick as successive thoughts of the mind."

It was clear to Scott that the prosecutor would be disappointed if he didn't get three first-degree convictions, subject to the death penalty.

Clayton scowled. "Defense talked about the shroud, shroud of innocence . . . Ladies and gentlemen, that shroud of innocence has now become a mantle of guilt . . . And what puts that mantle in place onto him . . . and ties it around him tightly? It's on the bands of DNA ..."

Tune it out, Scott told himself; let the prosecutor's lies tumble feebly in front of him like pebbles flung into a pond by a little boy.

Clayton exhorted, "So don't you turn your back on the evidence in this case just because someone says you've got a heavy burden . . . you have to do your duty. Thank you."

The stillness in the courtroom was bone-weary.

Judge Gerst announced that four of the jurists would be selected as alternates, who would now be sent home without deliberating. "I want to assure all of you . . . if somebody says I think my name was put in the box five times or something, all of your names, all of your names are put in the box one time."

Gerst's jocular protests raised Scott's suspicions. Shouldn't the defense be allowed to confirm that the box really did contain only one copy of every juror's name?

The names of the four alternate jurors were drawn from that mysterious box. As the names were called and the discarded jurists stood up, Scott's heart sank. What an amazing coincidence that the people now being excluded from the jury had seemed the most attentive. He remembered from the selection questionnaires that the job of one of them involved taking apart nuclear reactors. Here was someone with a logical and objective mind. Another excluded juror had taken a correspondence course on law, and another a college course that covered forensics and human DNA identification.

But Scott tried to forget his nagging doubts. The State of Arizona had done everything it could to bias the jury against him, but its case didn't hold water.

36: Thanksgiving

NOVEMBER 25, 1996

All the next day, a Friday, Scott heard nothing. He supposed that was good. The jury must be carefully debating each of the 23 charges. Still, he almost wished they'd reached their verdicts, to spare him a weekend in his cell, in gut-wringing suspense.

One minute he imagined an angry mob, accepting Clayton's shallow arguments to find him guilty of all but the most obviously false of the charges. The next minute he could imagine the voice of reason prevailing. They were taking time to think it through. Maybe this was his last weekend in jail, trying to remember every detail of the faces of Hallie, Lindsey, and Melissa.

Monday morning passed in slow motion. Just after lunch, they told Scott to get ready. When they led him back to the courtroom, Mike Reeves wore his familiar, inscrutable mask. No matter how much Phil Seplow joked and reassured, he looked nervous. Phil said the jury had actually reached their verdicts within a couple of hours on Friday. The court waited until now to deliver them for reasons of "scheduling."

A quick verdict was often a bad sign, Scott knew, but it was impossible to believe the jury wouldn't acquit him. Judge Gerst had instructed them that the State had the burden of proving guilt beyond a reasonable doubt in each charge. And anyone could see there was plenty of reasonable doubt.

Scott supposed the Clerk of the Court had already seen the verdicts; still he could read nothing in her face. She walked up to the jury foreman and accepted the verdict forms. At last, Scott allowed himself to look directly at the jury, these people who'd been given absolute power over his life. He didn't like the sober look of the foreman.

The Clerk would read the verdicts in chronological order, so the first verdicts were for Mona Barnett, who'd testified that she'd never seen Scott. These would be easy.

"Guilty," the clerk read.

Scott's heart jumped. Impossible.

The Clerk of the Court kept reading verdicts concerning Mona Barnett. Each charge was pronounced in ugly, clinical terms: vaginal intercourse, oral contact with penis, penile penetration of anus.

"Guilty." "Guilty." "Guilty."

Scott wished he could wake up from this nightmare, but he knew better. If the jury could find him guilty in the Barnett case, he had no hope for the others. He forced himself to keep listening, almost in a trance, as the clerk droned through the long list.

"Guilty," she read, again and again. Of every charge of kidnapping and sexual assault against Nancy Caporaso, Meredith Porter, and little Amy Perry.

Guilty of attempted murder in the cases of Nancy Caporaso and Meredith Porter.

And of the murders of Margaret Christorf, Belinda Cronin, and Michelle Morales, guilty in the first degree, and subject to the death penalty.

The jury was polled to confirm their verdicts. In their minds there was no reasonable doubt. Twenty-three charges; twenty-three guilty verdicts.

Seplow and Reeves were patting Scott on the shoulder and saying something about appeals. No words made sense. The liars won. They could even execute him. The best he could hope for was the rest of his life in prison.

The jurors were excused, believing that justice had been served. They hugged affectionately and hurried home for Thanksgiving weekend with their families.

37: "He Wasn't Trying to Kill Me"

APRIL 30-MAY16, 1997

Even in the windowless courtroom, Scott could smell spring. In the five months that had passed since the verdict, he'd gotten used to the role of convicted felon. Most of the time he kept his anger at a safe distance.

Now, over the next couple of weeks, he'd be tried again, this time for assaults against Emily Caldwell, Nicole Churchill, and Alison Brooks. Caldwell had been picked up for prostitution the year before at the same place where she got in the car with the suspect; Churchill took heroin on the day of the attack; and Brooks was a teenager with a habit of lying. All three were victims whose word was so questionable that most D.A.s would never bring them before a jury. Even worse, Maricopa County investigators had hypnotized these witnesses in an attempt to gather additional evidence. And to top it off, Churchill and Brooks had also testified at the first trial—where their testimony had apparently helped convict Scott of unrelated crimes.

It seemed like a waste of taxpayers' money to have another trial at all. The State had convicted him of three capital murders and 20 other felonies; at the very least, he'd be in prison for life without parole. Were they trying him on these additional cases out of revenge because he refused to plea bargain? Or did Romley and Company just hope to ride the wave of the public's willingness to believe Scott capable of any atrocity? The County Attorney team could handily improve their conviction records by pinning more unsolved cases on him. "Clearing the books," as Phil Seplow called it.

Scott told himself these charges didn't matter. The first trial was the important one. Even so, he guessed that, when this jury acquitted him, he would feel a bit less hopeless.

Seated at the defense table, armed guard at his side, Scott felt an ache of déjà vu. The cast of characters was familiar: Judge Gerst would again preside. Bill Clayton would argue for the prosecution. Phil Seplow would defend Scott, with Mike Reeves handling cross-examination on the DNA evidence. Mom sat behind Scott in the audience.

Again Judge Gerst wore a mask of fatherly solemnity as he told the jury, "You have to make a conscious decision to keep an open mind until you've heard everything."

People selected for this jury were not supposed to have heard about Scott's prior convictions, but he wondered how they could possibly not know of his reputation as "baby-seat killer/rapist," unless they never watched the news.

Scott thought he was totally desensitized to this ritual, but his stomach churned to hear Bill Clayton's stale tricks during his opening statement: again portraying the victims as innocent little girls, then exaggerating the violence of the crimes and vehemently proclaiming Scott guilty of every cruel act. Although none of the women had needed medical treatment for physical injury, the State was prosecuting Scott not only for sexual assaults and kidnappings but also for aggravated assault against Emily Caldwell and for the attempted first-degree murder of Alison Brooks.

As he had at the first trial, the prosecutor asserted in advance that he was likely to make mistakes. "Let me tell you now I may misstate an address or license plate number or a person's name."

Scott had no doubt that Clayton was again covering his ass for ignoring the facts.

Once more, Clayton claimed that the suspect's DNA evidence would match Scott's with a rareness of ". . . it's either 1 in 8 million or 1 in 11 million."

Scott tried to detach himself. He couldn't afford to get mad. To convince people that he wasn't a monster, it wasn't enough to behave normally. He needed to show the patience of a saint.

Now it was Phil's turn to give his opening statement. "You've heard a lot of stuff, a lot of unpleasant stuff during Mr. Clayton's opening statement," he began. "So if there are any of you thinking, 'Okay, this guy's guilty,' you haven't heard any evidence." The defense attorney went on to counter Clayton's melodramatic accusations with bland musings, sometimes academic in his word choice. But at last Seplow got to the key issue, the victims' unreliability. He emphasized that, in key instances, the victims changed the information they gave to different investigators over time. And Seplow reminded the jury that, even if they thought Scott might have committed one of the crimes, that didn't implicate him in all of them, a caution the jury in the earlier trial had obviously ignored.

Yet again, Seplow's comments understated the glaring differences among the cases, which were committed from 3 miles apart to over 14 miles apart.

"You know," Seplow concluded, "One of the young girls who viewed the lineup talked about being 60 percent sure, not even 80 or 85 percent sure. . . I submit to you you'll find that reasonable doubt is more than 60 percent. Thank you."

Even though truth and logic were on his side, if Scott were sitting on the jury listening to Seplow, he would not have been impressed.

Emily Caldwell was the only victim who hadn't appeared at the first trial. Now in her mid twenties, Caldwell testified that on the evening of February 23, 1991, she visited her stepmother's boyfriend, from whom she'd borrowed $20 or $30. She was running late to meet her boyfriend and missed the last bus. As she walked south on 16th Street between Thomas and McDowell, a man pulled up in his car and kept asking if she wanted a ride. Finally, she said, "I was like, if you're going to talk to me, or something, pull over . . . ."

Asking a guy to pull over onto a side street so you could *refuse* a ride sounded preposterous to Scott.

Caldwell said she eventually got in the car and he drove. They stopped at a convenience store for him to buy a drink. While she waited, Caldwell went to the pay phone and tried to reach her boyfriend. The suspect bought her a soda.

Scott remembered that Caldwell told police the guy himself was drinking a wine cooler. That was significant. In some of the other "baby-seat" crimes the suspect drank soda, but in no other case did he drink alcohol.

As the man drove further out of town, Caldwell said, he seemed to know she was afraid. "You know, he grabbed my hair and kind of wanted me to come closer to him, but it was almost like he was going to comfort me and tell me, 'Everything's okay,' and 'I'm not going to hurt you.' "

Well, now, Scott nodded, by the victim's own account, it hadn't been the bloodthirsty attack that Clayton wanted the jury to imagine. Scott had to give her credit for not playing along with Clayton.

Then she revealed even more: "I don't remember a whole lot of conversation. It was something to the effect that—that he would pay me for—for sexual favors or—or I could clean his house. . ."

Aha! She'd never mentioned the bid for "sexual favors" before. Clayton must have been sweating under his dapper black suit.

Quickly, Caldwell added that she refused the sexual favors.

When the man stopped the car, it was dark, but she could see the lights and hear cheering from a BMX racetrack behind them. She moved to get out, but he pulled her back into the car ". . . he . . . told me I was a whore and 'Did you really think we were going to go to my house?' "

She tried to honk the horn to attract attention. Infuriated, he dragged her into the back seat, ". . . and some things are clearer now than they were when I first talked to the detectives, and other things I don't remember at all now."

At least she admitted it, Scott thought. But how could the jury know when her memories were accurate and when they were not?

The man took off her clothes, and when he pulled off her socks, "there was the money that my stepmother's boyfriend gave me . . . And I was, like, 'That's my money.' "

The money in her sock was a detail the police reports hadn't mentioned.

Then the man was on top of her and she couldn't move. He penetrated her vaginally and tried to penetrate her anus. When he was done, he got out the passenger door to zip up his jeans. She slipped out on the driver's side and ran behind the car. She saw that his license plate began ADW. "And then I believe I told them 5—515 or –915."

No! Scott looked over at Seplow. She'd told police at least twice that it was either ADW515 or –519. Now she was making her recollection sound closer to Scott's plate number, ADW015. The difference was crucial, since the actual Arizona plates numbered ADW519 had gone missing from a used car lot sometime between February 11 and March 7, 1991. Caldwell was raped February 23, possibly by whoever stole those plates. Seplow nodded, scribbling furiously.

He picked up a rock and told her to run, "and it glanced across my chest."

The prosecution was charging that the stone-throwing amounted to aggravated assault, which involved using a dangerous instrument or deadly weapon to put the victim "in reasonable apprehension of immediate physical injury." But Caldwell put that charge firmly to rest. "He wasn't trying to kill me with those rocks, you know. He was making me run . . ."

What happened later at the police station, Scott remembered from the reports, was that detectives confronted Caldwell with the fact that she'd been arrested for prostitution 14 months earlier, exactly where she'd accepted a ride in this incident. Those charges had been dropped because she'd been only 16 at the time.

Today, Caldwell testified that detectives were rude and intimidating to her, doubting that she'd really been raped, so she declined to press charges.

Prompted by Clayton's questions, Caldwell said she remembered being interviewed by Detective Dimodica "a few months after that."

Seplow objected; in fact, over a year passed between the crime and Caldwell's statements to Dimodica. And Dimodica, who apparently assumed she was a victim of the hypothetical "baby-seat rapist," recorded details that were different from those she'd given police the year before.

As in the other "baby-seat" cases, the suspect Caldwell described generally resembled many men in the Phoenix area. She'd told police the guy had unusually long fingernails, but she didn't mention that today. That would have helped rule out Scott, who'd bitten his nails all his life, as anyone who knew him could have testified. One trait she consistently described—which also exonerated Scott—was that the man who raped her had very muscular calves on an otherwise flabby build. Scott's weight fluctuated, but, when he was at his fittest, his build was on the wiry side of average. No one would describe his calves as outstandingly muscular.

Caldwell described the suspect's car as a four-door, between beige and tan.

"Hard top?" the prosecutor probed.

Scott supposed Clayton wanted her to say that it might have been a convertible, since that was the only way that the jury could be conned into believing that the car resembled Scott's, with its black vinyl top.

But Caldwell answered frankly. "Yeah, a hard top."

Clayton showed her photos of Scott's Caprice, and asked her if was "similar" to the suspect's. She agreed that it looked "similar," which really wasn't identifying the car. Then, as she looked at a photo of the interior with its wood-grain detailing, Caldwell remarked that she did not remember wood-grain in the suspect's car.

Clayton hurried to show her a photo of the license plate on Scott's Caprice. He asked if it was similar, "aside from numbers."

"Aside from numbers," for Pete's sake!

Not surprisingly, Caldwell agreed that Scott's plate was "similar" to the suspect's.

Next Clayton questioned Caldwell about the lineup back in June 1992, 16 months after the crime. Eyewitness identification even a few *weeks* after a crime was considered questionable. And then, Caldwell had not identified Scott at all. She said that Scott's face looked like the man who raped her, but that the legs of one of the other men in the lineup looked more like the rapist's. But instead of eliminating Scott as a suspect then and there, the County Attorney's Office counted her statements as identifying him.

As Caldwell responded to the prosecutor's questions, it was clear to Scott that she'd been coached. "I was fairly certain that it was him. . . . It was a high percentage—70, 80. . . ."

But as Seplow had emphasized in his opening statement, she'd actually said 60%. Not much better than flipping a coin!

Clayton showed Caldwell photos of that lineup and asked her to identify Scott.

Scott steeled himself. Just in case Caldwell didn't know that Scott, seated at the defense table with a guard hanging over him, was the man she was supposed to identify today, showing her his picture gave her one more clue.

Sure enough, Clayton said with his habitual display of righteous indignation, "The person who did this to you, who committed the sexual offenses against you, is that person here in the courtroom?"

"Yes, he is."

The jury sat breathless, as if some truth was being revealed.

When she "identified" Scott, a couple of jurists shook their heads and made notes. Behind him, Mom let out an angry breath. He wished Phil could at least cross-examine Emily Caldwell while her testimony was still fresh in the jury's minds, but Judge Gerst dismissed them for "a nice weekend."

Four days later, with Caldwell back on the stand, Seplow's cross-examination focused on details Caldwell had apparently changed to suit the prosecution's case. She'd previously described the drink caddy in the car used in the crime as tan; in court she'd said it was "tan or brownish," which made it sound like a possible match for the maroon caddy in Scott's car.

But most important was her description of the car's color. Phil probed, "You never mentioned anything about the top being any different color than the body of the car; is that true?"

Caldwell thought that she'd said something about the top being a different color, but she couldn't remember when.

Fat chance, Scott thought. If she had, the officer in question had for some reason never filed a report.

Then Phil got to the truth of her so-called identification at the lineup. He read from the police report. "Well, at the time of the lineup you said you were 60 percent sure . . . do you recall that?"

She did not.

"Would you agree that 60 percent is a lot less than 80 percent?"

"It's a bit less; a lot less, no."

Next Phil asked her about the photo of the license plate on Scott's Caprice, ADW015. "You did tell Officer Hoeve at the time that you met with him that there was a license plate number, possibly ADW515 . . ."

"I believe I said ADW151 or 915."

Scott gasped. That was not what she'd told police and not even what she'd testified. But instead of pinning her down, Phil just moved on!

Seplow circled back to the lineup, quoting her own words: "I am confused, it looks like number two's legs and number three's face."

Caldwell answered that "The officer assured me that physical things change, body weight and such, but to go with the one that looked facially like what I remember . . ." At that, she must have realized that her identification was tainted if the officer had encouraged her to identify Scott. "I didn't mean to give a wrong impression there," the young woman corrected hastily.

Phil stepped down with a straight face, but Scott knew he was grinning inside.

It his redirect examination, Bill Clayton swept all the contradictions in Caldwell's statements under the rug and appealed to the jury's sympathy: "As you sit here today, what is your belief about who did these things to you?"

Caldwell rallied. "I believe it is the same person that I identified in the lineup, which is sitting here in front of me, Scott Lehr. I recognized him and I recognize him now. . ."

Damn, she sounded sincere, Scott thought. The County Attorney's office probably did have her convinced that Scott was to blame.

The following afternoon, Clayton called for testimony from a nurse, Pat Jenkins,* regarding the case of Alison Brooks, which would not be addressed for several more days. Scott had found that frustrating about the first trial too: that witnesses for the various cases sometimes testified out of order, making it even easier to confuse the cases.

Nurse Jenkins was eager to talk, and she identified photos of Brooks's injuries, which she described as "reasonably fresh bruises and scratches . . . a large hematoma on her head and also injury from being dragged on the ground."

Clayton asked the nurse if there were any other injuries not shown in the photos, to which she responded, "I know that there was dried blood on the inner thighs . . ."

Shady, Scott thought. By her own report, Alison Brooks was having her period, and that was the source of any blood on her thighs. Jenkins must have known that, but she didn't mind hinting that Brooks's genital area had been torn.

When Seplow approached to cross-examine the nurse, she eyed the attorney suspiciously.

Responding to Phil's question, Jenkins agreed that Brooks said she'd had unprotected sex with her boyfriend within 72 hours before the incident.

Phil asked if the dried blood on Brooks's thighs had been from menstruation.

Jenkins suddenly lost her memory.

Scott couldn't understand how seemingly decent people thought they were doing the right thing by giving deceptive testimony. Hadn't they ever been falsely accused of anything?

As testimony began on the case of Nicole Churchill, Scott wondered whether he'd hear anything that hadn't been said at the first trial. When Churchill testified at the first trial, she'd been in jail for drug possession. Now she was serving time for fraud. Again, Scott suspected that she'd been offered a reduction in her sentence if she would help convict him.

According to Churchill, the car used in the crime "was like a beige or tan-colored car, a different—lighter-colored top on it."

She'd again made it clear that it was a lighter top, ruling out Scott's car. He knew that the lighter top did match the car of Richard Donohue, plate ADW-777, whom police had questioned as a possible suspect. Back then, Churchill had agreed that Donohue's photo looked like the assailant, although she wasn't positive. Even so, she'd been at least as confident in her identification of Donohue as she was in her so-called identification of Scott in the lineup over a year later. That was the same Richard Donohue who'd later served as foreman of the grand jury that agreed to charge Scott with these crimes.

When Clayton asked about the suspect's height, she went further than the prosecutor wanted: "His stature did not seem all that large to me . . . what I call medium height . . ."

Scott was six foot one, and Clayton changed the subject.

Churchill added that the man said his name was Dave. That was interesting, too. A couple of guys meeting the description whose names really were Dave had been briefly considered as suspects.

Clayton was building up to the dramatic in-court identification. Again, the prosecutor helped her out by first showing her lineup photos of Scott.

Then it came. "The person who assaulted you, is that person here in the courtroom today?"

Scott sat frozen. Some dumb, unquenchable optimism still made him hope that she'd look him over and admit, "To tell you the truth, I can't remember." Mona Barnett had the guts to do that, but every other victim who testified jumped on the bandwagon to accuse him. And each time, no matter how full of holes her testimony had been, once she pointed to him, he felt every juror glare at him in horror.

"Yes . . . It's that gentleman right there, the large one in the gray suit."

Scott closed his eyes.

While the jury was still distracted by her accusation, Clayton brought up the issue that might, more than all the contradictions in her statements, torpedo Nicole Churchill's testimony. "In 1991 on the day that this happened, were you having some medical problems having to do with using drugs?"

Churchill stated that she was using methadone and heroin, but that she had not used any drugs on the day of the assault, because she'd missed her methadone clinic. She testified that, although she felt ill, missing her methadone "Didn't have anything to do with my perception of anything."

Clayton asked how drug use affected her memory.

"I have never—in myself, I've never noticed it has."

Seplow must have been salivating to cross-examine Nicole Churchill. In response to his questions, she admitted that she had taken heroin on the morning of the crime, contradicting her testimony.

Before Churchill stepped down, Judge Gerst read a question from the jury: "You did point out the defendant as your attacker. How sure today are you of that?"

"Sure," the woman said emphatically.

Clayton requested that Churchill be transported back to prison in Tucson as quickly as possible.

The following afternoon, Clayton called Alison Brooks to the stand. She was a 19-year-old of average size, but Clayton addressed her as a child. "Can you count back and tell us what your age was on October 23, 1991?"

"I was 13." Brooks's account paralleled what she'd testified at the first trial. Clayton showed her the photo of Scott's Caprice, asking if "there might be something different, or about the same."

Brooks instantly agreed, "The car is the same. I don't remember if it had the dark top on it or not."

Scott was beyond exasperation.

Then Clayton showed her photos of the interior, and she said that the wood grain was the same. "The drink caddy looks the same, but this one is maroon. I don't know, it might have been."

"It might have been"?

When Clayton questioned Brooks about the rape, he primly asked her whether she was familiar with the female vagina and the "male part of the anatomy."

Clayton asked, "Do you remember any conversation about not wanting to have sex with him, and that it might hurt or it did hurt, or something to that effect?"

"Yes. He asked me if I'd never done that before, had sex before, and I said no."

Scott bet Clayton hoped the jury would believe she had not.

Brooks said that after raping her, the man "picked me up off the ground by my neck with his hand, both hands, and he slammed me down on the ground and started choking me and beating my head against the ground. . . . I blacked out . . . I woke up . . . and he started to choke me again, and I had reached my left hand up and I put it on his arm; 'Please, please don't.' And I think that I passed out again, it's not really clear . . ."

Now, wait, Scott thought. She'd told Officers Sweeney and Dimodica that she asked the suspect to stop choking her, and he stopped. It was a crucial detail, since the prosecution was pretending this was a case of attempted murder. Also, she'd walked to the Granatelli building immediately after the episode, so she was not seriously disoriented.

Clayton moved on to showing the jury the composite portrait, for which Brooks had directed the drawing. The drawing did resemble Scott, but at the time, Brooks had denied that the sketch looked like the man who assaulted her.

On his cross-examination, Phil Seplow brought out the facts that Alison Brooks had intercourse with her boyfriend the night before the assault; that she'd first told police that the suspect had pulled her through a window into his car, which she latter admitted was a lie; and that she'd once falsely accused her mother's boyfriend of assaulting her.

Phil had to counteract the attempted murder charge. "The assailant, as far as you know, while you were lying there unconscious, never struck you so when you woke up you had any bruises . . .?"

He had not.

"Didn't run over with the car or anything like that?"

"No."

On the following day, Clayton called Dr. Webster, the emergency room physician who examined Alison Brooks. Clayton had Dr. Webster tell the jury about Brooks's injuries. He listed a hematoma on her head and scratches on her side and back. "She was having her menses at the time and she had some dried blood on her inner thighs. . . . She also had some contusions on her neck, also."

Scott snapped to attention. He didn't remember anything in the reports about bruises on Brooks's neck.

On cross, Seplow had in hand the Dr. Webster's notes from that examination. "As a matter of fact, in those documents you never write anything about any bruising to the neck; is that correct?"

"That's right," the doctor admitted.

When Clayton called Philip Earl Keen, M.D., chief medical examiner for Maricopa County, Scott was puzzled. At the first trial, Keen had testified about autopsies, but Scott didn't remember Dr. Keen being involved in any of the cases on trial now.

Clayton's ploy was soon clear: Alison Brooks had only a few abrasions after the assault, yet the State was claiming attempted murder. Clayton had called Doctor Keen to tell the jury about how the body "responds to injuries or application of pressure points."

Clayton displayed photos of Alison Brooks's injuries. Keen summed it up. "What you've described is absence of a skull fracture, absence of a laceration, presence of probable bruise."

"A *probable* bruise?" Scott shook his head.

Clayton doubled back. "Let me add more to that . . . along with the injury to the back of the head, there had been application of force or pressure around the neck, and then the person being applied to the ground with the person's hand around the neck, and that would be the right hand of an adult male . . . . What is the physical or physiological aspect of what is going on with this particular person, this 13-year-old?"

Keen graphically described what strangulation would be like. "The placing a hand around the neck . . . applying pressure in those areas will cause the blood pressure to go down . . . and you momentarily lose consciousness. . . ."

Clayton asked how long it would take for death to occur.

Three minutes, the doctor said, "to be close to death."

On cross-examination, Phil exposed the absurdity of Keen's testimony. "Now, you did no examination on this particular case; is that correct?"

Dr. Keen confirmed that he had not.

"And you're basically just answering questions and hypotheticals; is that correct?"

The doctor agreed.

Scott hoped to heaven that the jury caught the point: Alison Brooks had never claimed that the guy tried to kill her and there was no evidence he had.

Having finished testimony from the victims, Clayton began to present DNA evidence. If this went like the first trial, Scott expected to hear the prosecution's "experts" present questionable exhibits aimed at leading the jury to think that, despite the many logical reasons why Scott could not have been guilty, scientific evidence incriminated him.

Clayton again swore in David Duplissa, criminalist from the Arizona DPS lab, who explained how he analyzed DNA samples. Scott saw the prosecutor suppress a shudder when Duplissa volunteered, "If these two bands ended up showing up in this lane, well, that would tell me that I might have mixed the two samples."

"Mixed the two samples"?! Extra bands, which had never been explained, had in fact appeared in some of the DPS's samples that were used to convict Scott in November.

Briskly, Clayton moved Duplissa on to explain how size standards and control samples were used. It angered Scott that one of the examples Duplissa used was an autorad from the case of Margaret Christorf. Was Clayton deliberately reminding this jury that Scott had been convicted of murdering her?

It was getting late, but Clayton kept Duplissa talking reassuringly about how widely DNA analysis was accepted in the scientific community.

That wasn't the point, as Scott had learned from Dr. Bakken at the first trial. The question was whether the DPS lab was conducting tests that were unbiased and reliable. But so far, Gerst had kept the defense from questioning the quality of DPS work.

When they reconvened on the afternoon of May 13, the trial was down to its last two days. Testimony on the DNA evidence lumbered on. Duplissa showed the jury the "known DNA profile for Scott Lehr" and shadowy DNA analyses from the case of Nicole Churchill. Churchill had been examined soon after the assault, and the sample should have been of high quality. But it was clear to Scott that the donor of the semen found in Churchill could not have been him, although DPS had tried to make it appear to match the DNA of the blood sample he'd given police five years ago.

When Clayton asked about a Mylar transparency including Scott's known sample, Duplissa admitted lightly, "What was basically done there was that type of alteration. The DNA band placement was the same relative to the adjacent size standards, but everything was—it was either blown up or it was slightly decreased a little bit."

In other words, Scott thought, they fudged it!

Nevertheless, Duplissa was willing to testify that the sample "could not exclude" Scott Lehr.

On cross-examination, Mike Reeves elicited from Duplissa that RFLP was relatively new to the forensic community when the tests for these cases had been done, and the DPS lab had performed the tests for this case during their first year of DNA analysis. Then Reeves got into the fundamental unreliability of the DPS's tests. In

1991 the National Research Council published "DNA Technology in Forensic Science" which provided guidelines for DNA laboratories. "Now, your laboratory has not adopted all of the recommendations contained within the NRC report, correct?"

"I'm not sure."

Responding to Reeves's questions, Duplissa confirmed that, even at its best, the DPS lab did not have the ability to produce a profile that positively distinguished one individual from another.

Reeves then led Duplissa to admit that the analyst had performed a "manual override" of the computer scored results, without letting the jury know.

"Now," Reeves pursued, "the computer is in place to provide kind of a second opinion as to whether or not match has occurred, right?"

"Well the computer is a way to make it as objective as possible. . ."

Reeves asked whether the analyst could override the computer.

Duplissa agreed, explaining how, in this case, the computer "marked the top band correctly; the bottom band it didn't see, so it put a mark somewhere else."

"The objective approach didn't work?" Reeves said, with an irony Scott thought was probably too subtle for the sleepy jury.

"Right," Duplissa nodded, as if the irony was lost on him, too.

"Instead," Reeves said, "You told the computer to put a mark down here on this faint marking, and you called that a band?"

"Yes," Duplissa agreed, as if faking a DNA match to convict an innocent man was no big deal.

Next Reeves prompted Duplissa to admit that even the control testings of DNA, which were supposed to give consistent results, varied widely.

Reeves summed it up, asking, "despite the astronomical number that you gave us, 1 in 11 million, truly, the best thing that we can say about this is Scott Lehr is not excluded?"

Duplissa hedged. "No, I would say there's very strong evidence that Mr. Lehr is the source of the semen."

On redirect examination, Clayton tried to salvage Duplissa's testimony, asking if the samples in his lab were available for retesting.

Duplissa agreed they were.

Scott's face flushed. That made it sound as though the defense could just run their own tests. But it didn't work that way. First of all, Scott was sure that either the samples did not come from where the prosecution said they did or the results were botched or mislabeled. Since DPS probably didn't have adequate samples to yield accurate results to begin with, what was to keep an unscrupulous staffer from simply taking blood from the sample Scott had given and saying it came from the rape kit? Second, the meager public defense budget did not include funds for DNA testing at a private lab. And finally, the legal burden of accurate testing was on the prosecution, not the defense.

And Reeves objected to Clayton's shifting the burden of proof to the defense and asked for a mistrial.

Judge Gerst looked nervous. ". . . as I recall, in the first trial we were basically at this same posture . . . . . I denied the motion for mistrial."

The State's final witness was another criminalist with the DPS crime laboratory, Terry Hogan. Scott remembered him too.

Hogan testified that he had done the DNA testing in the case of Alison Brooks.

Since Brooks admitted she had sex with her boyfriend the day of the assault, Scott wondered how Hogan was going to claim to match the sperm in her rape kit to Scott's DNA. Then he saw: they'd distorted or "demagnified" the evidence in what Hogan called a "demonstrative exhibit."

Scott noticed that the sample in the rape kit was extremely faint on the autorad.

Clayton questioned Hogan about his test results, building up to Hogan's claim of a visual match between the suspect's and Scott's DNA as well as match by "computer image analysis measurement."

On cross-examination, Reeves asked, "Were you asked to test the DNA of Alison Brooks's boyfriend?"

Hogan could not recall.

Then Reeves asked Hogan about one of the rape kit samples that he had just claimed to match to Scott.

Hogan agreed that there was no second band, as would have been necessary for a match to Scott.

"So," Reeves raised his voice dramatically, "this autorad cannot be used for purposes of matching, excluding or including Mr. Lehr?"

"We considered it inconclusive . . ."

"Well you're just guessing at this point . . . right?"

"Well, I don't know if a second band would show up . . . But I'm saying it's consistent with what we would expect."

Reeves had him there. "As a scientist you're not supposed to expect anything, are you?"

OK, Scott sighed. After three long days of testimony on DNA, Reeves had shown the jury that DPS could not guarantee accurate test results. And when it came to "matching" DNA from the Brooks and Churchill cases to Scott, they faked it by telling the computer to identify bands where they knew bands occurred in Scott's profile.

The prosecution and defense rested. Scott wished Phil had called at least one witness. Sure, the prosecution's case was flimsy. But if the jury didn't hear anything good about Scott, wouldn't it be easy for them to assume he was capable of these crimes?

The following afternoon, as Scott waited for the jury to be brought in for closing arguments, he looked around the dreary, wood-paneled courtroom one last time. Would he leave with better memories than at the first trial?

As before, the prosecution got to give two closing arguments but the defense only one. Even six months later, an angry nausea came over Scott when he remembered this moment from the first trial. Testimony had to follow an elaborate set of rules, but, in the closing arguments, Clayton threw away the rulebook. According to everything Scott had read, that was not accepted procedure. The prosecutor was not supposed to manipulate the jury's emotions like a Hollywood courtroom drama, but to present logical arguments.

Again Clayton began by cozying up to the jury and proceeded to confuse them with inaccuracies or downright falsehoods.

Again, Clayton argued that the jury should take the reliability of the DNA evidence on faith, despite the sloppiness that Reeves's cross-examination had exposed. "Scientists who work in that field know their job," the prosecutor asserted piously. "Don't be fooled. . . ."

Describing the stones tossed at the Emily Caldwell as "a dangerous instrument," Clayton claimed that Caldwell said, "I was afraid that if the rock hit me in the head, it would kill me."

No; she'd testified the very opposite, Scott remembered: "He wasn't trying to kill me with those rocks, you know."

Finally, Clayton worked in Dr. Keen's testimony about choking. Keen had admitted his testimony was theoretical, but irrelevance didn't stop Clayton from speaking as if Brooks really had been strangled: "Twenty seconds or so until that little body goes limp. . . . Alison Brooks was a 13-year-old little girl. . . . Alison Brooks was crying, begging, and the choking continued."

Shit, Scott thought. Twice in the police reports Brooks had contradicted Clayton's fabrication; she asked the guy to stop choking her, and he stopped.

Clayton ended with an indignant "They are no longer allegations. They are proven to you. Find him guilty. Thank you."

Scott watched Seplow stand to face the jury. He had been strong on cross-examination for this trial, and the attorney looked relaxed as he began his closing argument. Maybe he would speak with more passion than he had at the first trial. Seplow reminded the jury that their duty was not to be influenced by sympathy. He continued, "Three young women experienced something that was not favorable . . . Prejudice . . . against multiple acts that are outlandish, outrageous . . . . that shouldn't be thrown upon the man who sits there unless a lot of other things happen during your deliberations . . ."

"Unless"! There Phil went again with his timid understatement!

"When I first addressed you . . . I presented to you that the presumption of innocence is still in this room, that the State has not met its burden, its hard burden of proof, to find this man guilty of anything."

Scott supposed that the jury could interpret that to mean that Scott was innocent only on a technicality.

Reminding the jury of inconsistencies in the victim's statements, Seplow focused on Nicole Churchill's drug use, Alison Brooks's history of lying, and the possibility that Emily Caldwell had actually agreed to prostitution. All of these were relevant to their credibility, but Scott hoped the jury wouldn't feel that Seplow was casting blame on the victims.

Seplow wound up towards his finish. "It's the State's burden to prove to you beyond a reasonable doubt that Mr. Lehr is guilty. . . . I submit to you the State has not done it. . . . you've got 60 percent from Ms. Caldwell. You've got an exclusion, a total exclusion from that top band, a total exclusion on that top band on Alison Brooks.

"And you've got Nicole Churchill who was injecting heroin on that day, who picked two other people out of a photo lineup, and at the time of the regular lineup said it looks like him. I submit to you, ladies and gentlemen, that when you go in there and deliberate, you do what you're supposed to do. You find Mr. Lehr not guilty. Thank you."

Clayton jumped up for his final attack. He fumed that not he, but Phil Seplow, had distorted the facts. "Look to the evidence . . . This lawyer is not an expert in DNA."

No, Scott thought wearily, and neither were the prosecution's supposed "experts."

Then, one last time, Clayton misrepresented the license plate numbers in the case of Emily Caldwell. ". . . there was ADW 915 in her head. . . . So that one number there was off. . . . Do you throw out everything she had to say?"

Yes, Scott thought wearily, you do throw that out, because the plate Caldwell had identified was not ADW 915, but ADW 515 or 519, a plate presumed stolen just before the crime.

And Clayton urged the jury to take offense at Phil's points about the victims' reliability. "Well, I guess women in prison can't be raped or people who have to have a crutch or drink alcohol, they can't be raped . . . . Tell him no . . . !"

But then it was over. Reeves shook Scott's hand and left. Phil was cautiously reassuring. Scott knew that unless the jury was fooled by the DNA evidence, they couldn't possibly buy the prosecution's arguments this time.

Early the next morning, Scott lay awake. The jury might have a verdict before the day ended, or it might take them days. He reminded himself that these verdicts didn't really matter.

It wasn't long after lunch when a couple of officers came for him. Scott's blood pressure spiked. If the jury found it so easy to decide, it was all or nothing.

Phil greeted him in the courtroom with a forced smile. The jury filed in. When Scott saw their faces, here serious, there sad, and there downright hateful—he didn't expect much. Still, it had to be better than the first trial.

At first, the foreman's voice caught nervously. Then as he read the verdicts, one by one, he seemed to enjoy his role as the voice of justice. And after every charge, he had nothing to say but "guilty."

They found Scott guilty, not only of the sexual assaults, but also of aggravated assault with a dangerous instrument against Emily Caldwell. They even convicted him of the attempted first-degree murder of Alison Brooks.

It was like going back to the first day he woke up in Madison Street Jail. Why him? When did the person he really was become invisible?

William W. Clayton, Deputy County Attorney, was all smiles. He seemed pleasantly surprised. After two weeks of testimony, it had taken the jury only a couple of hours to find Scott guilty of all

14 charges involving three women, not one of whom would be considered a credible witness.

38: "Die, Sucker"

AUGUST 8, 1997

"Mitigation"—allowing Scott's legal team to crawl around, asking family and friends to plead to Judge Gerst that Scott did not deserve to be executed. Scott wasn't interested.

After the first trial, hearing verdicts of guilty of every crime on Bill Clayton's list, Scott was probably what shrinks call "depressed." But he'd still held onto a crumb of hope that the second trial would begin to set things right. Lightning wasn't supposed to hit twice. After the second trial, Scott let go of hope. In its place he felt a bottomless anger.

And this mitigation seemed like another temptation to make a deal with the Devil. Scott hadn't even been able to stomach the County Attorney's terms for a plea bargain. How could he turn around now, to save his skin, and whine, "I am not responsible for the crimes, but this is why I would have committed them. Please excuse me"? No. He was innocent, and he wasn't going to lie about it.

Now Seplow advised Scott to reveal the abuse and loneliness he'd suffered as a child. But Scott wasn't going there, not even if he could believe that Judge Gerst would give a damn. He would not make a public spectacle of his family's pain, and he would not make excuses.

And why beg for life in prison? Every day felt like slow hell. He couldn't look forward to another 40 years alone in a cage. He was tired of being jerked around, like an animal on a chain. It would be all or nothing. Either he walked free, or he'd become a murder victim of the State of Arizona.

In July, Judge Gerst held a mitigation hearing. Bill Clayton was in the courtroom to urge Gerst—as if he needed urging—to throw the book at Scott. Phil Seplow and Mike Reeves were there to make a case for leniency.

In his familiar way, Clayton stood up and railed about the brutality of the crimes, distorting facts or downright making things up.

Mike Reeves called as witness Dr. Charles Woods, the psychiatrist who'd interviewed Scott a few weeks before. At that time, Scott remembered feeling contempt for the guy, who seemed to consider it "paranoid" that Scott, having recently been found guilty of dozens of crimes he didn't commit, did not trust people.

But now Dr. Woods was introduced as an objective expert witness, who'd worked with such notorious killers as Gary Gilmore. Although Woods personally favored the death penalty for some offenders, he recommended against the death penalty for Scott. The psychiatrist added, "It is very important for we, the people, to think very long and hard before we decide to take a life."

Scott was sorry he hadn't given Dr. Woods more credit.

At that, Clayton stood up and tried to make Dr. Woods' recommendation sound superficial. And when Clayton asked him outright, Woods replied, "I was of the opinion that he was a person who, yes, might very well lie to me. I was of the opinion that he was a person who has lied in the past."

Scott wasn't sure what "lies" Dr. Woods was referring to. No matter. Scott suspected that that comment about dishonesty shattered the psychiatrist's argument for leniency.

What else was there to consider in Scott's favor? He'd read the letter Mom sent Judge Gerst. "I believe in Scott's innocence," she wrote, pointing out Scott had never been in trouble, let alone hurt anyone. And she went on to document the many reasons for reasonable doubt that the jury somehow failed to consider. She added, "It could be that the death penalty is more about being just plain mean. Maybe we are becoming more like the people we condemn and abhor than we want to admit."

Scott knew his mother was smart, but he'd never guessed that she could write so movingly. If he was ever allowed to touch her again, he would hug her with all the pride he'd never been able to express.

His cousin Donna also wrote a letter, focusing on what a "terrific father" he was. "People everywhere would comment about how cute the girls were dressed and what a nice dad they had. . . . Scott would cook very delicious meals and they would sit at the table and have dinner together and talk about events of their day. . . . Scott would read to Hallie and Lindsey ... Their home was filled with love, discipline, and respect for each other."

There were letters to Judge Gerst from a friend and coworker of Mom's who'd known Scott as a hard-working and helpful young man, and from Aunt Sandy, who said what a "warm and caring" person Scott was and how much his daughters missed and loved him.

But Scott suspected that this hearing was a mere formality. Judge Gerst's mind had been made up before he called the first trial to order.

Another month passed. When they came and told Scott he'd be sentenced the following day, they gave him a plastic razor for the occasion. He'd always kept himself clean and well-groomed, but what did it matter now? Gerst would sentence him either to death or to life in prison. As he looked in the murky metal mirror in the cell, the anguished face staring back already looked more like a tortured animal than a 38-year-old father.

Scott shaved his face. His hands trembled so hard he barely kept from cutting himself. Alright, then. They wanted a cheap crime drama; he'd give them their deranged serial killer. His breath constricted by rage, he kept shaving, onto his head. When he stopped, he was nearly bald. Finally he looked as bad as the County Attorney's office, the Honorable Judge Gerst, and two juries believed he was.

The next morning in the holding cell behind the courtroom, he couldn't wear a suit brought by Mom. Now that he was convicted, he had to hear his sentence in jailhouse stripes.

Being led into the courtroom was like having to come out of a warm, dark cave into bitterly cold winter sunlight. Sitting at the defense table, this place of shattered hopes, brought tears to his eyes.

A crowd had turned out to see the baby-seat rapist-murderer sentenced. Scott made Mom promise to stay away. No mother should have to witness this, and he wasn't sure he'd be able to keep his mouth shut. Elaine hadn't come; he hadn't really expected her. Scott spotted Steve, a coworker and friend of Mom's, who smiled kindly. And Dee Dee was there, with her boyfriend Dan.* Scott was happy to see his sister with the guy; it was impressive that Dan was willing to share this with her. Scott smiled at them, and a tremor passed over Dee Dee's face. He'd momentarily forgotten about his appearance. Dee Dee—not easily moved—looked flat-out shocked by his shaved head and prisoner's stripes.

The air was almost festive. There were people who looked like reporters, and others he recognized as witnesses and victims' family members. There was the mother of Belinda Cronin, holding up a framed photo of the murdered woman like an icon.

And lurking in the back was Scott's first wife, Trish, and her weird husband. What made her want to watch this in person? Scott would have thought she could get enough enjoyment by reading about it in the paper. Guess she wanted one more horrendous thing to tell the twins about their father. His poor, beautiful babies.

Acknowledging that Judge Gerst had already determined the sentences, Bill Clayton called some of the victims and their family and friends who wished to speak. Clayton added piously that it would be "helpful to them in their healing process."

Belinda Cronin's mother spoke bitterly of her family's loss, ending, "But you, Scott Lehr, be reminded with every breath you take, may every bite of food, may it choke the life from your body and may every time you close your eyes to sleep you feel . . . fear. May you be haunted with Belinda's spirit on every day that you're on this earth and thereafter . . ."

Scott set his face in a blank stare. Although it hurt the hell out of him to hear her curse him for another man's crimes, he knew the State of Arizona had authorized her to blame him.

Then Michelle Morales's sister spoke, through tears. "You, Scott Lehr, robbed away my only sibling. I will never be an aunt and my kids will never know the joy of having cousins. How do I begin to explain my devastating loss to you, Scott Lehr, a man with no conscience . . . I feel resentment that your children are safe when my daughters have to live with constant memories of murdering beasts such as yourself . . ." Her friends embraced her.

At her resentment of his innocent kids, Scott felt his anger rise.

Bill Clayton read a letter from Alison Brooks. Scott braced himself for another stream of abuse, but Brooks surprised him. "Even though he is a very sick man, I don't think that his life should be taken from his family like he took from the other families and children."

Scott wondered whether, somewhere in her heart, Brooks knew he was innocent.

Finally Gerst asked Scott to come forward. "Is your name Scott Alan Lehr?" With his lips frozen in an icy parody of detachment, Judge Gerst looked as if he'd enjoy taking a gun to Scott himself. Sternly but ceremoniously, Gerst went through every charge for the two trials, adding with apparent satisfaction after each, "It's now the judgment of the Court that you are guilty of that count, and that judgment is entered of record."

Finally Scott was allowed to sit. After summarily listing the letters he'd received attesting to Scott's character, the judge asked whether Phil Seplow had anything else to present on Scott's behalf.

Seplow renewed his challenge to the State to demonstrate a compelling interest in taking another life. "The killing of the defendant obviously doesn't bring back a life, nor people who love the defendant, those people are now going to suffer the same type of trauma that some of the people talked about in court today."

That didn't seem to make an impression, but he kept talking. Scott thought Seplow was making it up as he went. He mentioned listening to a tape as he drove into court that morning. " . . . One of the songs was, 'Hard Rain's Going to Fall,' and the one line that stood out was, 'The executioner's name is always well-hidden.'

And all of the other reasons we have given you, Your Honor, there is not really much more I can add."

Seplow's argument rang hollow in the presence of so much hatred.

Gerst turned to Scott and asked him if he wanted to say anything.

Scott was tempted. His heart cried out, "I'm innocent; damn you!" But there was no point. He kept himself still. He'd give them nothing else to twist against him.

Some of the victims and their friends and family held hands as Judge Gerst read the sentences in chronological order.

The judge pronounced that the circumstances for the crimes were aggravated by previous conviction of violent felonies. That was circular; the only felonies involved were all the other "baby-seat" crimes. Gerst read a separate sentence for every charge in the two trials: 14 years for kidnapping, 35 years for kidnapping with one prior felony conviction. Gerst kept adding "the maximum period." He was throwing everything he had at Scott for each count.

Scott thought the judge's rasping voice would fill the courtroom forever. For the 36 counts involving kidnapping and sexual assaults, Gerst sentenced him to several life sentences, plus something like 950 years in prison. The judge added that all of the sentences would run consecutively.

Then Gerst began his "special verdict" regarding the murders of Margaret Christorf, Michelle Morales, and Belinda Cronin. Although little was known about the crimes, the judge was sure that they were committed in "an especially cruel manner." He read, "A murder is especially cruel if the defendant inflicts mental anguish before the victim dies." To take life was always cruel, Scott believed, but from the known evidence, the murders of Christorf, Morales, and Cronin did not seem crueler than most.

Against those "aggravating circumstances," the judge was supposed to weigh mitigating circumstances. The mitigating circumstances that Seplow had presented were undeniable: that Scott was a good father who provided for his family; that he was a good husband and a good son to his mother; that he had no prior criminal record; that he had no prior accusations of violence of any kind; that a psychiatrist testified that the death penalty was unwarranted in Scott's case; that Scott been a model prisoner at the county jail; that Scott had not been a predator in jail and would not be a predator in prison; that there was lingering doubt as to whether Scott had actually committed the murders; and that, if Scott were executed, more victims would accumulate — his mother, his sister, his wife, and his daughters; that only one family member out of all the victims requested that Scott receive the death penalty; that Scott never knew his father; and that the only male influence in Scott's childhood was not a good one.

Gerst curtly denied that any of the other factors gave reason for leniency. The Honorable Stephen A. Gerst sentenced Scott Lehr to three deaths by lethal injection.

People in the victims' circle applauded, cried quietly, and hugged each other.

Phil Seplow made a gesture of comforting Scott, but the man seemed to be sleepwalking himself. Mike Reeves calmly collected his papers from the table, but a hue of sadness welled behind his professional façade.

Scott felt as if he was already dead and floating over the courtroom. Looking behind him, he remotely saw Dee Dee hold her stomach as if she was going to throw up.

The next day's headline in *The Arizona Republic* echoed the words of a friend of Belinda Cronin. "Die, sucker," she spat. "The sooner the better."[61]

39: "Arizona Death Penalty History"

Several pages on the Arizona Department of Corrections Web site offer information about the Death House, which is maintained at the State Prison Complex in Florence where Scott Lehr has been imprisoned since 1997.

Visitors to the page learn that the Florence Death House has been the scene of executions in Arizona since 1910. Ninety-nine men and one woman have been executed. As of December 2014, 119 men and two women still waited on Arizona's Death Row.

The web site features a list of the last meals requested by the condemned. As they prepare to die, the prisoners' wishes for food vary widely. Daren L. Bolton, executed June 19, 1996, had no meal request. Arthur Martin Ross, executed in 1998, asked for "3 grilled cheese & fried egg sandwiches, macaroni & cheese (lots), pint of mint chocolate chip ice cream, 2 cans of Pepsi." Before his execution in 1997, William Lyle Woratzeck asked for "16 oz top sirloin steak (medium rare), French fries, onion rings, 1 dozen deep-fried butterfly shrimp, 1 whole cherry cheesecake, 1 case Pepsi Cola, 1 pot of coffee." Whether or not the last meal requests are fully granted is not stated.

According to the Web site, hanging was Arizona's method of execution until 1931. Beginning in 1934, lethal gas was used. Prisoners have been executed by injection since 1992. Material that was on the site in 2010 that has recently been deleted stated that, a few minutes before their assigned execution time; prisoners are brought into the injection room and strapped to a gurney. Intravenous tubes are inserted into their arms. Through those tubes the condemned are injected first with the sedative sodium pentothal. Next, Pavulon is injected to stop breathing and paralyze the muscular system. Finally, a potassium chloride injection will cause the heart to stop. The Department of Corrections added,

"Death by lethal injection is not painful and the inmate goes to sleep prior to the fatal effects of the Pavulon and potassium chloride."

This information about lethal injection was rendered obsolete after key manufacturers refused to supply drugs to be used in executions in the United States. Pro-death-penalty states including Arizona have resorted to using experimental drugs. On July 23, 2014, Arizona's most recent execution, Joseph Wood was injected with midazolam and hydromorphone. It took 15 injections of the drugs to kill Wood, who lay on the gurney gasping for two hours before dying.

40: A Wider Pattern

The jury who found Scott Lehr guilty of the murders of Margaret Christorf, Michelle Morales, and Belinda Cronin could not have been confident of the justice of their verdicts if they had realized the commonness of such crimes. It's likely that the jury did not know that the modus operandi of the murderer (or murderers) was not unusual—contrary to the claims of prosecutor Bill Clayton.

Ann Rule wrote of similar tragedies in *The Stranger Beside Me* ". . . there are, sadly, hundreds of young women killed each year in the United States. Many of them are strangled, bludgeoned, and raped. The method of murder was not distinctive enough to assume that any one man was responsible for a particular group of victims."[62]

A similar case in Arizona, for example, is the May 18, 1989, murder of Ruby Reid, which closely resembles what is known about the slaying of Margaret Christorf. Reid was last seen walking home from a Tucson bar around 11:30 p.m. Her body was found three days later in a desert area on the outskirts of the city. Twenty-two-year-old Christopher John Spreitz confessed that he drove Reid to the desert area, raped her, and killed her by crushing her head with rocks.

In November 2010, 50-year-old Patrick Ryon was arrested for the murder and sexual assault of Allison Marie Mims back in 1980. Mims' remains were not discovered until 1987—in the area where Michele Morales's body would be found in 1992.

Beyond the flimsiness of the cases presented against Scott Lehr by the State of Arizona, there is, in fact, persuasive evidence that they condemned the wrong man to death for the murders of Christorf, Morales, and Cronin. For an unknown killer—or killers—continued to murder women in the Phoenix area under chillingly similar conditions. The following are a few such unsolved murders that have occurred after June 1992, when Lehr was imprisoned.

On February 14, 1993, a woman's body was found near Pima Road and Dynamite Boulevard in north Scottsdale. The victim was identified as Renata Bateman, who had been known to work as a prostitute near 43rd and Glendale Avenues. Bateman died after being "hit in the head numerous times with a blunt object."[63] She was last heard from on January 13, 1993, when she called her boyfriend to say she was with someone she had met before. A slender 29-year-old with shoulder-length brown hair, Bateman was wearing jeans, a blue denim jacket and white tennis shoes when she was killed.

The body of 19-year-old Stacy Rae Morris was found on June 1, 1993, "in a dump area"[64] five miles west of Interstate 17 along Carefree Highway. This was the very same road along which the body of Michelle Morales was found the year before, on the other side of the Interstate. Like Morales, Morris died of blunt force injuries. Stacy Morris disappeared after leaving her apartment at 9440 N. 32nd Ave. on foot on the night of May 28, saying that she intended to stay with friends nearby. Morris's apartment was a little over a mile from the Circle K where Michelle Morales was last reported alive.

On the evening of May 24, 1996, Jennifer Lueth, 19, and Diana Shawcroft, 20, lingered outside a Glendale convenience store after buying cigarettes and soda. The cashier saw the young women conversing with a white man, age 31-33, with dark-blond hair and some facial hair. The women got into a blue or black early-1980s Chevy pickup truck with the man. Their bodies were found August 24, some 100 miles north, near Tule Mesa, Arizona. Police have withheld details of how Shawcroft and Lueth were slain. Like murder victims Margaret Christorf and Michelle Morales, Lueth and Shawcroft were last seen in front of a convenience store.

In January 1999, 11-year-old Mikelle Biggs disappeared while waiting on the sidewalk for an ice cream truck in her Mesa neighborhood. After hundreds of people searched without finding any trace of the girl, she was presumed to have been kidnapped and murdered.

Summer Sizemore left her home at 15th Avenue and Dunlap in April 2001. The 36-year-old, who lived with her boyfriend, reportedly "went out to get something" and intended to return soon. Sizemore's body was found a few days later about 25 miles to the south, in a grassy area near Chandler Blvd. and Gilbert Road. Sizemore died of blunt force trauma, according to investigators, who believe she may have been killed elsewhere, like Belinda Cronin. Also like Cronin, Sizemore struggled with substance abuse problems.[65] Sizemore's apartment was only three miles from the apartment to which Belinda Cronin never returned.

On September 19, 2002, Arleen Cilione celebrated her 60th birthday. A small, youthful-looking woman, Cilione joined coworkers for a couple of drinks at Donna's Hut, a Prescott tavern. She left Donna's Hut on foot shortly after 9:00 p.m. but never arrived home. Motorists found Cilione's body on January 8, 2003, in a wooded area off Highway 89, 10 miles southwest of Prescott, in the region where Meredith Porter was assaulted over ten years before. Police have not released details about the murder.

In April 2007, 81-year-old Raymond R. Sawyer confessed to having strangled his wife 25 years earlier and leaving her body in the desert only 2.8 miles from where the body of Margaret Christorf was found in 1991. After killing his wife, Frances, who was 45, Sawyer left her body with her blouse open and her pants pulled down to her knees, a detail hauntingly similar to the way in which Christorf was found.

41: 130004

20015

"Hey, Scott; suicide check!" they tease.

He laughs, but sometimes he goes days without talking to anyone. The prisoners can't see each other from their cells, but some talk constantly, to their neighbors, to themselves, to their television sets. The mentally healthy find ways to socialize through the steel cell doors, even playing games of chess. They make chessboards out of legal folders, number the squares, and call out their moves to opponents.

For over 17 years, Scott Lehr has lived in the Arizona State Prison's Browning Unit in Florence. He is inmate number 130004; all communications must include this ADC number.

The Browning Unit, a Special Management Unit (SMU), was designed to handle the "worst of the worst," prisoners considered a constant threat to staff and other inmates. However, Scott observes — and many experienced guards would agree—that death row prisoners are one of the easiest groups of inmates to handle. Most prisoners put so much time and energy into fighting their death sentences that they have little interest in making trouble. The few who have lost hope are the ones who cause most of the problems.

The unit includes four wings. As you approach the sliding door opening onto wing 3, you'll see "Condemned Row" stenciled in black letters over the door. Through that door on opposite sides of the hallway are the entrances to G, or "George," cluster and H ("Henry") cluster. Both clusters are divided into six "pods" of ten cells, stacked in two layers of five, housing a total of 60 condemned prisoners per cluster. Each pod of ten inmates is a microcosm, separated from the other pods on death row. All prisoners are locked in individual 8' x 12' cells at least 22 hours a

day. Furniture is riveted to the walls or floor. There are a narrow
bunk, toilet, sink, small desk, and hard seat. It's up to inmates to
keep their cells clean, and most do. Prisoners are allowed to leave
for showers, to help clean the pod, or, up to four days a week, to
take two hours of recreation in the small designated pens.
Scheduled visits from attorneys, family, or friends and trips to the
medical unit are other rare occasions for getting out of their cells.

Unlike the stereotypical dungeon popularized by movies, the
Browning Unit is new and clean. Low, gray clusters of buildings
sprawl in a baffling constellation in the desert, enshrouded by
barbed wire fences. Modern though the facility may appear, in
Scott's words, it's "a sensory-deprivation unit." There are no
windows that inmates can see. Walls are of colorless cement
block. A Plexiglas-domed skylight at the top of the pod admits
some natural light, but that sunshine never reaches the cells. Only
the outdoor recreation cages allow prisoners to enjoy a view of the
sky.

For death row prisoners there is little human contact. During
recreation, they can talk to other inmates in nearby pens.
Otherwise, conversations must be shouted through the perforations
in the steel cell doors or the thick glass windows in the visitation
room. Prisoners are required to keep cell walls clear of photos,
posters, or any other decorations.

Some inmates never have a visitor. Many break down under
these conditions. They are given antipsychotic drugs that make
them sleep all the time.

If there is a positive side to be found in inmates' isolation, it is
that their maximum security unit protects them from violence at
the hands of other prisoners. With all their deprivations, SMU
prisoners suffer less in some ways than those in Sheriff Joe
Arpaio's Maricopa County jail, where Scott was imprisoned
before being convicted. In Scott's view, "Arpaio's jail is one place
that can be said is worse than death row."

Scott has adjusted as well as anyone can to living out the prime
of his life in a cell. "I've had so many years to think and to come to
terms with what has transpired in my life, that basically I'm numb.

I've closed off my emotions to the pain that I once felt so strongly. And I did this as a form of defense; a human can only take so much suffering, and then they either snap, or they shut down emotionally, for their own protection."

All Browning Unit prisoners wear garish, carrot-orange jumpsuits, which are hot and scratchy. During the humid rainy season of late summer, the "swamp cooling" evaporative cooling system adds to the natural humidity, and prisoners awaken soaked in sweat.

Death row prisoners are allowed to own a 13-inch color television set, a walkman radio/cassette player, and an electric razor. No typewriters, computers, or personal telephones are allowed. They may have six cardboard storage boxes of belongings, five magazines, ten cassette tapes, and ten books. Hardcover books are forbidden; authorities decided they pose a security threat. Prison staff remove any staples from magazines. Gifts sent by well-wishers will not be given to prisoners; books or magazines must be mailed directly from approved distributors. Everything else must be bought from the prison store, where each week inmates can order stationery, hygiene items, and snack food. Money for these purchases must be provided by family or friends. And many of those on the unit have been shunned or simply forgotten by their families.

In less secure units in the Arizona State Prison, prisoners who behave well may be engaged in work, crafts or educational programs. They can earn a few cents an hour or complete their GED in some cases. In the Browning Unit, such productive ways of occupying time are banned. Prisoners needing to be active can "walk the dogs," pacing back and forth in their cells for hours. Even with a TV, walkman, and family and pen-friends to correspond with, Scott's "dogs" still get plenty of exercise.

One year it was decided that Arizona's death row prisoners should work for their keep—or put on a show of working. "Gun-gangs" of eight to ten men were taken out into the desert to plant a garden. Whether they could actually grow anything in the dry sand was not a concern. In their heavy jumpsuits, prisoners were forced to work at temperatures that could reach 110 degrees for up to six hours, plus the time they stood waiting to be shackled and unshackled at each end of their shift. Armed guards on horseback supervised inmates wielding hoes and rakes, potentially lethal weapons. After one summer when a fight broke out between a couple of gardening prisoners and a few others collapsed from heatstroke, the death row work crews were quietly discontinued.

Breakfast is delivered in a brown bag at 5:00 am, although lights aren't turned on until 6:00. Dinner is at 4:30 or 5:00 pm. Meals have been cut back to two a day. Lights go off—or are dimmed enough to sleep; the cells are never dark—between 10:00 and 10:30 every night. The exact time is at the whim of whoever's working the control tower. If lights are still on by 10:20, some inmates will make a racket in protest.

Within those constraints, each prisoner has his own daily program. Scott follows a unique sleep schedule to give himself uninterrupted time. After breakfast he goes to sleep on most days. On Mondays, Wednesdays, and Fridays, he'll first walk in the indoor recreation pen, a box 12' wide by 22' long, and then take a shower before sleeping.

When the lights go out at night, no more loud conversation or unnecessary noise is allowed. Scott's pod mates enforce this rule themselves, more harshly than the staff would, giving one another peace and quiet time. Most of the day, they are fairly respectful of noise levels, allowing Scott to sleep during the day. He knows he is lucky to be in this pod.

He'll usually wake up around 2:00 in the afternoon, when swing shift starts and staff come around to collect the trash. After dinner he might take a nap and then watch baseball or basketball games and do correspondence. If there's a good drama or documentary on TV (he favors BBC productions on PBS), he'll watch that instead of the games, keeping track of the scores during commercials. The prison cable television is on until midnight on weeknights, 2:00 am on weekends.

Night is Scott's time to read and write. After the overhead lights are dimmed, he'll work through the night with a 30-watt reading lamp attached to the wall, aimed at the end of his bunk. There he reads lying down, or writes sitting cross-legged, with a firm chess board on his lap, until the others wake for breakfast.

Scott usually accompanies his reading and writing with music from his Walkman. He came of age during the disco era, and now he usually listens to the local jazz station. If the right tune comes on the radio, maybe the Rippingtons, Fourplay, Dave Kos, or Gato Barbieri, he'll stand up to take a dancing break.

It's easy, he says, to be lazy under the forced passivity of prison. There is no job to get up for; you don't have to cook your own meals or wash your own clothing. Yet despite having to cope with illness, what most people would consider the worst imaginable social life, and the despair of knowing that society has judged him unworthy to live, Scott has used his time on death row well. He says he has been "catching up on all the reading that I should have done when I was younger and free but had no interest in at the time." The prison library limits borrowers to one book a week, but family and friends help take up the slack by sending Scott mail-order books. All but the precious few books that he's allowed to keep in his cell he gives to other inmates, donates to the prison library, or sends to friends.

Scott's taste in reading is both broad and discerning. He never had much interest in "true crime" writing, and now he lives surrounded by real crime stories. He prefers the classics, as well as serious contemporary literature. In fiction, Emily Bronte, Oscar Wilde, Ernest Hemingway, F. Scott Fitzgerald, Herman Hesse, Albert Camus, John Steinbeck and Joyce Carol Oates are some of his favorites. He says, "I think that you can learn a lot from good fiction, but it's also a great way to escape reality in a place like death row. Escape is essential to good mental health in here." Edgar Allan Poe and Charles Baudelaire are his favorite poets. He also reads history and classical philosophy, particularly Boethius, Seneca, Lucretius, and Marcus Aurelius. "If you'd have told me twenty years ago that I would be reading. . . ancient Roman philosophy, I'd have laughed at you," he observes.

The lack of basic art supplies hasn't kept Scott from creating stationery for his correspondence. He'll draw a design or cut out a picture from magazine and have the paper xeroxed in the prison library. He also recycles postcards and greeting cards into beautiful new cards. Over the years he has written hundreds of pages of letters to people from all over the world. In the past, some correspondents sought him out after reading about him on the Arizona Department of Corrections Web site. He also wrote to pen-pal organizations and newspapers in Italy with a brief statement about himself. Responses have come from a few who believe he's guilty and want to satisfy their morbid curiosity about what a serial killer is like. There have been hostile kooks as well, writing to berate him and to gloat that he will be executed. But through the years, compassionate people have written, and some have become genuine friends through correspondence. Now he limits his correspondence mainly to a couple of pen friends who have exchanged life stories with him for over 15 years.

Over time, Scott has schooled himself as a writer, most recently of essays and poems. "I enjoy it as a challenge of my creative spirit but don't see it really as a labor of love. Writing is a lot like work—hard work!—and if I didn't enjoy the sense of personal growth and understanding that accompanies the act of composition, I'd give it up in a heartbeat and just be a reader like most normal people. Writing is good for me, and that's why I continue to do it."

Although crushingly routine, life is not the same on the pod from one day to the next. One of the prisoners will suddenly yell out into the silence that a certain show is on TV, or another will want to share what a pen-friend wrote to him. However, conversation on the pod usually stems from the news: who's on trial now, or who's being sentenced, but most of all, cops. Everything that's reported about cops, prosecutors, or judges is scrutinized and debated ad nauseam.

According to Scott, no matter how well a prisoner may deal with keeping up with, or letting go of, the outside world, everyone in the Browning Unit knows he's been condemned to die.

However, as the years pass while legal appeals are exhausted, execution may seem only a distant possibility. Most prisoners think more about their current deprivations than the eventuality of one day being marched to a quick and public death.

Thirty men have been executed in Arizona since Scott's imprisonment, but he personally has spoken to only two or three of those. "Nothing much changes around here near or at the time of an execution for the rest of us," he says. "We've been isolated and distanced from it all . . . We watch the news coverage of it on TV, and the inmates who knew the poor fellow will sometimes reminisce about some humorous anecdote of times back in CB-6, but that's about it. I think that everyone has his own way of dealing with these reminders of his own possible fate, much the same as anyone does who sees or comes close to death experiences."

Most of the time, Scott says, "We all get along fine and help each other out as best we can, but there are also times when, either no one is talking to each other because of some silly disagreement; or we're screaming obscenities at one another for some disrespect—actual or perceived. In time all's forgiven, and we're back to playing chess again . . . We do help each other out a lot. Legal information is exchanged; help is given to those who cannot read or write; food and coffee are bought and passed among those with no family or friends on the outside. No one is ever left to do without anything if it can be helped."

In September 2000, Yvonne Lehr died unexpectedly. It hit hard to lose the mother who had sacrificed so much for him and never stopped believing in him, who devoted her last years to trying to help him and his daughters.

Scott was diagnosed with diabetes in March 2000. In honor of the first anniversary of his mother's death, he fasted 24 hours, despite the danger that fasting posed to him as a diabetic.

Scott says that, like any other adversity, the effects of having to live on death row are "entirely dependent upon your attitude." While he has good days and bad, "I have not let this place get the best of me yet, and in fact I have experienced a great deal of personal growth throughout this ordeal. I'm not the man who was arrested over 22 years ago.

"I became more introspective. Instead of trying to understand the outside world and how it relates to me and my life, I began to analyze myself more and to discover who I was and how I fit into the rest of the world. It's a complete reversal of perception."

When asked about what he might do for a living if he were exonerated and released, Scott Lehr thinks he might go back to being his own boss in his old business of tree service. "What I miss most . . . is solitary places with beautiful landscapes where I could go to meditate in tranquility. And the more time I spend locked away like this, the more I like being alone with myself. That must sound strange, I know, but it's the truth."

In April 2004 he wrote, "It is always much more difficult to be locked up at this time of year than at any other. Springtime is in the air! The smell of flowers, the vibrant feel of cool days changing to warm. I can smell the desert in bloom. We had a good stretch of rain here about a week ago; and when that happens in March or April, the desert literally explodes into color. It's a very lovely sight to behold. The rest of the year I couldn't care less about the desert, with all the cacti, rocks, and assorted critters, who only come out at night anyway. I would just as soon be as far as humanly possible from it. And, I suppose, that is a fairly accurate way to describe prison: 'As far as humanly possible' from all things beautiful. But the springtime desert will not be ignored, and it can be sensed from behind all the barbed-wire fencing, concrete barriers, and the maze of cinderblock walls, making one's 'debt to society' all the more expensive for a few long weeks."

Since he has been incarcerated, Scott's twin daughters have married and he's become a grandfather. His ex-wife, Elaine, has not remarried.

42: Justice Delayed

2015

On January 30, 2002, the Arizona Supreme Court ruled on Scott Lehr's appeals regarding his convictions and sentences. The prosecution's position was argued in the name of Arizona Attorney General Janet Napolitano (who by the end of 2002 had been elected Governor of Arizona and in January 2009 was appointed Secretary of the Department of Homeland Security by President Barack Obama).

The Arizona Supreme Court's opinion uncritically accepts the evidence presented by the prosecution. Its sketchy summary of the "facts" of the cases is rife with the errors provided by the prosecution. To name a few examples, the opinion repeats the erroneous testimony that Emily Caldwell identified the license number ADW915 or -515, rather than the number she confidently reported to police on at least two occasions, ADW519 (a plate that was missing from a salvage lot at the time of the crimes) or -515. The opinion repeats the prosecution's false assertion that Meredith Porter was "badly injured," and it does not mention that Porter first told police that the suspect drove a gray pickup truck, not the Nissan sedan that was later claimed as a link to Scott Lehr.[66] The Supreme Court's summary of Scott Lehr's testimony in the 1996 trial oozes hostile bias: "Nonetheless, he denied ever meeting any of the victims. He did not offer to explain how his DNA could be linked to four of the women or how his fingerprint was found at the scene of one of the attacks." The fingerprint in question is the indistinct partial fingerprint in the Nancy Caporaso case that had first been determined not to be Scott's.

Despite its bias in favor of the prosecution, the Arizona Supreme Court did find that Judge Gerst erred in preventing Scott

Lehr's defense team from adequately cross-examining the State's witnesses concerning DNA evidence. In addition, the Court found that Gerst should have allowed the defense to present evidence regarding the DPS crime lab's work. Consequently, the Court reversed the murder convictions and other verdicts in the cases of Margaret Christorf and Michelle Morales, along with all charges in the case of Mona Barnett, who had testified that Scott Lehr was not the man who assaulted her.

Ruling that Judge Gerst's errors were "harmless" all the same, the Arizona Supreme Court claimed that the errors did not influence the jury's verdicts in the remaining cases. This was despite the fact that the questionable DNA testing was central to prosecutor Bill Clayton's case. The Supreme Court upheld the death sentence for the murder of Belinda Cronin, although the only possible connection between Scott Lehr and the victim had been the subjective testimony by a family acquaintance that a second-hand ring found in the Lehrs' home resembled one belonging to Cronin.

The Court let stand all the remaining verdicts and sentences. Although it found that Meredith Porter's pretrial identification of the defendant was "arguably unduly suggestive," it nevertheless asserted that her description of the assailant was "accurate and detailed." (The Court's opinion failed to note that Porter described to police a blue-eyed man with protuberant ears, who did not resemble brown-eyed Scott Lehr.)

Still led by Rick Romley, the Maricopa County Attorney's Office responded to the reversals by choosing to retry Lehr for the murders of Michelle Morales and Margaret Christorf.

In June 2002, the United States Supreme Court ruled in *Ring v. Arizona* that the capital sentencing laws of Arizona and four other states were unconstitutional because judges, rather than juries, held the power to impose death sentences. Following that decision, some 30 of Arizona's death-row prisoners, including Scott Lehr, were to be resentenced by juries who would decide whether aggravating factors were relevant.

In March 2009, the Maricopa County Attorney's Office retried Scott for the crimes against Mona Barnett, Michelle Morales, and Margaret Christorf. Although the jury was asked to resentence him for the murder of Belinda Cronin as well, they were not allowed to consider whether the 1996 guilty verdict was warranted in the Cronin case.

Bill Clayton headed the prosecution—in his last case before retiring. Scott refused to be present at the 2009 retrial because Maricopa County regulations required that in the courtroom he wear a stun belt capable of delivering a 50,000-volt shock. Over the objections of the defense, the Barnett, Morales, and Christorf cases were tried together. The bulk of the testimony was from Alison Brooks, Nancy Caporaso, Amy Perry, and Meredith Porter, witnesses unrelated—but highly prejudicial—to the cases of Barnett, Morales, and Christorf. Even Nicole Churchill's and Emily Caldwell's testimonies from the earlier trials were read to the jury, although Caldwell had adamantly refused to participate in the retrial. Despite the wealth of contradictory details, the State again claimed to have DNA evidence that implicated Scott—even in the case of Michelle Morales, where any scant, degraded DNA evidence had supposedly been consumed by testing for the first trial, where it had yielded inconclusive results. (The State's claim in 2009 was that DNA was sampled from the sticks left over from the rape kit swabs from the first trial.) When five jurors applauded the testimony of prosecution witness David Duplissa, some even rising to give a standing ovation, only one of the biased jurors was removed from the jury.

Predictably, this tainted jury found Scott guilty on all charges and again sentenced him to death for the murders of Morales and Christorf. They sentenced him to life in prison for the murder of Belinda Cronin. On appeal, those decisions were promptly upheld by the Arizona Supreme Court. Scott is now awaiting a decision on his final State appeal, a motion for post-conviction relief. If his appeal should be denied, only a successful appeal through the Federal system could save him from execution.

In March 2002, Ray Krone was exonerated for a Phoenix murder for which he'd been sentenced to death in Maricopa County. A Postal Service employee and Air Force veteran with no criminal record, Krone had been convicted in 1992 of murdering Kimberly Ancona. The prosecution's case had rested on "expert" testimony that claimed to match Krone's teeth to bite marks on the victim. The jury found Krone guilty despite testimony from his roommate that Krone was at home asleep at the time of the crime. After Krone spent ten years in prison, his innocence was established when DNA evidence linked the crime to Kenneth Phillips, a registered sex offender who lived within a block of the murder scene. Phillips's fingerprints and hair had also been left at the scene of the crime, but that evidence had not been brought to the attention of the jury.[67] In 2005, Maricopa County awarded Krone a $1.4 million settlement.[68]

Those involved in convicting Scott Lehr have continued to make the news. In October 2010, former Detective Michael Johnson denied allegations that he had tried to influence a witness in a case involving the shooting of an unarmed man by a Phoenix police officer.[69]

Sheriff Joe Arpaio has been beleaguered by controversy. His practices have been condemned by Amnesty International as violating basic standards of human rights,[70] and the U.S. Department of Justice sued the Maricopa County Sheriff's Office for refusing to provide access for a civil-rights investigation.[71] "There's no such thing as 'abuse of power'—there's no law against that," Arpaio has insisted.[72]

According to a 2003 *Arizona Republic* article, "Phoenix police crime lab technicians blundered nine cases while analyzing DNA evidence to be used against murder, rape, and aggravated assault suspects" in 2001.[73] Susan Narveson, who had supervised the lab that performed DNA tests for Scott Lehr's first trial, was also the administrator of the Phoenix police crime lab at the time of the errors. Narveson responded that "It's an honest mistake made with the best intentions."[74]

Judge Stephen A. Gerst, who in 1997 meted out maximum sentences to Scott Lehr, drew attention to himself in 2004 when he handed Bishop Thomas J. O'Brien, convicted of leaving the scene of an accident that killed a pedestrian, the remarkably light sentence of probation and community service.[75]

And in 2008, William Clayton received a Lifetime Achievement Award from the Arizona Prosecuting Attorneys' Advisory Council for securing more than 10 successful death penalty verdicts during his career.

Acknowledgments

Information on the crimes and ensuing investigations was provided primarily by Phoenix Police Department and Maricopa County Sheriff's Office documents. Details of the trials came from transcripts of legal proceedings concerning The State of Arizona vs. Scott Alan Lehr.

This book could not have been written without the late Yvonne Lehr, who contributed her collection of documents, along with her passion for finding justice for her son.

A debt of gratitude is extended to Scott Lehr for his vast recollection of events and people and for his keen intelligence and enduring sense of humor. His conversations with other participants have necessarily been approximated from memory.

Warm thanks are due to others who cannot be named here for their insight and moral support.

Notes

1 Dennis Wagner, Judi Villa, and Patricia Biggs, "Phoenix Worst in Solving Rapes," *AZCentral.com,* November 3, 2002, http://www.azcentral.com/news/articles/1103clearance-rape0.html.

2 Ibid.

3 Michael Baden, M.D., and Marion Roach, *Dead Reckoning: The New Science of Catching Killers* (New York: Simon & Schuster), 247.

4 Ibid.

5 Ibid., 237.

6 Carol Sowers, "Study: Arizona Among 10 Worst States for Errors in Death Penalty Cases," *AZCentral.com,* February 11, 2002.

7 Stephen G. Michaud with Roy Hazelwood, *The Evil That Men Do: FBI Profiler Roy Hazelwood's Journey into the Minds of Sexual Predators* (New York: St. Martin's Press, 1998), 91-92.

8. Jim Walsh, "Serial Rapist Likely to Strike Again," *Arizona Republic,* February 28, 1992.

9 Jeanne Boylan, *Portraits of Guilt: The Woman Who Profiles the Faces of America's Deadliest Criminals* (New York: Pocket Star Books, 2001), 11.

10 Frederick Bermudez, "Rapist-Slayer Prowling Freeways," *Arizona Republic,* February 27, 1992.

11 Frederick Bermudez and Jim Walsh, "Father of 3 Suspected in Serial Rapes, Killings," *Arizona Republic*, June 27, 1992..

12 Frederick Bermudez, " 'Too Much' in Cases Was Alike," *Arizona Republic,* June 27, 1992, sec. A.

13 Tony Ortega, "Joe Assumes Deposition: Arpaio Tries to Distance Himself From Pronouncements About Punishing Inmates," *Phoenix New Times*, http://www.phoenixnewtimes.com/webextra/arpaio/media/052997.html.

[14] Barry Graham, "Star of Justice: On the Job with America's Toughest Sheriff," *Harper's*, April 2001, 61.

[15] Ibid.

[16] John Dougherty, "Jailhouse Blues: Pack'em In and Take Away Their Rights. That's Sheriff Joe Arpaio's Philosophy," *Phoenix New Times*, November 24, 1993, http://www.phoenixnewtimes.com/webextra/arpaio/crime/112493.html.

[17] Tony Ortega, "Boxer Rebellion: When It Comes to Sheriff Arpaio's Underwear Policy, Taxpayers Are Taking It in the Shorts," *Phoenix New Times*, http://www.phoenixnewtimes.com/webestra/arpaio/media/110295.html.

[18] Eugene Scott, "Temperatures Rise to 145 inside Tent City," *AZCentral.com*, July 3, 2011, http://www.azcentral.com/community/phoenix/articles/2011/07/03/20110703tent-city-temperatures-rise-145.html.

[19] John Elvin, "High-Profile Sheriff Makes Inmates Look Like Pinkos," *Insight on the News Newspaper*, June 24, 1996, http://findarticles.com/p/articles/mi_m1571/is_n24_v12/ai_18400880/

[20] "Sheriff Runs Female Chain Gang," *CNN.com*, October 29, 2003, http://www.cnn.com/2003/US/Southwest/10/29/chain.gang.reut

[21] "About MCSO: Welcome to the Maricopa County Sheriff's Office," http://www.mcso.org/submenu.asp?file=aboutmcso&page=main, accessed June 11, 2002.

[22] Fred Francis, "Too Tough-On-Crime Lawman: Sheriff Brownshirt," quoted in *MediaWatch* 08/01/1994, page 3, https://secure.mediaresearch.org/news/mediawatch/1994/mw19940801p3.html.

[23] Tony Ortega, "Joe Assumes Deposition: Arpaio Tries to Distance Himself From Pronouncements About Punishing Inmates," *Phoenix New Times*, http://www.phoenixnewtimes.com/webextra/arpaio/media/052997.html.

[24]Gary L. Stuart, *Innocent Until Interrogated: The True Story of the Buddhist Temple Massacre and the Tucson Four* (Tucson: The University of Arizona Press, 2010), 175.

[25] Gregg McCrary with Katherine Ramsland, *The Unknown Darkness: Profiling the Predators among Us* (William Morrow, 2003, HarperTorch, 2004), ch. 5, "The Buddhist Temple Massacre," 160-163, quoted in Stuart, 15.

[26] Brian Downing Quig and A. Scintilla, "Temple Murders News Blackout Ends," http://www.dcia.com/blackout.html (Accessed August 22, 2002).

[27] Ibid.

[28] Stuart, 59.

[29] Stuart, 18.

[30] Russ Kimball and Laura Greenberg, "Trials and Tribulations," *Phoenix,* December 1993, 101.

[31] Ibid.

[32] Ibid., 102.

[33] Stuart, 134.

[34] Tom Fitzpatrick, "Romley Misdealt This Hand," *Phoenix New Times,* February 16-22, 1994, 5.

[35] Stuart, 261.

[36] Stuart, 130.

[37] Kimball and Greenberg, 104.

[38] Stuart, 131.

[39] Kimball and Greenberg, 105.

[40] Stuart, 148.

[41] Stuart, 156.

[42] Kimball and Greenberg, 106-107.

[43] Stuart, 151.

[44] Brent Whiting, "Only 'Imbeciles' Doubted Guilt of 'Tucson 4.' Temple Jury Told," *Arizona Republic,* May 26, 1993.

[45] Tom Fitzpatrick, "Dealing with a Confessed Serial Killer," *Phoenix New Times,* January 13-19, 1993, 6.

[46] Randy Collier, " 'Major Errors' in Probe of '91 Temple Slayings: Ex-Sheriff, Aides Faulted in Report," *Arizona Republic,* November 18, 1993, A4.

[47] Stuart, 185.

[48] Stuart, 207.

[49] Stuart, 187-188.

[50] Manson, "Man Jailed for Year Sues," *Arizona Republic,* May 1, 1993, B8.

[51] Pamela Manson, "Judge Hails Deal in Jailing of Wrong Man," *Arizona Republic,* January 29, 1994, B.

[52] Ibid.

[53] Manson, "Man Jailed for Year Sues."

[54] Randy Collier, "Confessions in Question: County to Review Past Cases Based on Crime Admissions," *Arizona Republic,* January 9, 1993, A4.

[55] Tom Fitzpatrick, "Dealing with a Confessed Serial Killer," *Phoenix New Times,* January 13-19, 1993, 5.

[56] Brent Whiting, "Killer Spared Death, Given 281 Years in Massacre at Buddhist Temple," *Arizona Republic,* February 12, 1994, sec. B.

[57] Mike Sager, *Scary Monsters and Super Freaks: Stories of Sex, Drugs, Rock 'n' Roll and Murder.* (New York: Thunder Mouth Press, 2003), 313, quoted in Stuart, 269.

[58] Fitzpatrick, "Romley Misdealt This Hand," 5.

[59] Frederick Bermudez, "3 Abductions but No Arrests in Phoenix," *The Arizona Republic,* October 19, 1992, sec. B.

[60] Jennifer Thompson-Cannino, Ronald Cotton, and Erin Torneo, *Picking Cotton: Our Memoir of Injustice and Redemption* (New York: St. Martin's, 2009) details the ordeal of a rape victim and the totally innocent man she helped convict when she confidently but erroneously identified him at a lineup and during two trials.

[61] Susie Steckner, "Killer Gets Death in 3 Slayings," *The Arizona Republic,* August 9, 1997, sec. B.

[62] Ann Rule, *The Stranger Beside Me,* updated 20th anniversary ed. (New York: Signet, 2001), 131.

[63] Silent Witness: Killer at Large," *The Arizona Republic,* April 23, 1993.

[64] "Silent Witness: Tips Needed," *The Arizona Republic,* June 20, 1993.

[65] "Detective Files: Summer Sizemore," Channel 12 News Today video posted on *AZCentral.com,* February 22, 2005.

[66]Introducing a new error, the opinion states that Margaret Christorf was "in her mid-thirties" at the time of the murder, when in fact she was 40.

[67] Dennis Wagner, "Exonerated Death Row Inmate Files $100 Million Lawsuit," *AZCentral.com,* April 21, 2003.

[68] Christina Leonard, "Cleared Man to Get $1.4 Million From County," *AZCentral.com,February 22, 2005.* April 6, 2005.

[69] Lynh Bui, "Nowakowski, Johnson Say Call to Officer Was Not Inappropriate,"
http://www.azcentral.com/members/Blog/PHXBeat/102492 (accessed November 11, 2010).

[70] Tony Ortega, "Human Plights: International Group Urges Immediate Stop to Arpaio Jail Practices," *Phoenix New Times,* September 18, 1997,
http://www.phoenixnewtimes.com/issues/1997-09-18/news3.html

[71] Yvonne Wingett and JJ Hensley, "Sheriff Joe Arpaio Sued by Justice Department in Civil-Rights Probe," *AZCentral.com,* September 3, 2010,
http://www.azcentral.com/news/election/azelections/articles/2010/ 09/02/20100902joe-arpai...

[72] Dan Nowicki, "Critics Call Arpaio Aggressive, Intimidating," *AZCentral.com,* August 23, 2009,
http://www.azcentral.com/news/articles/2009/08/23/20090823arpa io0823.ht...

[73] Carlos Miller, "Phoenix Police Lab Errs on DNA," *AZCentral.com,*
http://www.azcentral.com/news/articles/0506phxlab06.html.

[74] Ibid.

[75] Michael Kiefer and Christina Leonard, "No Jail Time for O'Brien," *AZCentral.com*, March 27, 2004.

www.ingramcontent.com/pod-product-compliance
Lightning Source LLC
Chambersburg PA
CBHW022349280326
41935CB00007B/131